CONTROLLING WOMEN

CONTROLLING
WOMEN

WHAT WE MUST DO NOW TO SAVE REPRODUCTIVE FREEDOM

KATHRYN KOLBERT & JULIE F. KAY

hachette
BOOKS

NEW YORK

Hachette Books

Hachette Book Group

1290 Avenue of the Americas

New York, NY 10104

HachetteBooks.com

Twitter.com/HachetteBooks

Instagram.com/HachetteBooks

First Edition: July 2021

Published by Hachette Books, an imprint of Perseus Books, LLC, a subsidiary of Hachette Book Group, Inc. The Hachette Books name and logo is a trademark of the Hachette Book Group.

The Hachette Speakers Bureau provides a wide range of authors for speaking events.

To find out more, go to www.hachettespeakersbureau.com or call (866) 376-6591.

The publisher is not responsible for websites (or their content) that are not owned by the publisher.

Print book interior design by Trish Wilkinson.

Library of Congress Cataloging-in-Publication Data

Names: Kolbert, Kathryn, author. | Kay, Julie F., author.

Title: Controlling women : what we must do now to save reproductive freedom / Kathryn Kolbert & Julie F. Kay.

Description: First edition. | New York : Hachette Books, 2021. | Includes bibliographical references and index.

Identifiers: LCCN 2021005512 | ISBN 9780306925634 (hardcover) | ISBN 9780306925627 (ebook)

Subjects: LCSH: Abortion—United States. | Women's rights—United States.

Classification: LCC HQ767.5.U5 K65 2021 | DDC 362.1988/800973—dc23

LC record available at https://lccn.loc.gov/2021005512

ISBNs: 978-0-306-92563-4 (hardcover), 978-0-306-92562-7 (ebook)

Printed in the United States of America

LSC-C

Printing 1, 2021

To Kitty's grandchildren, Ari, Sylvia, and Zoe
and Julie's children, June and Fiona

CONTENTS

Introduction 1

1   Gender, Sex, Race, and Power: Why Abortion Matters 6

2   A Texas-Sized Win: *Roe v. Wade* 20

3   A High Five from the Supremes:
The Surprising Story of *Planned Parenthood v. Casey* (Kitty) 38

4   A *Roe*-Shaped Piñata:
Five Decades of Abortion Litigation in the US 63

5   Dr. Jekyll and Representative Hyde:
The Battle over Government Funding for Abortion 70

6   The Kids Are Not All Right:
States Limit Teen Access to Sex Education,
Birth Control, and Abortion 86

7   Death by a Thousand Pinpricks:
Attacks on Clinics and Doctors Move Abortion
Further Out of Reach 100

8   In-Your-Face Politics: Abortion Bans Inflame the Debate 116

9   A Wolf at the Door:
New Supreme Court Majority Puts Procreative and
Sexual Freedoms at Risk 130

10   Meanwhile, Across the Pond: A Human Rights
Approach to Abortion (Julie) 146

11   New Tactics, New Triumphs: Now It's Time for Big Ambitions 168

12   Give Me an *A!*: Abortion Access for All   183

13   And the Nominees Are . . . : Ten Steps Forward   200

14   Fueling an Audacious and Inclusive Movement:
     Reproductive Freedom in the Twenty-First Century   219

Acknowledgments   231

Authors' Note   235

Notes   237

Index   283

INTRODUCTION

*This is a story about control. My control.
Control of what I say. Control of what I do . . .
Are we ready?*

JANET JACKSON, "CONTROL"

WEDNESDAY, MARCH 4, 2020, was like a homecoming on the plaza of the Supreme Court. It was the day the Court would hear oral argument in *June Medical Services v. Russo*, a challenge to a repressive Louisiana abortion law. The two of us lingered in the crowd, overlooked by two marble statues: a female figure, *Contemplation of Justice*, and a male figure, *Guardian of Law*.

Embracing old colleagues, we posed for photos and were handed brightly colored placards declaring that all women have a right to abortion. It was so unseasonably warm that we didn't need the turquoise beanies handed out by supporters. Still, we grabbed them as a souvenir of our days as lawyers at the Center for Reproductive Rights during its early years.

Once inside the Court's marbled hallways, we waited to be let up the sweeping staircase and into the courtroom. We reminisced with one of the parties in the case, Michael Rothrock, about his mother, Robin, a Louisiana abortion clinic owner whose strong sense of justice and quick wit had made her one of our favorite clients in our legal battles. We embraced colleagues from the ACLU's Reproductive Freedom Project,

1

who had lined up outside the Court at four a.m. that morning in order to get one of the few seats inside. After wishing good luck to the attorneys from the Center for Reproductive Rights arguing the case, we passed through a final set of metal detectors and followed the federal marshals to our assigned seats.

"Oyez, oyez, all rise."

Underneath the conviviality and ritual lay a grimness and fear. Here we were at the Supreme Court, fighting to save abortion rights. Again. Would this be the case where the Court overturned *Roe v. Wade* (*Roe*), the 1973 decision that legalized abortion nationwide?

We had both been here many times before. Kathryn—Kitty—had convinced the Supreme Court to preserve abortion rights in *Thornburgh v. American College of Obstetrics and Gynecologists* in 1985. Six years later, back before the Justices and armed with a bold legal strategy, she successfully persuaded the Court to preserve *Roe*'s core principles in *Planned Parenthood v. Casey* (*Casey*). That same year, she cofounded the Center for Reproductive Rights (the Center), the leading reproductive rights nonprofit law firm where Julie and hundreds of other attorneys over the years would be trained in cutting-edge litigation and advocacy to advance reproductive freedom.

In the immediate years following *Casey*, each of us worked on a number of other reproductive rights cases that the Center filed in state and federal courts. Julie moved to Ireland and argued against that country's total ban on abortion at the European Court of Human Rights, while participating in efforts to liberalize abortion laws worldwide. We had closely followed and supported Supreme Court arguments in many other abortion and women's rights cases. We had marched and voted and then marched again. Wash, rinse, repeat.

Every time the Supreme Court hears an abortion case, it brings out crowds and marches, increased public debate, and anticipation that this time might be the end of the abortion protections first established in *Roe*. As the Court has steadily become more conservative, and more anti-abortion, women's rights supporters have become increasingly anxious about "saving *Roe*"—with good reason.

Fixated on the Supreme Court, legislators in red states continuously lob opportunities for the Court to consider laws that are passed simply to provide a chance to turn back the clock on *Roe*'s protections. These anti-abortion trial balloons demonstrate utter contempt for existing law—for example, by banning abortion within the first trimester—and are so blatantly unconstitutional that they would not be put on a first-year law school exam. Yet they serve the purpose of firing up a zealous anti-abortion base and, more importantly, might lure the conservative courts to further narrow abortion rights.

American politics have become more polarized in the past decade, and the chasm that separates the two sides of the divide on abortion is unrivaled. Abortion rights have been fought over in courtrooms, hospitals, and parking lots. The vitriol and violence associated with abortion access—from clinic blockades to bombings and assassinations of doctors and clinic staff members in their homes, workplaces, and churches—have few parallels. In Congress, at state and local levels, and worldwide, there is little to no compromise on abortion.

Although *Roe* dramatically liberalized access to legal abortion in 1973, since then, politicians of every stripe have moved to limit abortion access in the majority of states. As a result, abortion rights and services have been disappearing before our eyes. For marginalized women and disproportionately for women of color, inequities in access to health care services overall impose limitations on the ability to obtain an abortion. Every time the courts or legislators allow a restriction on abortion, the impact falls even harder on women who struggle for basic services as a result of structural racism, poverty, or youth. These restrictions also perpetuate negative stereotypes about women's identities, lifestyles, and cultural traditions.

For decades we have been litigating, discussing, and strategizing together about the best ways to protect and expand reproductive freedom. *Controlling Women* is the result of our work together in courthouses and conference rooms, on planes and trains, and over meals and drinks with groups large and small, working to define a way forward for gender equity, all as conservative forces push us backward.

Courts have played a central role in defining the scope of abortion access. As we have been fighting to protect *Roe* and its progeny, abortion protections have been whittled away with alarming precision. A new ultra-conservative majority now dominates the Supreme Court, placing these rights on the edge of a cliff. Nearly a third of the states have laws to abolish legal abortion that could immediately be triggered at the moment *Roe* is overturned, or soon thereafter. On the bright side, several blue states have state constitutions or laws further protecting abortion rights—a set of suspenders for when the Supreme Court loosens the belt on *Roe*.

This legal history has shaped abortion rights and strongly influenced both the progress and the setbacks of our movement; it provides valuable lessons for the future. But it's not all about *Roe*, nor just about abortion litigation. Importantly, we've learned that we cannot allow vital reproductive freedoms to twist and turn on the vagaries of legal decisions or the whims of Supreme Court Justices. Neither can these important freedoms depend, like *Roe*, solely on concepts of privacy. We need to think more boldly and broadly if we are to advance gender equity and human rights.

We are lawyers and also activists, so we know that multiple strategies are needed. Therefore, we also propose diverse ways to gain access to abortion and a wider range of reproductive freedoms. These strategies are influenced by the stories we will share about women and girls who have faced barriers to making private and intimate decisions about their health and lives, and the courageous medical practitioners providing services in the face of government-imposed obstacles, violence, and acrimony from abortion opponents. *Controlling Women* offers an opportunity to dream bigger, think differently, and bring in new allies.

Abortion rights go hand in hand with a broader agenda that decries the racial inequity, homophobia, and transphobia that are so intertwined with misogyny. We recognize that transgender men and non-binary people (TGNB) also seek abortions. Therefore, where possible, we use gender neutral language. Nevertheless, we emphasize throughout that misogyny, discrimination, and control of women are the foundation of anti-abortion sentiment.

It is clear to us as feminists that reproductive freedom is vital in order for everyone to be able to live their fullest lives, join the workforce, control their family size and timing, and have the best chance of participating equally in all aspects of society. *Controlling Women* aims to lay bare what's at stake and to create a widespread understanding of what we must do now to bring reproductive freedom in from the cold.

CHAPTER 1

GENDER, SEX, RACE, AND POWER
WHY ABORTION MATTERS

I am not free while any woman is unfree, even when her
shackles are very different from my own.

AUDRE LORDE

THE ISSUE OF abortion at its core is a question about control. It's about
who holds the power to make fundamental judgments for others. Although people may disagree on many key life decisions—whom to
marry, what religion to follow, or how to educate our children—rarely
are strangers allowed to have authority over others' intimate life decisions as they are when it comes to pregnancy.

Abortion is a common medical procedure. Approximately one in
four women in the US will have an abortion by age forty-five. While
the majority of women in the US will never themselves need an abortion, nevertheless it is a defining issue in the gender wars in the US
and worldwide. For decades, abortion has served as a litmus test for US
Supreme Court Justices, presidential candidates, members of Congress,
and even candidates in local school board elections.

Neither of us has ever personally needed an abortion, and at this
stage in life we never will. But we have dedicated decades to litigating,
lobbying, and planning for the expansion of abortion rights. For most
of that time, the future of *Roe* was the dominant question: Would *Roe*
remain the law, or would new conservative Supreme Court Justices decimate it?

6

Why does abortion matter so much and to so many? What is really at stake in the abortion debate and for whom? What is underlying a debate that on its surface is too often portrayed as women's rights versus fetal rights? Is this fight really about protecting religious or moral values or women's health, or is something bigger imperiled by denying women control over their bodies and their decision making? What does it say about a country's values when it bans or severely restricts access to legal abortion?

The debate over abortion in America and, indeed, worldwide, has largely been discussed in terms established by the anti-abortion movement. If, as the saying goes, imitation is the sincerest form of flattery, then the abortion rights movement should be pleased to see its opponents adopt a "pro–women's health" rhetoric in recent years. But the abortion debate is not about the safety of a routine medical procedure. Abortion is safer than childbirth, and safer than many other routine health services that are regularly performed in clinics and outpatient centers across the country, such as colonoscopies and dental surgery. If women's health were truly the goal, then the expansion of the Affordable Care Act and Medicaid, greater support for research and services for cancer and heart disease (the leading causes of death for women), and greater access to mental health care would be the top priorities.

Nor is opposition to abortion really about the protection of life. Many who claim to be "pro-life" oppose policies that protect life, such as elimination of the death penalty, gun control measures, and expansion of affordable health care. Similarly, the belief that life begins at conception and that the state needs to protect "innocent life" or fetal rights is not the bona fide reason why abortion is such a contentious issue. If it were all about protecting "babies," there would be more emphasis on reducing infant mortality, which is at crisis levels, particularly for infants born to Black women, impoverished women, and teens.

Jerushah Duford, the granddaughter of televangelist Reverend Billy Graham, agrees. She recently challenged anti-abortion evangelicals to redefine "pro-life" to apply to more than fetuses. "I genuinely wish the Democratic Party would have a greater value for life inside the womb,"

Duford said. "Yet I equally wish the Republican Party would place a greater value on life outside the womb. You cannot choose just one and define yourself as pro-life."

Despite many protestations to the contrary, abortion is not predominantly a religious issue. Certainly, religious beliefs or words from the pulpit can influence a person's opinion of abortion. As part of a reproductive imperative, many religions espouse "be fruitful and multiply" as a direct commandment. And some religious groups remain pretty solidly anti-abortion: about three-quarters of white evangelical Protestants (77 percent) think abortion should be illegal in all or most cases. In contrast, the significant majority (83 percent) of religiously unaffiliated Americans say abortion should be legal in all or most cases. But abortion views are more complicated than a split of the God-fearing versus the godless.

For instance, while the political movement against abortion is fueled by leaders of religious groups, particularly Catholic, Mormon, and evangelical churches, individuals of faith can, and often do, hold beliefs that conflict with those of their religious hierarchies. Of course, women of all faiths have abortions—when it comes time to make a personal decision, religious beliefs can be more nuanced.

Additionally, religions of the world are not uniformly anti-abortion in their beliefs, even though the loudest or most politically powerful anti-abortion religions often drown out other voices. Many mainstream Protestants—Methodists, Episcopalians, Presbyterians—members of Reform and some Conservative Jewish communities, and Buddhists, for example, believe that in certain situations abortion is either mandated or the preferable moral option in difficult circumstances. Those who oppose abortion support only some religious views (their own) and too often use "religious liberty" as a hatchet to ensure that others with contrary positions are unable to act on them. In the process, they diminish not only reproductive freedom but also the religious freedom of those whose views conflict with their own strident beliefs.

No one in the abortion rights camp is arguing that religious women must have abortions against their will. It's about options and choice: "Not the church, not the state, women must decide our fate" and "If you don't support abortion, don't have one" are chants that echo through rallies. Indeed, the right to pray and believe as you wish is protected by the free exercise clause of the First Amendment, and like most abortion rights activists, we respect that mandate.

AT ITS CORE, the abortion debate is an embodiment of the conflict between traditional and more modern concepts of gender roles. In its darkest corners, the abortion debate is about controlling when and with whom sex is appropriate, and when and with whom one has babies. A woman is unfairly branded by the sexual and procreative decisions she makes: married or spinster, saint or sinner, Madonna or whore, selfless mother or welfare queen.

For hundreds of years, until the last several decades, gender roles were clearly defined and enforced by law. A man was expected to make key family decisions, enter the world of work, and provide financially for his wife and children. A woman's role was to bear children and be the primary caretaker of her husband and children, often while working outside the home and providing financially for her family as well. Legally, men had an exclusive right to own property and make all important decisions for their wives and families. Women could not even retain the wages they earned. And those who did not fit into the gender binary were overlooked or ostracized.

As Justice William Brennan explained in *Frontiero v. Richardson*, one of Justice Ruth Bader Ginsburg's early victories from her days at the ACLU,

> There can be no doubt that our Nation has had a long and unfortunate history of sex discrimination. Traditionally, such discrimination was rationalized by an attitude of "romantic paternalism" which, in practical effect, put women not on a pedestal, but in a cage. Indeed, this paternalistic attitude became so firmly rooted in our national consciousness that, 100 years ago, a distinguished Member of this Court was able to proclaim:
>
> > Man is, or should be, woman's protector and defender. The natural and proper timidity and delicacy which belongs to the

> female sex evidently unfits it for many of the occupations of civil life. The constitution of the family organization, which is founded in the divine ordinance as well as in the nature of things, indicates the domestic sphere as that which properly belongs to the domain and functions of womanhood. . . . The paramount destiny and mission of woman are to fulfil the noble and benign offices of wife and mother. This is the law of the Creator.

The vestiges of this patriarchal legal system remained in place well into the early 1970s, when RBG and other women's rights advocates successfully dismantled much of it. While many sexist legal structures were invalidated or diminished, gender bias in the law endures, particularly when it comes to abortion restrictions. Moreover, some of the cultural expectations of women and men have had greater staying power and are deeply entwined with views on abortion.

The research confirms that those who oppose abortion are more likely to be married, have larger families, and participate in religions that perpetuate traditional gender roles. A wide range of conservative groups that draw on doctrines of evangelical or fundamentalist Christianity espouse these traditional views of men and women's differing roles in society and see opposition to abortion as an important part of those values. Childbearing is the goal of heterosexual marriage, with each partner expected to play an ascribed role: woman as mother and caretaker, man as breadwinner and spiritual guide. For example, the beliefs of People of Praise, the insular religious group to which Supreme Court Justice Amy Coney Barrett belongs, include "a strict view of human sexuality that embraces traditional gender norms and rejects openly gay men and women." Despite Justice Barrett's prominent role in the workplace, her religious community is run almost entirely by men and dictates that a husband's responsibilities include "correcting his wife should she stray from the proper path." These gender stereotypes not only limit women's choices they also hamstring men by reinforcing a gender binary that limits choices for everyone from the moment a baby is assigned a pink or blue onesie.

Notably, this traditional view, which places motherhood on a pedestal, applies nearly always only to white women. Since the founding of our nation and the days of slavery, Black women were expected to help white women with childbirth and parenting, while their own roles as wives and mothers were entirely disregarded. Equally problematic, Black mothers, particularly those who are poor, have been devalued and penalized. For centuries, they have been subjected to rape and forced or coerced sterilization, disproportionate removal of their children through child endangerment laws, prohibitions on interracial marriage, and inequitable enforcement of welfare rules. They have also been targeted unfairly with criminal prosecution for drug use and other behaviors during pregnancy.

To counter this systemic racism and exclusion of Black women, we must, as law professor Dorothy E. Roberts argues, expand "the meaning of reproductive liberty beyond opposing state restrictions on abortion to include broader social justice concerns." Reproductive rights are only truly accessible when women of all races are able to make the decision to choose to have a family. While polling shows that the majority of Americans support abortion rights, nonetheless many fail to recognize how out of reach abortion and reproductive health care are for the most vulnerable women, and how imperiled those rights now are for all women, particularly for women of color.

As Roberts and others in the reproductive justice movement have counseled, reproductive freedom cannot be just about access to contraception and abortion. Decisions about whether to start or add to one's family cannot exist in a vacuum. Women also need access to full maternal care, child care, and other family friendly policies at work as well as the ability to live in safety, provide an education for their children, and have the social and economic means to raise them.

In contrast to those with views that would limit reproductive freedom, research confirms that abortion rights supporters embrace the reality that women work outside the home, expect or hope that both parents will share child-rearing responsibilities, accept sex before marriage, and support LGBTQ+ identities, marriage, and parenthood without bias. They believe the availability of abortion is crucial to ensuring that women can determine their own path in life when facing an unplanned pregnancy. The question becomes whether a pregnant woman or one raising a child can make the same choices that men or other women who have no caretaking responsibilities make: where and when to work, get an education, marry, and participate in community organizations and religious life, or not.

We recognize that being a parent can be a tremendously fulfilling part of life: we have both experienced enormous happiness in mothering even as we are aware of how oppressive cultural expectations around motherhood may be. If a woman is not able to control when, whether, and with whom she has children, her ability to fully participate in all aspects of life is limited. In short, abortion matters because it is about dignity, equality, and the chance to fully participate in and control the direction of one's life.

As Justice Ginsburg noted when urging the Supreme Court to ground abortion rights in the Fourteenth Amendment's Equal Protection Clause rather than the right to privacy, as was ultimately done in *Roe*,

> the conflict . . . is not simply one between a fetus' interests and a woman's interests, narrowly conceived, nor is the overriding issue state versus private control of a woman's body for a span of nine months. Also in the balance is a woman's autonomous charge of her full life's course . . . her ability to stand in relation to man, society, and the state as an independent, self-sustaining, equal citizen.

Justice Ginsburg knew this from her own life experience as a lawyer during a time when women, particularly mothers, were rare in the profession. Her deep understanding of the legal framework of gender stereotyping further informed her certainty that this was not a debate that could be reduced to woman versus fetus—a uniquely false dichotomy since, of course, the fetus is entirely dependent upon the woman.

Although Justice Harry Blackmun, the author of *Roe*, initially grounded the abortion right in privacy, by his later years on the Court he agreed with Justice Ginsburg that abortion restrictions were grounded in outmoded assumptions about gender roles that implicated the Equal Protection Clause of the Constitution.

FOR SOME WOMEN, the question of abortion is how to balance employment, education, or other life goals with being a parent. For others, the question is whether to become a parent at all, or how many children to have. Nearly 60 percent of women who have abortions are already mothers at the time they seek abortions, and most need to continue to work, whether or not they have another child.

Evidence shows that there are a diverse range of reasons that influence an individual's decision to seek an abortion or continue a pregnancy to term. The factors that shape the decision are as varied as the individual's situation. Does she have the support of a partner or family, or is she on her own? Does she face financial constraints or housing or food insecurity? How will having a child affect her ability to hold onto her job or advance in her workplace, especially when data show far less career advancement for women with children? Does she have responsibilities for her existing children or other family members? Does she believe she is too young or too old to have a child? Does the fetus have anomalies that will severely affect its quality of life or demand care that the family cannot afford or manage? Will carrying the pregnancy adversely affect the woman's health or future fertility? Or does she simply not want a child at this time in her life? For many women, a dearth of quality, affordable child care and paid maternity leave can also affect their choice.

We know that restrictions on abortion and contraception most severely affect those who have the least access to health care and social supports, particularly low-income women, who are disproportionately Black, Latinx, Indigenous, and Asian American Pacific Islanders (AAPI) and face structural racism. Teenagers, rural women, immigrants, and those living in abusive relationships encounter additional barriers as well. Too often people with disabilities are viewed as being asexual and face public policies that ignore their sexual and reproductive health and their right to parent. All these communities have less access to health services, healthy birthing options, and supportive work with benefits, such as paid sick and maternity leaves or affordable child care. Particularly for low-income women or families, an additional child can conscript them to poverty or hardship.

Of course, not all women who choose motherhood or opt to be stay-at-home mothers oppose abortion. Nor are all women's decisions agonizing or filled with conflict or shame. Many are relieved when they choose abortion and believe it is the best decision for them at the time. The most important point is that these decisions are personal, are theirs to make, and should not be dictated by others or prescribed by the state.

Those who regard motherhood as a woman's most exalted or sole role in life view unwanted pregnancy as simply a bump on the road to greater fulfillment or, alternatively, a blessing like no other. But this blessing is not for all. Scratching the surface reveals the anti-abortion movement's belief that parenthood belongs only to those in heterosexual marriages. In addition to their opposition to abortion, Concerned Women of America, a leading anti-abortion group that "promotes Biblical values and Constitutional principles through prayer, education, and advocacy," believes that sex is only for procreation within marriage. They therefore oppose the use of contraception by young and unmarried women, subscribing to the myth that birth control and abortion will encourage promiscuity or sex without consequences. Importantly they also decry "normalizing same sex and queer attraction and transgenderism" and define homosexuality as "unnatural." Prohibiting LGBTQ+ sex and marriage lies at the core of their social and political views.

As a lesbian mother of two children, Kitty directly saw the ideological links between controlling access to abortion and placing restrictions on sexual relations and childbearing outside of heterosexual marriage. Kitty and her wife, Joann, had been together for over thirty-five years and raised two grown children by the time legal marriage became an option for them. But in the early 1980s, when they decided to have children together, the notion that lesbian, gay, bisexual, transgender, and queer people could be good parents was a radical one, and people on both sides of the political aisle were uncomfortable with it. In recent years, as a result of dramatic cultural shifts, we've seen greater acceptance of

LGBTQ+ parenting as well as the recognition that everyone is entitled to equal justice under marriage and civil rights laws. However, such inclusive views are not universally accepted, and abortion opponents continue to take the lead in pushing against these societal trends.

THE ABILITY TO choose abortion enables women to have control over their bodies or, in legalese, to preserve their bodily integrity. The slogans, T-shirts, and bumper stickers say it best: "My Body, My Choice." "Keep Your Laws Off My Uterus." "Freedom Is For Every Body." As Justice Blackmun recognized in the case Kitty brought, *Planned Parenthood v. Casey*, the Supreme Court as early as 1891 had held that "no right is held more sacred, or is more carefully guarded by the common law, than the right of every individual to the possession and control of his own person, free from all restraint or interference of others." Philosopher John Stuart Mill, in his seminal work, *On Liberty*, phrased it similarly: "Over himself, over his own body and mind, the individual is sovereign," and "each is the proper guardian of his own health, whether bodily or mental and spiritual." Mill's words certainly apply to pregnant women as well.

The very idea of forced pregnancy is a dystopian terror for most women, *The Handmaid's Tale* come to life. Even a "normal" pregnancy produces uncomfortable and often debilitating symptoms over many months including nausea, heartburn, swelling, extreme fatigue, shortness of breath, anemia, urinary tract infections, and back pain. Any pregnancy can affect a woman's physical health in a variety of dangerous ways. Medical complications can include high blood pressure, gestational diabetes, and hyperemesis (extreme vomiting). Forced pregnancy can exacerbate the adverse physical effects and may cause severe mental distress. The latest data show that the mortality and morbidity rates in the US for childbirth exceed that for abortion.

Importantly, the rights protecting bodily integrity that abortion supporters seek can safeguard any woman from those who try to interfere with her reproductive decision. As the Supreme Court found in *Casey*, "[r]esearchers on family violence agree that the true incidence of partner violence is probably . . . four million severely assaulted women per year."

In these abusive relationships violent efforts to influence women's abortion decisions are all too commonplace. Parents also may push their daughters into having abortions against their will. Abortion clinics are particularly sensitive to these dynamics and frequently separate patients from their partners, and teenagers from their parents, to ensure that abortion is an entirely voluntary decision.

Although no one should be prohibited from obtaining an abortion, equally reprehensible are the realities of forced abortion and forced sterilization. Appallingly, state and local governments have a long history of forcibly sterilizing women, particularly women with disabilities, institutionalized women, and women of color. In one of the most despicable Supreme Court decisions of all time, Justice Oliver Wendell Holmes upheld a Virginia law that had allowed, after a court hearing, forced sterilization of disabled women at state mental institutions in order to promote "the health of the patient and the welfare of society."

These practices still continue today, as seen in the allegations of forced hysterectomies on immigrant women at ICE's Irwin County Detention Center in Georgia in 2020. Reproductive rights advocates have stated their opposition to policies and practices such as these, but often not loudly enough. Some have faced legitimate criticism for not making this issue a priority or dedicating sufficient resources to opposing horrific actions that are carried out primarily against women of color and women who cannot advocate on their own behalf.

The notion that one should not be required to sacrifice one's body in service of another has long been a part of America's fundamental legal beliefs. Our laws do not require anyone to donate a kidney to save the life of a family member. Parents are not mandated to donate blood or bone marrow to save their children. Courts have long supported this view. In fact, only three states even require people to aid others in any situation. For example, no one is required to be a Good Samaritan and stop on the highway to save another's life, unless you are in Rhode Island, Minnesota, or Vermont. And even those states only require you to do so to a reasonable extent and without danger to yourself or others. In the same way, pregnant women should not be forced to sacrifice their own health or life to carry a pregnancy to term.

WE HAVE SEEN many advances in reproductive medicine over the last forty years. While new devices and technologies allow individuals a greater ability to have bodily self-determination and autonomy, they do not automatically usher in reproductive freedom. As soon as these new technologies arrive, they become the target of anti-abortion policies that create difficulties and delays for all.

Beginning in 1960, with the Food and Drug Administration's (FDA) approval of the birth control pill, new medical advances have improved the efficacy of and access to contraception. More recent options include intrauterine devices (IUDs) and contraceptive injections like Depo-Provera. In the late 1990s, FDA approval of emergency contraception or "the morning-after pill," a higher-dose hormonal medication that can help prevent pregnancy if taken within a few days of unprotected sex, led to reduced likelihood of pregnancy when contraception is un-available, was forgotten, or fails. Medication abortion approved around the same time offers another safe option for abortion through the first ten weeks of pregnancy; it does not require surgery or anesthesia and may allow a woman to complete the procedure at home on her own.

Each new advance has ushered in new government restrictions to push reproductive freedom further out of reach for many. The com-bination of the sexual revolution, availability of contraception, and feminism's push toward greater recognition of women's roles in the workplace created a wave of progress. Yet as always with women's rights, one step forward, two steps backlash. Abortion poses a grave threat to those who embrace male dominance and traditional gender roles. Al-lowing women a degree of sexual autonomy dangerously unravels the male-based authoritarian system. Not only does this remove power from men in some fundamental ways, it also destabilizes those women who have benefited by conforming to patriarchal ideals and who have an obvious stake in their position as mothers and caregivers. As Gloria Steinem remembers,

> It took us a while to figure out . . . but patriarchy—or whatever
> you want to call it, the systems that say there's masculine and fem-
> inine and other bullshit—is about controlling reproduction. Every

economics course ought to start not with production but with re-
production. It is way more important. And it becomes even more
political when there's racism and caste or class, because the impulse
to preserve [power] means you have to control who has children
with whom, and how many.

As we witnessed in the decades following *Roe*, conservative crusaders
have been relentless in trying to reverse the gains made from the 1960s
onward. Anti-abortion forces have isolated and stigmatized abortion
and successfully put up harmful hurdles to women's access. By narrowing the debate around abortion to women's rights versus fetal rights,
and demanding "fair" coverage of both sides of the debate of this "controversial" issue, abortion opponents have minimized the real-world
consequences of impeding women's access to contraception, abortion,
and maternity care in order to push the notion that sex is only moral if
undertaken for procreation by married straight couples.

Abortion is an issue that has been isolated from other gender equity
matters. Indeed, in coalitions to advance gender equity or health care,
access to abortion is often the first concession made. Particularly when
the reproductive rights of indigent women, marginalized women, or
women of color are at issue, abortion rights may be readily tossed aside
even by pro-choice supporters, either for political expediency or as an
unnecessary, dangerous bow to religion.

The recent outpouring of feminist activism against an established
and powerful political opposition has been inspiring and is cause for
optimism. From the miles of pink pussy hats marching nationwide in
rebuke of Trump's blatant sexism to the millions of #MeToo posts calling out workplace misbehavior that generations of women had been
forced to accept as part of doing business, the younger generation gets
it and is demanding more.

Their more modern call for a new framework for advancing reproductive freedom requires a focus on achieving true gender equity. We
can no longer rely on the Supreme Court's grant of privacy rights in
order to obtain the right to dignity, liberty, and full participation in
society for all. Today's feminists know that fighting for gender equity

without racial or LGBTQ+ equity unacceptably ignores the intersectionality of the lives of women of color and queer people and leaves true
equality off the table. It's why abortion really matters.

As we will spotlight throughout our discussion of our decades of
abortion rights work, relying heavily on individual privacy rights to
empower us to control those decisions most vital to our lives and well-
being has severe limitations. It ignores historic inequality and structural
racism and allows the government to shirk its responsibility to take affirmative steps enabling all individuals to reach the goal of reproductive
freedom. A human rights framework fits far better than the traditional
American reliance on individualism.

It is time for a new direction.

CHAPTER 2

A TEXAS-SIZED WIN
ROE V. WADE

> We are for every woman having exactly as many chil-
> dren as she wants, when she wants, if she wants.
>
> THE JANE COLLECTIVE

ROE V. WADE is a household name synonymous with abortion rights
and among the most widely known Supreme Court decisions. Yet its
holding is as complicated as the woman at its core. The case began quietly enough in March 1970, when two young, gutsy attorneys, Sarah
Weddington and Linda Coffee, challenged a Texas law that banned all
abortions except those necessary to save a woman's life. The law had
been on the books and largely unchanged since 1854. Because Texas
had made it a crime to "procure an abortion" or "to attempt one,"
any person performing the abortion or helping someone to obtain one
would be liable for two to five years in jail.

Weddington and Coffee filed their challenge to the law on behalf of
Jane Roe, a pseudonym to protect the identity of Norma McCorvey, an
unmarried pregnant woman from Dallas who wanted a safe abortion
but couldn't afford to travel to New York to obtain one. Her lawyers,
who were working pro bono, soon requested class certification, asking
the Court to allow McCorvey to represent herself and other women in
similar circumstances.

Years later, McCorvey's involvement in the debate over abortion would take many twists and turns. She switched from being an

anonymous icon for reproductive freedom to a national spokesperson for the anti-abortion cause, undergoing a public baptism by the director of the anti-abortion group Operation Rescue in a Dallas swimming pool in 1995 and proclaiming that she deeply regretted her involvement in the lawsuit that legalized abortion. Upon her deathbed in 2020, McCorvey admitted what many had suspected for years, that she had been paid by an anti-abortion group to speak out against the case that bore her pseudonym. Despite what many saw as the anti-abortion leaders' exploitation of a troubled woman, McCorvey had bravely and crucially represented the interests of Texas women facing unintended pregnancies when it mattered most.

Following the filing of *Roe*'s complaint, James Hubert Hallford, a licensed physician repeatedly prosecuted for performing abortions, asked to join the case. Hallford was one of the first physicians to serve as a plaintiff representing the rights of his patients, now a common practice.

ABORTION OPPONENTS TALK about the 1973 decision in *Roe* as a magic moment when a group of progressive Supreme Court Justices tore the blindfold off justice and ushered in an era of unfettered abortion rights. Yes, *Roe*'s legalization of abortion was a Texas-sized win and the turning point for access nationwide. Its history is more nuanced and thorny, however, and the decision, particularly its aftermath, less liberating than once thought. Nearly fifty years after *Roe*, access to abortion remains impeded and inequitable for many.

When Kitty gives talks about abortion, she often reads a letter from Sherry, an Illinois woman who had an illegal abortion in the days before *Roe*. Sherry survived rape only to be further humiliated and assaulted by an exploitative, unqualified, illegal abortionist. Her own doctor and one "considerably less reputable" had both refused to help her because they feared criminal penalties. Hopeless and terrified, Sherry attempted to induce an abortion by throwing herself down a flight of stairs, scalding the lower half of her anatomy, and pounding on her abdomen with a meat mallet, leaving her "very black and blue and about a month more pregnant." In desperation, she finally turned to an illegal abortionist.

What she remembered most was walking up "three flights of darkened stairs and down a pitchy corridor . . . not knowing whether [she] would ever walk back down those stairs again." The man, visibly drunk while operating on her, offered $20 off the $1,000 fee for a "quick blow job." In the end, more than the degradation she felt—her "gut-twisting fear of being 'found out' and locked away for perhaps twenty years"— more than the life-threatening infection she was ultimately hospitalized for, it was "the dank dark hallway that stayed with her and chilled her blood still." In Sherry's words:

> I saw in that darkness the clear and distinct possibility that at the age of 23, I might very well be taking the last walk of my life; I might never again see my two children, my husband, or anything else of this world. . . .
>
> Thirty years later, I still have nightmares about those dark stairs and that dark hall and what was on the other side of that door. I resent them. I resent more than any words can say what I had to endure to terminate an unbearable pregnancy. But, I resent even more the idea that ANY WOMAN should, for ANY REASON ever again be forced to endure the same.

Sherry survived, but, tragically, thousands of women in similar circumstances did not. Throughout the 1950s and '60s, women with financial means had access to legal hospital-based abortions in limited circumstances. The only option available to less affluent women needing to end a pregnancy was to self-abort or seek an illegal abortion. Although it is difficult to measure accurately, researchers estimate that during those two decades, at least 200,000 and possibly as many as 1.2 million women sought back-alley procedures.

Some of these women died. In 1930, abortion was listed as the official cause of death for almost 2,700 women but decreased considerably in later years. The Guttmacher Institute, a research and policy organization committed to advancing reproductive health worldwide (where Julie serves as the chair of the Internal Review Board), found that "by

1965, the number of deaths due to illegal abortion had fallen to just under 200, but illegal abortion still accounted for 17% of all deaths attributed to pregnancy and childbirth that year."

When the results were not fatal, women still faced significant health consequences, including infection or perforated uteri, which often led to a loss of fertility. The fear and stigma of criminalization coupled with the fact that illegal abortion was largely performed by unregulated and untrained providers often meant that women suffered abuse or psychological trauma, like what Sherry experienced.

Women who could not find an illegal provider or afford services bore children who were unintended and in some cases unwanted. They gave up some of these children for adoption. Others they raised and loved. But too often an unintended pregnancy forced a woman to abandon her own plans for her education or employment, or compelled her into marriage with mixed results.

Not all women faced the impact of unwanted pregnancy equally. For decades the Guttmacher Institute has closely tracked the consequences of abortion restrictions and bans. Their research shows that prior to *Roe*, poor women, disproportionately Black and Latinx, faced a greater risk of death and injury from illegal abortion: "In New York City in the early 1960s, one in four childbirth-related deaths among white women was due to abortion; in comparison, abortion accounted for one in two childbirth-related deaths among nonwhite and Puerto Rican women." The laws prohibiting abortion had dire consequences that we too often forget or ignore because abortion has been safe and legal for so long. But these grim circumstances were what motivated some advocates in the early 1960s to help women obtain safe, albeit illegal, abortions, while others worked within the system to eliminate bans on abortion and enact more liberal laws.

A tight-knit group of women in Chicago formed a collective called Jane to help women find people willing to provide illegal abortions in safe conditions without risk of exploitation or abuse. Their advertisements in student and alternative papers were relatively subtle: "Pregnant? Don't want to be? Call Jane." This collective of activists performed thousands of abortions between 1969 and 1973, using clandestine tactics that preserved the anonymity of the collective and the medical and nonmedical abortion providers who worked with them.

In that era, religious leaders also supported women seeking abortion services. An underground network of ministers and rabbis—many of whom had been active in the civil rights movement—helped women locate safe abortion services. While some worked individually to help members of their congregations, others joined groups like the Clergy Consultation Service that quietly referred women to illegal abortion providers they had found to be safe.

In addition to taking matters into their own hands, supporters of abortion rights began to press for legalization in receptive state legislatures. In 1962, the American Law Institute (ALI)—a panel of lawyers, scholars, and jurists that drafted model statutes on a range of topics—proposed liberalizing the law through a "Model Penal Code on Abortion," which permitted abortion in cases where the pregnant woman's life or health would be at risk, when the pregnancy resulted from rape or incest, or when the fetus had a severe anomaly.

Building on the ALI's prestigious reputation among state legislators, groups like Planned Parenthood, the National Organization of Women (NOW), and the National Association for the Repeal of Abortion Laws (NARAL) stepped up political pressure on receptive state lawmakers. As a result of this pressure from the nascent women's movement, key states began to liberalize their abortion laws. In 1967, Colorado became the first to adopt reforms, in response to an initiative by freshman legislator Richard Lamm, who had become aware of the harmful effects of illegal abortion while living in Peru. Lamm went on to serve three terms as governor. By 1970, four states had joined Colorado—Alaska, Hawaii, New York, and Washington—in repealing their abortion bans and allowing licensed physicians to perform abortions before fetal viability, usually between twenty-four and twenty-eight weeks of pregnancy, when the fetus is capable of independent survival.

While Alaska, Hawaii, and Washington restricted abortion access to their own residents and Colorado required hospital protocols, New York was open to any woman who could afford to travel. New York

became the unofficial "abortion capital of the country." Two years after abortion had been legalized in New York, and just a year before
the Supreme Court's decision in *Roe*, more than a hundred thousand
women traveled to obtain a legal abortion in New York City. Some
arrived from as far away as California, Arizona, and Nevada, while the
majority traveled between five hundred and a thousand miles. But even
with legalization, the *New York Times* noted that the quality of services
varied considerably: a "juxtaposition of good medicine with bad, of al-
truism with exploitation, of efficiency with incompetence, of humanity
with cruelty."

New York became a refuge for women needing abortions from across
the US. Less fortunate women would forgo paying rent or buying gro-
ceries in order to afford getting to New York early enough in pregnancy
to be eligible for a legal abortion. Wealthier women could also take
advantage of England's liberal abortion laws and purchase an advertised
package that included round-trip airfare, passports, vaccination, transportation to and from the airport, lodging, and meals. In other states,
abortions also were available to a small number of individuals who were
able to navigate byzantine hospital protocols. Overall services remained
unattainable for many women nationwide, particularly women of color,
low-income women, teenagers, and those who could neither navigate
hospital protocols nor afford travel.

The experience in New York and the other states that legalized abortion demonstrated the significant and largely unmet demand for safe
and legal health care. In response, lawyers supportive of abortion rights
began to bring legal challenges to abortion bans. Milan Vuitch, a doctor
who had been criminally prosecuted for performing illegal abortions,
asserted that the Washington, DC, law that allowed abortion only in
cases where there was a threat to the life or health of the woman was
unconstitutionally vague. In 1971, in *United States v. Vuitch*, the Supreme Court upheld the DC law but interpreted the term "health" to
include psychological as well as physical well-being, essentially allowing
legal abortion in Washington, DC, whenever a doctor believed it was
necessary to protect a woman's physical or mental health. Both before
and after *Vuitch*, state and federal courts nationwide—in California,

Illinois, Wisconsin, and South Dakota—had found similar restrictive laws to be unconstitutionally vague, laying the groundwork for *Roe*'s acknowledgment only two Supreme Court terms later, that legal abortion would protect a woman's health and well-being. By 1972, the year before *Roe* was decided, a total of seventeen states had legalized abortion in some circumstances.

BECAUSE *ROE* CHALLENGED criminal bans on abortion, the suit named as defendant Henry Wade, a renowned district attorney from Dallas who had prosecuted Jack Ruby, the man who shot President Kennedy's assassin, Lee Harvey Oswald. There is no record of Wade being vehemently anti-abortion, unlike many governors who would be named as defendants in later cases involving abortion.

Lawyers for Jane Roe and Dr. Hallford, who had intervened in the case, argued that the Texas law was unconstitutionally vague, as had been previously argued in *Vuitch*, positing that it was impossible to know what specific actions were subject to prosecution. More importantly they claimed that a pregnant woman's right to end her pregnancy was grounded in the concept of personal "liberty" embodied in the Due Process Clause found in the Fourteenth Amendment. They also invoked the personal, marital, familial, and sexual privacy rights protected by the Bill of Rights or its penumbras.

Eight years earlier in *Griswold v. Connecticut*, the Supreme Court had held that a married couple's right to use contraception is protected by a "penumbra," or zone of privacy guarantees that emanate from the First, Third, Fourth, and Ninth Amendments in the Bill of Rights, even though the Constitution never explicitly mentions privacy. By 1972, the Court had extended this right to use contraception to unmarried women in *Eisenstadt v. Baird*.

Winning a ruling from a three-judge District Court that the Texas law violated the Ninth Amendment and was unconstitutionally vague, the matter proceeded directly to the Supreme Court. The Court then consolidated the matter with a companion case from Georgia, *Doe v. Bolton* (*Doe*).

In January 1973, after Weddington appeared at two rounds of oral argument, the Court issued its seminal decisions in *Roe* and *Doe*. Joined by six other members of the Court, Justice Blackmun wrote the 7–2 majority decision. Just three years earlier, President Nixon had appointed Blackmun to the Court upon the recommendation of Chief Justice Warren E. Burger, a childhood friend of Blackmun's from Minnesota. Having failed to obtain confirmation of two previous picks to fill the vacancy created by the resignation of Justice Abe Fortas, Nixon had been looking for a noncontroversial choice who could be easily confirmed by the Democratically controlled Senate. Blackmun fit the bill. He was a corporate lawyer from a large law firm in Minneapolis, who went on to be general counsel to the Mayo Clinic and then a federal appeals court judge.

The mild-mannered Justice would forever have his name associated with *Roe*. Shortly after the decision was issued, he became a target of protests, vitriol, and hate mail. He told reporters, "It's a new experience for me to . . . be picketed and called Pontius Pilate, Herod, and the Butcher of Dachau and accused of being personally responsible for 500,000 deaths in the past year." Through the decades, Justice Blackmun received death threats from abortion opponents including the Army of God, a terrorist organization responsible for the murders of abortion doctors. In 1985, a bullet shot into his DC apartment shattered glass over his wife, Dottie. The next morning, "a man called Blackmun's office and told his assistant: 'I hope the bullet gets him next time. . . . That murderer deserves to die and he deserves to go to hell.'"

Justice Blackmun also received praise from those who knew how instrumental his voice had been in advancing abortion rights, from women who obtained safe abortions to religious, political, medical, and academic leaders. The Center for Reproductive Rights held a dinner in his honor in New York and established an endowed Blackmun Fellowship to train young lawyers—including Julie—to work on reproductive rights litigation. At the dinner, he presciently noted that the struggle for reproductive rights was a lifelong endeavor, opining that the evolution of the law often took "two steps forward and one back," an admonition that has remained with Kitty as the increasingly conservative Court has marched Blackmun's ruling backward and eroded its protections.

In 1973, when writing the majority opinion in *Roe*, Justice Blackmun was by no means an outlier. The six Justices who joined the *Roe* majority spanned the political spectrum. Justices William J. Brennan Jr. and Thurgood Marshall were the Court's two most liberal at the time. Justice William O. Douglas, appointed by President Roosevelt, served on the Court for thirty-six years and was deeply committed to civil liberties, particularly free speech. Justices Potter Stewart and Lewis Powell Jr. were at the center of the Court's jurisprudence and known as pragmatic moderates. Chief Justice Burger, who would be considered moderate by today's standards, was the most conservative of the Justices joining the majority.

In sweeping language, the majority took note of how an individual's opinion about abortion is formed:

> One's philosophy, one's experiences, one's exposure to the raw edges of human existence, one's religious training, one's attitudes toward life and family and their values, and the moral standards one establishes and seeks to observe, are all likely to influence and to color one's thinking and conclusions about abortion.

But Justice Blackmun noted the Court was charged with making its decision based on the Constitution, devoid of emotion or bias.

The threshold question was whether the plaintiffs had legal standing—were they the appropriate parties to bring the case? As a general rule, a person bringing a federal lawsuit must demonstrate that there is an actual controversy at all stages of litigation. But by the time her case reached the Supreme Court, Roe herself had carried her pregnancy to term and placed the baby up for adoption. Nevertheless, the Court allowed Roe to pursue her claims on her own behalf and those of other pregnant women, carving out an exception for pregnancy, since gestation almost always takes less time than litigation.

The Court also held that Dr. Hallford, who was subject to criminal prosecution, had standing to challenge the law, again on his own behalf and on behalf of his pregnant patients who wanted abortions. This ruling would become central to abortion litigation in the ensuing decades. It provided an avenue for legal challenges without requiring women to engage directly in litigation during or immediately after a crisis pregnancy or to risk revealing their identities. Unfortunately, by 2020, antiabortion lawyers and Supreme Court Justices were taking aim at this doctrine by seeking to require pregnant women to become plaintiffs, as Roe herself had been.

Justice Blackmun reiterated that while the Constitution does not explicitly mention any right of privacy, case law as far back as 1891 had "recognized that a right of personal privacy, or a guarantee of certain areas or zones of privacy, does exist under the Constitution." This privacy right "is broad enough to encompass a woman's decision whether or not to terminate her pregnancy." Significantly, the Court held that the right to make decisions about abortion was not created out of whole cloth. Rather it grew from a long line of previous Supreme Court cases in which intimate and important decisions such as marriage, procreation, contraception, family relationships, and child-rearing were protected. And importantly, the Court held that the rights at stake were *fundamental*.

The use of the term fundamental has particular meaning for lawyers and, in a nutshell, creates a three-step waltz for them to follow:

- First, *Roe* recognizes that abortion rights are entitled to the highest level of constitutional protection, the same as free speech or religious freedom, and therefore any government restrictions must be viewed with a skeptical eye. Lawyers call this *strict scrutiny*.
- Next step, after a woman asserts that her rights have been violated by a state or federal law, the government bears the burden of proving that the law is justified because it promotes a *compelling* state interest. Justice Blackmun held that the state's compelling interests varied throughout pregnancy.
- And, big finish, the state also needs to show that the law is the *least restrictive* way to further that compelling interest. Is there

another way to reach the purported goal other than by restricting abortion?

When *Roe*'s strict scrutiny standard is used, it is very likely that plaintiffs
will be successful at challenging laws affecting abortion—the bottom
line is that *women win*.

Nevertheless, even under *Roe*'s most protective standard, the Court
was clear that a woman's right to an abortion is not absolute. The state
could assert "important interests in safeguarding health, in maintaining
medical standards, and in protecting potential life." These state interests
were not uniform or stationary but changed throughout pregnancy and
became compelling at differing points.

During the first trimester of the pregnancy, the *Roe* Court held, a
state may require that an abortion be performed by a doctor, with the
abortion decision and its implementation "left to the medical judgment
of the pregnant woman's attending physician." Beginning in the second
trimester, the state could enact laws and regulations that safeguard a
woman's health or establish medical standards, such as requiring that
doctors and clinics be licensed in the same way they are for other medical procedures.

The Court drew a line at viability. At that point, the protection of
fetal life became a compelling state interest and states could ban the
procedure. Yet significantly, the Justices agreed that even after viability,
abortion must be permitted if the doctor decides that the abortion is
necessary to preserve *the life or health* of the woman. Thus, throughout
pregnancy, the woman's health and life must always take precedence
over the state's interest in the preservation of fetal life.

There was a great deal of discussion behind the scenes concerning
when a state's interest in protection of fetal life was compelling and
thus would justify a ban on abortion: at the beginning of the second trimester of pregnancy (thirteen weeks), at "quickening" (between sixteen
and eighteen weeks), or at viability (usually between twenty-four and
twenty-eight weeks). Recognizing the difficulty of a one-size-fits-all approach, Justice Marshall pushed for the latest of the three options—fetal

viability—so that a doctor could make a medical determination on a case-by-case basis.

The state of Texas had argued that life begins from the moment of conception and that the state "has a compelling interest in protecting that life" from the very beginning of the pregnancy. Ultimately the Court declined to take a position on when life began because "those trained in the respective disciplines of medicine, philosophy, and theology are unable to arrive at any consensus, [therefore] the judiciary, at this point in the development of man's knowledge, is not in a position to speculate as to the answer."

In 1983, Justice O'Connor addressed the viability line question, noting that recent studies showed fetal viability moving earlier and earlier in pregnancy:

> The *Roe* framework, then, is clearly on a collision course with itself. As the medical risks of various abortion procedures decrease, the point at which the State may regulate for reasons of maternal health is moved further forward to actual childbirth. As medical science becomes better able to provide for the separate existence of the fetus, the point of viability is moved further back toward conception.

But numerous medical experts and scientists in subsequent cases challenged Justice O'Connor's supposition, acknowledging that while increasing numbers of babies born as early as twenty-two to twenty-four weeks survive, fetal lung development prevents survival before then. In later rulings Justice O'Connor acknowledged that while advances in neonatal care had moved viability earlier, that did not justify abandoning *Roe*'s reliance on viability.

ON THE SAME day as *Roe*, with the same 7–2 lineup of Justices, the Court handed down a second significant abortion decision, the oft-overlooked, rhyming case of *Doe*. While *Roe* provided the major framework for abortion rights, *Doe* clarified that doctors would have great latitude to make health care decisions for their patients and specified how states could regulate abortion going forward.

The case was brought by a low-income married woman from Georgia who had been denied an abortion when she was eight weeks pregnant and twenty-three others, including doctors, nurses, clergy, and advocacy organizations. Mary Cano, who was the anonymous Mary Doe, changed her position on abortion after the decision was handed down, just like Norma McCorvey.

Georgia's law had initially been proposed to liberalize abortion restrictions. It permitted abortion when a physician determined in "his best clinical judgment" that the pregnancy endangered a woman's life or health, the fetus "would likely be born with a serious defect, or the pregnancy resulted from rape." Regardless of the stage of pregnancy, the law required that the abortion be performed in a hospital accredited by the Joint Commission on Accreditation of Healthcare Organizations (JCAHO) rather than in a doctor's office or clinic. Significantly, a woman had to gain approval from a gaggle of doctors that included her personal physician, two consulting physicians who examined her, and a committee at the hospital where the abortion was to be performed.

Arguing on behalf of Doe was Margie Pitts Hames, a civil rights lawyer from Atlanta. Though lesser known than Roe's attorney Sarah Weddington, Hames continued to be the chief advocate for reproductive rights in Georgia for her entire career. Hames had "developed the first stirrings of consciousness against both abortion restrictions and racial discrimination in her youth when a schoolteacher stated that the only acceptable time for an abortion was 'when a black man raped a white woman,'" a racist statement that led her to question the anti-abortion beliefs she had been taught as a child.

In *Doe*, the Court upheld the state's requirement that doctors use their best clinical judgment to determine if the abortion is appropriate. But the Court made clear that the doctor's judgment "may be exercised in the light of all factors—physical, emotional, psychological, familial, and the woman's age—relevant to the wellbeing of the patient. All these factors may relate to health."

Although the *Doe* Court gave doctors significant oversight of a woman's abortion decision, it crucially recognized the many overlapping factors that go into an individual abortion decision and acknowledged the significance of abortion in preserving women's health and well-being writ large. Abortion opponents frequently condemn this passage in *Doe*, as they lament that the Court has "effectively made abortion legal through all nine months of pregnancy for almost any reason" and castigate women, who they claim make frivolous decisions about abortion. Anti-abortion legislators frequently use these common refrains to justify a wide range of abortion restrictions, from waiting periods to parental consent and bans on so-called partial birth and sex-selective abortion.

The *Doe* Court also found that allowing an abortion only if performed in a JCAHO accredited hospital—rather than in a doctor's office or clinic—was invalid because there was no evidence that a woman's health could be protected only by having the abortion in a hospital, never mind a JCAHO accredited one. However, *after* the first trimester, Georgia could adopt standards for licensing all facilities where abortions are performed "so long as those standards are legitimately related to the objective the State seeks to accomplish," such as the protection of women's health.

The Court saw no need for the swarm of doctors overseeing the woman's decision. Approval by a hospital committee was not required for other surgical procedures, the Court noted, and to do so for abortion patients would unduly restrict their rights. Again demonstrating its trust in doctors if not in women, the Court noted its belief that a woman's interests were already safeguarded by her own personal physician and thus there was no need for the committee or for the additional certification by two practitioners. The Court (yet again) safeguarded doctors' interests by finding that the requirement would unduly infringe on the physician's right to practice. In each of these matters, the Court demonstrated a faith in doctors' decision making and a need to keep them safe from criminal sanctions; for women—not so much.

ROE AND DOE received a hero's welcome from abortion rights supporters, who recognized them as lifesaving decisions for thousands of women whose forebears had been harmed by illegal abortion. But the opinions garnered criticism from both those who oppose abortion and, to a lesser degree, those who supported legalization. The Court's dissenting opinions offered a stunning and some might argue misogynistic condemnation of *Roe* and *Doe*. Justice Byron White and Justice William Rehnquist were outraged that the Court was permitting a woman to choose abortion for whatever reasons were appropriate to her own life circumstances or to protect her health. Justice White's contempt for and suspicion of women as frivolous and anti-child comes through as he writes: "[D]uring the period prior to the time the fetus becomes viable, the Constitution of the United States values the convenience, whim, or caprice of the putative mother more than the life or potential life of the fetus."

Justice Rehnquist wrote separate dissents rejecting the majority's reliance on the right to privacy. In years to come, Justice Rehnquist would stick tight to his belief that choosing abortion was not a fundamental right because it was not enumerated in the Constitution or otherwise "rooted in the traditions and conscience of our people." He relied upon the long history of laws banning abortion before the adoption of the Fourteenth Amendment as proof that the Amendment drafters could not have intended it to permit abortion (although conveniently forgetting that abortion actually was legal when the Constitution and the Bill of Rights were adopted). In his view, abortion restrictions should be permitted as long as a legislature had a rational reason for passing them.

Although they rejected Justice Rehnquist's view of the Constitution, some abortion rights supporters also wished that the Court had left it to state legislatures to determine the parameters of legal abortion. These critics believed that if left to the political process, eventually there would have been near total liberalization of abortion. This approach to legalization, the theory went, would have resulted in less backlash because the change would have developed more organically from democratically elected state officials rather than being imposed by a federal court. There appears little evidence for this. The movement against abortion began before *Roe* in response to state legislative initiatives and was largely funded and driven by religious institutions whose opposition was equally vociferous whether rights were granted by the legislatures or the courts.

But others had a different critique of *Roe* as being too radical a departure from settled law and thus leaving its foundations susceptible to being maligned or overturned. Justice Ginsburg at a lecture at New York University in 1992 questioned whether *Roe* had grown abortion rights too fast or too far: "Doctrinal limbs too swiftly shaped, experience teaches, may prove unstable. The most prominent example in recent decades is *Roe v. Wade.*" Maybe, she suggested, if the Court had only gone so far as to just strike the extreme Texas law, the whole abortion debate might have proceeded more smoothly.

We are skeptics of this argument and believe there could have been very little forward motion on abortion rights that would have avoided opposition. *New York Times* Supreme Court reporter Linda Greenhouse and Yale Law professor Reva Siegel have responded persuasively, noting that the initial backlash was a response to pre-*Roe* legislative reform, not to the *Roe* opinion itself: "very few people either then or now actually read it. And of course in 1992, in *Planned Parenthood v. Casey*, the Court shifted the balance toward state regulation, and that didn't exactly lower the temperature of the abortion debate."

The ensuing years have revealed *Roe*'s real Achilles heel, one that was obvious to feminist activists when Weddington and Hames approached the all-male bench: the right to choose abortion or childbirth was not squarely within women's dominion or grounded in gender equality. In the lead-up to the Supreme Court hearing *Roe* in 1972, women's rights activists and attorneys had asserted that the right to make procreative decisions was based not simply on the liberty provisions of the Fourteenth Amendment and the Ninth Amendment but also on the Fourteenth Amendment's equality clause.

As discussed in Chapter 1, in order for a woman to participate equally in all aspects of society, she must be able to decide the direction of her life. The ability to control whether, when, or with whom she becomes pregnant is central to women's equality.

The Court's reverence for the men of medicine, rather than the women making decisions about their lives, is not surprising. At the time

Roe was decided, public opinion was firmly in support of allowing abortion to be decided by the woman in consultation with her doctor. Justice Blackmun, who had served as general counsel of the Mayo Clinic, was deeply attuned to protecting physicians. But beyond that, the opinion is a reflection and product of the times in which it was written.

By the early 1970s, the legal guarantees of women's equality that we now take for granted had not yet been established. For example, a woman could be fired for becoming pregnant, a husband could not be prosecuted for sexually assaulting or raping his wife, and sexual harassment in the workplace was not illegal. Eight years before *Roe*, the Supreme Court had recognized that married couples' right to use birth control was protected by the Constitution but extended that right to unmarried women just one year before *Roe*.

Although the Court never explicitly grounded the right to choose abortion in the Equal Protection Clause of the Fourteenth Amendment, in later years, Justice Blackmun recognized that the right to abortion was central to women's equality. In his opinion concurring in part and dissenting in part in *Casey*, he explicitly recognized that, "By restricting the right to terminate pregnancies, the State conscripts women's bodies into its service, forcing women to continue their pregnancies, suffer the pains of childbirth, and in most instances, provide years of maternal care." He went on to acknowledge that the assumption a woman could simply be forced to accept the "natural" status of motherhood rested on sexist notions of gender roles that ran afoul of the Equal Protection Clause. While he remarked that such assumptions about women's place in society were "no longer consistent with our understanding of the family, the individual, or the Constitution," it was too late. The abortion rights ship had set sail with privacy rights on board and gender equity left behind.

In the decades following *Roe*, organized and well-financed opponents of abortion used a variety of effective strategies to both limit women's access to abortion and undermine *Roe*'s jurisprudence. By 1985, abortion opponents had secured the support of the Reagan administration, which for the first time directly urged the Supreme Court to overturn *Roe*, in Kitty's first Supreme Court case, *Thornburgh v. American College of Obstetricians and Gynecologists.* While Kitty was successful in winning the case, its 5–4 margin (a far cry from *Roe*'s 7–2 vote count) signaled to the nation that the Supreme Court was only one vote away from reversing *Roe*. Thereafter, nominees to the Supreme Court were vetted by how likely they would be to vote to save or reverse *Roe*.

Four years later in 1989, when the Supreme Court considered *Webster v. Reproductive Health Services,* both sides of this contentious debate agreed that *Roe* was in hot water, as the Court now likely had five votes favoring its reversal. Although Justice O'Connor upheld the Missouri abortion restriction at issue in the case, she refused to address the key question of whether *Roe* would remain the law. Three other members of the Court would have preferred to limit *Roe* to render it essentially meaningless, while one other would advocate to explicitly overturn it, with the result being to "return to the States virtually unfettered authority to control the quintessentially intimate, personal, and life-directing decision." In his dissent, Justice Blackmun presciently warned of *Roe*'s demise, noting that the rights guaranteed by *Roe* "survive but are not secure."

By the early 1990s, a case was winding its way from Pennsylvania that would give the Court another opportunity to overrule *Roe* and once again give the states the ability to criminalize abortion. As Kitty and her colleagues asked the Court to hear *Planned Parenthood v. Casey,* the future of legal abortion hung in the balance, with the prospect of returning to the days when Sherry, and women like her, resorted to illegal, back-alley abortions.

CHAPTER 3

A HIGH FIVE FROM THE SUPREMES
THE SURPRISING STORY OF
PLANNED PARENTHOOD V. CASEY

At the heart of liberty is the right to define one's own
concept of existence, of meaning, of the universe, and
of the mystery of human life.

JUSTICE ANTHONY M. KENNEDY
IN *PLANNED PARENTHOOD V. CASEY*

KITTY'S STORY:

Arguing before the Supreme Court is informed by the lessons of *Sesame Street*: you need to learn to count, and the only number that matters is five—the necessary votes for a majority. In the summer of 1991, when President George H. W. Bush nominated Clarence Thomas to be an Associate Justice of the Supreme Court, abortion opponents were jubilant. His confirmation would provide the fifth vote on the Court to overrule *Roe*, a goal they had been working toward for nearly two decades.

An unabashed conservative with limited judicial experience, Thomas was tapped to replace Justice Marshall, a judicial lion and the first African American to serve on the Supreme Court. While on the Court, Marshall had developed a solid record in support of reproductive rights. Thomas, in contrast, posed a real threat to these freedoms.

The Senate Judiciary Committee, overseeing Thomas's confirmation, surfaced credible and disturbing allegations that Thomas had repeatedly sexually harassed law professor Anita Hill when she had worked for him at the Equal Employment Opportunity Commission. The committee, an all-male, all-white group, initially dismissed Hill's revelations. As public pressure to allow Hill to testify mounted, a group of resolute congresswomen—Barbara Boxer, Nita Lowey, Eleanor Holmes Norton, Pat Schroeder, Patsy Mink, and Jolene Unsoeld—strode up the Senate stairs to demand that Hill be heard. A powerful photo of the women's ascent appeared on the front page of the *New York Times* and tipped the scales in Hill's favor. Two days later, the Senate committee allowed her to testify.

Hill spoke convincingly about how Thomas, her boss, had asked her out on dates and ignored her refusal to see him socially. He had launched into workplace discussions about sex and would describe to her the graphic pornography he favored, including rape scenes and women having sex with animals.

Joining millions of viewers from across the nation, Julie and I both watched, riveted, as the proceedings unfolded on live television. Julie had traveled to DC for a reunion weekend with a group of college friends. As the Senate took the unusual step of holding hearings through the weekend, Julie watched from a crowded bar, where the gender lines quickly became clear. Although Julie had grown up in the hotbed of Boston sports enthusiasm, this was the first time she witnessed politics as a spectator sport. The Senate's obvious contempt for Hill was horrifyingly echoed by many of the bar's young, bro-culture customers.

While Julie watched the proceedings from a DC barstool, I was glued to the hearings as I worked the phones, urging women's groups and prominent members of the African American community to oppose the nomination and lobby Pennsylvania Senator Arlen Specter, a key member of the Senate Judiciary Committee. In the past, I had voted for and supported Specter. Although a Republican, he regularly voted in favor of abortion rights.

But now, known for his "sharp elbows and porcupine-prickly personality," the aptly nicknamed Snarlin' Arlen became the lead apologist for Thomas. Accusing Hill of perjury, Specter was an effective, albeit dispiriting inquisitor. Specter was not her only antagonist on the

Committee, yet Hill remained calm and composed in the center of the storm.

Chairing the Judiciary Committee, then senator Joe Biden refused to allow a second EEOC employee, Angela Wright, and other witnesses to testify about Thomas harassing them as well. In a private telephone interview with Senate staffers, Wright had relayed strong allegations against Thomas that corroborated Hill's testimony—including that he had arrived uninvited at her apartment one evening and on another occasion had questioned her about her breast size. It was certainly not one of Biden's finest moments; feminists rightly held him to task when during his 2020 presidential campaign he offered Hill only a tepid apology.

For Julie and me, along with so many others who had worked with survivors of sexual harassment and abuse, this type of disturbing workplace behavior occurs all too frequently. Hill's public testimony, with its detailed recollection, was remarkably credible. But to the nearly all-male Senate, it was at best a distraction; at worst, it was what Thomas angrily called "a high-tech lynching" by the committee.

Throughout the confirmation hearings, Thomas worked hard to avoid answering whether he would support the reaffirmation of *Roe*. While recognizing that the right to privacy protected contraception, he declined to go further. Specifically, he testified that he had never discussed *Roe* while in law school or debated its contents in the seventeen years since it was decided. Further, when asked about his public remarks at a Heritage Foundation event where he praised an article that invoked natural law to cast abortion as immoral, he denied that his comments would shed light on his position on abortion.

The votes of Republican senators along with the support of southern conservative Democrats assured Thomas's ascension. The full Senate voted 52–48 on October 15, 1991, to confirm him to the Supreme Court.

Just six days later, the US Court of Appeals for the Third Circuit issued its opinion in the abortion rights case I had been litigating for over two years. *Casey* would reach the Supreme Court less than a year later and become what Justice Stevens called "the most important abortion case that the Court has decided since *Roe v. Wade*."

I HAD BEEN fighting for abortion rights as both a lobbyist and a lawyer with the Women's Law Project in Philadelphia for over a decade. In the 1980s and '90s, Pennsylvania was a breeding ground for anti-abortion sentiment and a pacesetter for other states.

Eleven years before *Casey*, in 1981, the state legislature had passed a series of abortion restrictions, including a requirement that a married woman obtain her husband's consent to have an abortion. By Christmas Eve, the bill had landed on Republican governor Richard Thornburgh's desk for his expected signature, but he surprised everyone, including his staff, and vetoed the bill. Years later, Governor Thornburgh told me that he heard from more Pennsylvanians about that abortion bill than any other issue except the Three Mile Island nuclear accident.

The victory was short-lived. The governor indicated he would support a revised version of the law that deleted the controversial husband consent requirement, and soon thereafter the legislature passed a new version that included a sampling of impediments—waiting periods, biased counseling mandates, and restrictions on late abortion—that took aim at the most vulnerable women who as a result of their poverty, youth, or other factors were least able to overcome these state-imposed obstacles. In practice these restrictions overtly discouraged women from obtaining abortions, increased costs, and delayed the procedure, making it more expensive and less safe since the costs and risks of abortion escalate as pregnancy proceeds. Abortion opponents were passing similar mandates in target states nationwide, creating test balloons to see what restrictions the increasingly conservative courts would uphold.

My cocounsel Tom Zemaitis, a smart, affable lawyer who worked at a large firm in Philadelphia, and I challenged the revised law, known as the Abortion Control Act of 1982, in *Thornburgh v. American College of Obstetricians and Gynecologists* (*Thornburgh*). The case worked its way to the Supreme Court by 1985, when the Court invalidated all of the impediments and by a 5–4 vote unequivocally reaffirmed *Roe*.

At the age of thirty-three, I argued the *Thornburgh* case in the Supreme Court, joining a handful of women lawyers who had argued abortion cases there, and had my first taste of how integral the abortion issue is to national politics. At the urging of the Reagan administration, the solicitor general had asked the Court to overrule *Roe*, permit states to outlaw abortion, and for the first time in history, take away a settled constitutional right. But thankfully the Court was not ready to go there at that time; they lacked a fifth anti-abortion-leaning Justice.

ABORTION OPPONENTS IN Pennsylvania were not giving up just because they had lost *Thornburgh* at the Supreme Court. Three years later, by a substantial and bipartisan margin, the Pennsylvania legislature passed yet another Abortion Control Act. This time, the law was drafted with the help of then Governor Robert P. Casey Sr., who had vetoed an earlier version because it wasn't harsh enough. Casey was a Democrat but put his zealous religious views first when considering abortion legislation.

To stop the new law from going into effect, Zemaitis and I launched the *Casey* case in federal district court in Philadelphia. Linda Wharton, a dedicated women's rights advocate recently hired by the Women's Law Project, joined us in representing a doctor who performed abortions along with five abortion clinics across the state, including Philadelphia's Planned Parenthood affiliate. Both the doctor and the clinics brought suit on behalf of themselves and their abortion patients. Governor Casey was the named defendant, as he was responsible for enforcement of the law.

By the time *Casey* was filed, I had taken a job as an attorney with the Reproductive Freedom Project of the ACLU in New York. Following years of work on behalf of abortion clinics in Pennsylvania, I was thrilled to join the national-level work at the esteemed and well-resourced ACLU. Janet Benshoof, the director of the project, had created a new position for me just months after I joined: I would spearhead the ACLU's efforts to defeat anti-abortion bills in state legislatures and in Congress. These bills were being introduced at an alarming rate, and the work pace was often frenetic. Some weeks I would take the train to New York, fly to DC, and then return to Philly. Other weeks I would fly to state capitals to try to defeat proposed abortion restrictions.

While I was traveling around the country, my life partner, Joann—now my wife—and our two young children remained in Philadelphia. My grueling travel placed a huge strain on Joann, a partner at a large law firm, as she assumed the lion's share of responsibility for the care of our young children. Without Joann's support as a lawyer and life partner it would have been impossible to continue the work I loved, as abortion advocacy became a family affair for us.

Legal cases that challenge the constitutionality of a state law start small in either the federal or the state system. Because the provisions at issue in *Casey* were so similar to those Zemaitis and I had challenged in *Thornburgh*, the team went back to federal district Judge Daniel Huyett III, who had ruled in our favor in *Thornburgh*, and asked him to place the law on hold until a trial could be held and the Court ruled. As expected, he quickly held a hearing and then issued an injunction. Abortion access in Pennsylvania was safe from the many restrictions at issue in *Casey*—for now.

Casey challenged five provisions of a law that had been specifically crafted by abortion opponents to sound reasonable. The first provision mandated that a doctor recite a litany of information intended to discourage a woman from having an abortion and then to wait twenty-four hours before the abortion could be performed. Like the nearly identical provision found unconstitutional in *Thornburgh*, the law forced women to travel to the clinic twice, sometimes over several weeks, since clinics did not perform abortions every day. Particularly for low-income women, teenagers, and those who lived far from a clinic, the two-trip requirement made abortion more expensive and delayed their ability to obtain necessary care.

The act's requirement to "go home and think about it" typecast women as fickle decision makers when it came to abortion. Perpetuating the stereotype of women as irresponsible and capricious is a tactic often used to undermine women's agency in making abortion decisions. One particularly egregious example of such mythmaking came in 1996, after Catholic bishops ran a full-page advertisement in the *Washington Post* claiming that a teen had sought an abortion in order to fit into her prom dress. Exposed as a fiction and rescinded by the Church a year later, the myth is still perpetuated by anti-abortion crusaders.

A second provision required a married woman to notify her husband that she was about to have an abortion. Evidence showed that more than

90 percent of married women already discussed their abortion choice with their husbands. But the law had an especially devastating effect on women living in troubled and dysfunctional marriages, particularly those in abusive relationships. This provision echoed the worst elements of an archaic legal system that well into the mid-1800s considered a wife to be her husband's property. Not only did this provision guarantee that a married woman had fewer rights than her single counterpart, by lumping all married women into one category it also overlooked the diverse realities of marriage—including domestic violence, infidelities, and estrangement—and even in the best of matrimonial circumstances created unnecessary and harmful delays.

The act further targeted a young woman's ability to make an abortion decision by requiring minors to obtain the consent of one parent prior to seeking an abortion. As an alternative, a minor could go before a judge and seek a court order allowing her to obtain an abortion without her parent's consent through what is known as a judicial bypass procedure. For teenagers who tend to ignore or be ignorant about the signs of pregnancy, or who delay seeking help out of fear or naiveté, obtaining a parent's consent or navigating the judicial bypass procedure risked parental abuse, unnecessary stigmatization, and additional dangerous delays.

Another provision included a requirement that the state must publicly disclose detailed information about each abortion. Only in very limited medical emergencies could a doctor be exempted from the law's strictures.

DURING THE THREE-DAY trial before Judge Huyett in the district courthouse in Reading, Pennsylvania, the legal team aimed to create a strong factual record that would help sway Justice O'Connor, should the case make its way to the Supreme Court. Justice O'Connor was the only woman on the Court at the time and was considered one of the swing Justices. To win, we would need to secure her vote. Because she was often concerned about whether a law would adversely affect individuals, we focused a large part of the trial testimony on the law's impact on women who lived in abusive marriages and teenagers who were estranged from their families.

The state of Pennsylvania, represented by lawyers from the attorney general's office, relied on unsubstantiated pseudoscience to argue that the law was necessary to protect women's health. Their chief witness, Vincent Rue, the creator of a cockamamie theory that has remained popular in anti-abortion circles, claimed that women suffered from what he named "post abortion syndrome," akin to post-traumatic stress disorder (PTSD), often suffered by war veterans and trauma survivors. He had devised this theory a few years earlier and was eager to bring it to the courts, but it had never been substantiated.

Rue testified as an expert about problem pregnancy decision making, marital family relationships, and psychological effects following an abortion, but on cross-examination I was able to prove that he was not a psychologist and that he had received his advanced degree from a school of home economics in North Carolina. Judge Huyett found that he had never conducted a controlled research study or been published in a refereed journal and that the American Psychological Association had found no scientific studies that support the existence of a "post abortion syndrome," as suggested by Rue. Judge Huyett found him "not credible" and that Rue's testimony lacked "analytical force and scientific rigor" and suggested "a personal bias." Nevertheless, over the following decades Rue would continue to spread his specious theories in numerous cases and even collected tens of thousands of dollars in fees from the state of Texas to testify in support of an abortion restriction there.

Ultimately Judge Huyett held that most of the provisions at issue in *Casey* were unconstitutional. He struck down the waiting period, biased counseling, husband notice, parental consent, and narrow medical emergency provisions. The Court upheld only the provisions requiring doctors to determine gestational age (already a routine procedure) and the requirement that doctors report information about their patients to the state, but only if the state kept the information confidential.

Predictably, Pennsylvania immediately appealed the ruling to the US Court of Appeals for the Third Circuit. The state was hoping it would be one of the first cases to reach the Supreme Court and be the test case to overrule *Roe*. About six months later a three-judge panel convened to hear oral arguments and make its decision.

I received a copy of the Appeals Court opinion by fax one crisp fall afternoon in mid-October 1991, the curled shiny pages arriving just six days after Clarence Thomas had been confirmed to the Supreme Court. I had argued the appeal before the Third Circuit in February of that year and was surprised that the Court had taken so long to issue its opinion. The Court of Appeals, like the nation, had awaited a change at the Supreme Court.

Like all experienced litigators, I had received my share of disappointing rulings. Yet I was truly shaken by the Circuit Court's reasoning. In a brazen and shocking move, the Court of Appeals had reversed eighteen years of settled legal precedent found in *Roe* and its subsequent case law, disregarding the judiciary's practice of giving deference to previous cases that involve similar facts or legal issues. Rather than wait for the Supreme Court to take the monumental step of overturning precedent, the three judges acted on their own, hacking away at the strict legal standard that had been the abortion law of the land for nearly two decades and consistently reaffirmed.

The Court upheld as constitutional all of the Pennsylvania restrictions except the husband notification provision. The provisions requiring minors to inform their parents, the medically harmful and unnecessary waiting period, and the medical emergency definition were all given the green light to impede access to abortion.

The Appeals Court announced a new "undue burden test" that would permit states to make abortion much more difficult to obtain, modeled on a test contained in an earlier dissenting opinion that Justice O'Connor had written in 1983. A third member of the panel, Judge Samuel Alito, went even further, and his opinion also upheld the husband notification provision. Judge Alito had been appointed to the Third Circuit by President George H. W. Bush and would join the Supreme Court fifteen years later after President George W. Bush nominated him to the seat vacated by Justice O'Connor.

That evening, I spoke to a group of young, mostly female college students at Hampshire College. I was very emotional when talking about the ruling and almost burst into tears as I explained that if *Casey* went to the Supreme Court, the case could be the likely vehicle for the new conservative majority to reverse *Roe*. More selfishly, I was panicked that my clients would have to decide whether we dared risk giving the Supreme Court the opportunity to do so. As I looked out over the audience, I was devastated by the prospect that this next generation might not have the right to abortion for which I had fought my entire career.

WITH JUSTICE THOMAS on the Court, most experienced court watchers, including those from anti-abortion groups, believed that there were now five votes to overrule *Roe*. Faced with an imminent and certain loss in the High Court, our team had two equally bad choices: we could move slowly by seeking consideration of the full Court of Appeals, delaying the inevitable reversal of *Roe* but enabling millions of women access to safe and legal abortions as the case wended its way to the High Court. Although going slowly would take our clients off the hot seat for now, there were numerous other cases pending in the lower federal courts that raised similar questions. Some were challenges to abortion restrictions like the Pennsylvania law. Other cases from Guam, Louisiana, and Utah challenged more onerous bans on abortion. Many state legislatures across the country, controlled by anti-choice majorities, were poised to pass new measures with the hope that their law would be the test case leading to the overruling of *Roe*.

Alternatively, we could speed up review as fast as possible so the case would be decided by June 1992, prior to the 1992 presidential election. The theory was that if *Roe* was overturned by June when the Supreme Court closed for the summer, abortion would become a key issue in the election. Since Democrats controlled both the US House and the Senate and there was a pro-choice majority in each chamber, the election of a pro-choice president would enable Congress to pass a nationwide law that offered women greater protections than what the Court would establish. We thought of this as the "go down fast but swinging" approach. It was up to our clients to hear the options and then decide for themselves.

The clinic directors and I were a close-knit group. The women tasked with deciding how to proceed understood better than most what was at stake for women facing unintended pregnancies. Some of them, like Sherley Hollos, Artis Ryder, Sue Rosselle, Rusty Stengel, and Carole Wall, had been providing health care to women for decades. Others, like my close friend Morgan Plant, the head of Planned Parenthood's lobbying arm, spent their time in Harrisburg, needling and cajoling politicians. They were fighters, and they wanted to win for the long run, not just this particular skirmish. Fully aware that the best shot at firming up abortion rights long-term was to win the presidential election in 1992 and pass a national law protecting women, they supported an appeal to the Supreme Court.

Because of an agreement I had made with him back in 1985 when *Thornburgh* went to the Supreme Court, it was Zemaitis's turn to argue *Casey*. But within a few weeks, he dropped off the team. He had recently taken a new job where his employer was not keen on him having such a public role in America's most divisive debate. As a result, I would take the lead at argument.

Later that week, with marching orders in hand, Wharton and I met with my colleagues at the ACLU to map out a detailed strategy. I, like my clients, wanted to put all the cards on the table and ask the Court to address *Roe*'s validity, rather than take a more legalistic view that focused on how the Court of Appeals had overstepped its role. We knew that we needed a way to easily explain to the American people why the case was so important. We settled on a radical but practical solution— ask only one question of the Court: "Has the Supreme Court overruled *Roe v. Wade* holding that a woman's right to choose abortion is a fundamental right protected by the United States Constitution?"

To this day, I think that the petition I filed asking the Supreme Court to hear our case is the best legal work of my career—mostly because it wasn't legal at all. In the form of a small, thirteen-page bound booklet that the Supreme Court anachronistically still requires, it was meant as an opening salvo in a campaign to make abortion a key issue in Congress and the 1992 presidential election. I had dictated the first draft with the help of David Gans, a phenomenal paralegal who had a nearly perfect recall of case citations and holdings—had he not later gone to law school, he would have been great at counting cards in Vegas. Andrea Miller, my assistant at the time, whom I often referred to as the other half of my brain, was able to cut through the legalese to help the public better understand what was at stake, a role she continues now as president of the National Institute for Reproductive Health.

On the morning I asked the Supreme Court to take the case, colleagues at the ACLU along with the leaders of major pro-choice groups assembled at the National Press Club in Washington, DC. Ira Glasser of the ACLU, Kate Michelman of NARAL, Faye Wattleton of Planned Parenthood, Ellie Smeal of the Feminist Majority, and others made clear that pro-choice organizations across the country were unified. For the next several months, these leaders repeatedly emphasized that the Supreme Court was poised to overrule *Roe* and that when they did so, Congress must pass a federal law protecting women, and a newly elected, pro-choice president must sign it into law.

With the papers filed, it became a waiting game—and wait I did. Like many families, I focused on the upcoming holidays, traveling to Ohio to visit with Joann's family over Christmas and then to Florida to celebrate my dad's birthday on New Year's Day. But even after the holidays, the Court kept putting off consideration of the request. Years later, I would learn that there were great internal struggles about how to handle the case.

Chief Justice Rehnquist, perhaps fearing considerable backlash if the Court overruled *Roe* before the presidential election, or perhaps just angry at what one journalist had called my "transparently political" framing of the question, began to unilaterally delay consideration, with the hope the Court would run out of argument slots in the spring.

Justice Blackmun's papers and other reporting offer a rare window into the controversy around granting consideration to *Casey*. According to their recounting, Justices Blackmun and Stevens's early entreaty to the Chief to bring to a vote whether the Court would hear the case went unanswered. Justice Stevens then made an unorthodox threat that forced the Chief's hand: for the first time in Court history, Justice Stevens, joined by Justice Blackmun, agreed to make public the Chief's delaying tactics by writing a dissent to the procedural order holding the case over for another week. Because this had never been done before, the Justices knew that the Supreme Court press corps would write about it and that the Chief would be seen as playing politics with the Court's docket. In response to this novel move, the Chief relented and listed the matter at the next conference, where the Court voted to accept review.

Normally the Court simply accepts the petitioner's framing of the question at issue. However, instead of accepting my stark question, "Is *Roe* still the law?" or the state's alternative, the Court took the unusual step of changing the legal questions to be considered. They adopted more moderate phrasing that asked whether the Court of Appeals had erred when it found most of the Pennsylvania law constitutional, thereby focusing attention on the individual provisions of the law rather than the continuing validity of *Roe*. *Casey* was set for argument on April 22, 1992, the last argument day of the term.

With their lifetime appointments, Supreme Court Justices are supposed to be impervious to public opinion and above the fray of political debate. As the sole unelected branch of the federal government, the Court is always sensitive about maintaining its legitimacy with the public and not being seen as ideologues. Yet while the Justices may have every intention of ignoring the dynamics of public opinion on controversial issues, it is unlikely that they can remain completely unaware of public sentiment.

With this in mind, grassroots abortion rights activists took the lead on rallying public support while the Supreme Court considered the case. The National Organization for Women organized a March for Women's Lives in support of abortion rights on the first Sunday in April, a few weeks before the argument. These were the days of landline telephones and shiny paper fax machines. Because the internet was not yet widely used and mobile phones were large, clunky, and rare, the organizing effort was more difficult than in today's connected climate. But NOW succeeded beyond all expectations:

At least half a million people marched from the White House to the Mall near the Capitol. . . . The crowd, perhaps the largest ever to march on Washington, was estimated by the police at 500,000 and by the organizers at 700,000. . . . They included mothers and daughters, Hollywood stars, teachers, preachers and doctors, Republicans for Choice, Catholics for Choice and two Presidential candidates, Bill Clinton and Edmund G. Brown Jr.

Joann and I were in DC that day with our children and took turns holding Sam's hand or pushing Kate along in her stroller as we marched. The mall was filled with people from across the nation sporting colorful signs and spirited posters in what felt more like a parade or celebration than a serious or angry political protest. A few of the most rabid anti-abortion activists with their bullhorns and grotesque pictures of bloody fetuses lined the parade route, but they were far outnumbered and ignored.

That afternoon, I climbed onto the large stage at one end of the mall to speak. While I have little memory of what I said, I can still remember that I was both extremely nervous and excited about the huge crowd. There were people as far as I could see, and perhaps for the first time, I let myself feel the enormity of what I was trying to do and how many Americans cared deeply about the rights at stake.

I BEGAN TO get blowback from experienced Supreme Court litigators who thought that my all-or-nothing approach was too risky and radical. Wharton and I had argued in our court filings that if the Court abandoned its practice of affording abortion the highest level of constitutional protection, then it would be overruling *Roe*. Almost all of the non–reproductive rights litigators thought that I should push for the adoption of an undue burden test, giving the Court a way to avoid full repudiation of *Roe*. In contrast, the reproductive rights lawyers, more keyed into the politics of the issue and the fact that abortion was treated differently from almost any other issue before the Court, wanted me to keep pushing the significance of eliminating the most protective standard of *Roe* as long as possible. If the Court was going to adopt a more restrictive legal standard, they certainly were not going to get my blessing to do so.

For about a week before oral argument, I camped out in a large suite at the Henley Park Hotel in DC, a stately if slightly worn hotel only a few blocks from the Court. A line to attend the *Casey* argument began to form outside the Supreme Court at nine a.m. on Tuesday morning, over twenty-four hours before it would begin. Gans, my paralegal, left to stand in line, unwieldy cell phone in hand in case I needed him. I called him at midnight with worried questions about the names and holdings in several Supreme Court cases, only to discover that thunderstorms had forced the Court to move the waiting line indoors, where everyone could camp out safely on the basement floor. Dependable as ever, he answered my questions as he, along with my clients, sat in sopping wet clothes and awkwardly close quarters with impassioned abortion opponents.

After a long sleepless night, I spent time in the morning guzzling coffee and donning my new black suit, white silk blouse, and flowered scarf. Most people who know me consider me something of a schlump. Luckily Joann, who had driven down from Philly with Sam the night before, has a much better sense of fashion. She had helped me pick out the conservative suit mandated by Court rules (well before pantsuits were in vogue) and that morning made sure I looked presentable, with hair, makeup, earrings, and scarf all in place. I put on the watch my parents had given me the day of the *Thornburgh* argument. It had brought me luck then, and I hoped that it would do so again.

As I settled into the lawyers' room at the Court, Marcia Coyle, the Supreme Court reporter for the *National Law Journal*, stopped by to say hello and asked if I had had anxiety dreams the night before. She reminded me that prior to *Thornburgh*, I had classically dreamed about standing up before the Court without my skirt on. But this time around I had had no anxiety dreams, mostly because I didn't sleep all that much.

The courtroom where Supreme Court arguments are held is small—only eighty-two by ninety-one feet—and more intimate than you might expect, given the gravity of its rulings and the power the Justices exercise there. Surrounding the room are twenty-four marble columns. The rich red carpets and regal upholstery may be more suited to a monarchy than a third branch of a democratic government. The Justices sit, emanating from the center in order of seniority, on a raised bench with red velvet drapes through which they emerge in formation at the start of the daily arguments, promptly at ten a.m.

There is a lectern and microphone facing the Justices, and a mahogany table for the opponents on either side. Unlike many more modern courtrooms, advocates are close enough to talk with the Justices, rather than orate at them. When the Chief Justice announced the case and invited me to start, with a bit of a quiver, I began:

> Whether our Constitution endows Government with the power to force a woman to continue or to end a pregnancy against her will is the central question in this case. Since this Court's decision in *Roe v. Wade*, a generation of American women have come of age secure in the knowledge that the Constitution provides the highest level of protection for their child-bearing decisions. This landmark decision . . . not only protects rights of bodily integrity and autonomy, but has enabled millions of women to participate fully and equally in society. . . .
>
> Government may not chip away at fundamental rights, nor make them selectively available only to the most privileged women.

After nearly eight minutes of uncomfortable and extremely rare silence from the bench, Justice O'Connor wondered whether I would address the individual provisions at issue in the Pennsylvania law. But I ignored her request and pushed forward, concentrating instead on preserving *Roe*'s framework of abortion as a fundamental right.

Next up came Justice Antonin Scalia, the Justice most wed to originalism, a controversial theory of constitutional analysis that looks to what the framers understood the Constitution's text to mean at the time of its drafting to determine its meaning today. He pushed me on where in the specific language of the Constitution and within our country's history and traditions the abortion right resided.

Justice Scalia and many of his fellow conservatives believed that the Fourteenth Amendment's Due Process Clause, which protected the right to marry, use contraception, and choose abortion, for example, should only be recognized in very narrow circumstances when there was a long history of laws that specifically protected these rights. Justice Scalia wanted me to concede that there was no long history of laws protecting abortion, and that in fact states had prohibited abortion from the mid-1800s to 1973, but I didn't take the bait. Rather, I argued that the Court needed to look generally at "whether the Nation's history and tradition has respected interests of bodily integrity and autonomy and whether there has been a tradition of respect for equality of women," the central and core values at stake, rather than whether the states specifically had outlawed or permitted abortion at any one point in time.

When Pennsylvania Attorney General Ernie Preate began, he argued that *Roe* need not be "revisited by this Court except to reaffirm that *Roe* did not establish an absolute right to abortion on demand, but rather a limited right subject to reasonable State regulations designed to serve important and legitimate state interests." This mischaracterization of *Roe*'s holding was immediately met by an incredulous Justice Blackmun, who asked Preate "whether he had read *Roe v. Wade.*" Some in the audience gasped, while others laughed. Preate stumbled several times over what he wanted the Court to do—adopt the Court of Appeals' undue burden test or allow states to adopt any rational regulations, including bans on abortion.

Next to argue was Solicitor General Kenneth Starr representing the administration's anti-abortion views. He was dressed in his formal morning coat with tails stiffly jutting out behind him. Morning coats are a holdover from when all attorneys arguing at the Supreme Court were required to wear them. They were required for solicitors general until 2009, when the first female solicitor general, future Supreme Court Justice Elena Kagan, was appointed to the position by President Obama. Starr was clearly at home in his suit, as he was in the Court. The tenor of the arguments shifted significantly as he approached the lectern.

First, Justice Stevens wanted to know whether the Justice Department had a position on when life began and whether the fetus is a person protected by the Constitution. Starr deftly avoided answering that, for if he asserted that the fetus was in fact a "person," then all states would be mandated to outlaw abortion altogether, a position too extreme even for this conservative Court.

Instead, Starr implied that under the rational basis test that the government sought, states would be free to ban all abortions, so long as there was an exception for those small number of abortions necessary to save a woman's life. In my view, this was the turning point in the argument, as the Justices starkly understood that the government's position would give states the ability to ban abortions, a position I hammered home on rebuttal.

With the argument over, I felt exhausted yet relieved. While I didn't think I had changed any minds, I had not made any concessions or major gaffes. I scooped up my papers and grabbed the quill feather set out for all advocates, then went out to meet my family and make my way to the swarm of reporters at the bottom of the Court steps. Governor Casey was in the scrum as well, and his security detail did their best to prevent me from reaching the microphones. But with a bit of help from Zemaitis and Planned Parenthood attorney Roger Evans, I wormed my way to the front with Sam at my side.

I continued to stress to the numerous reporters that nothing less than the continuing legality of abortion was at stake. The following morning, the *New York Times* printed substantial excerpts from the arguments in a two-and-a-half-page spread that started on the front page, highlighting that the Court was poised to overrule *Roe*.

WHILE THE NATION waited for the Supreme Court decision to be handed down, my colleagues and I at the ACLU Reproductive Freedom Project had another major decision on our minds. Janet Benshoof had long wanted to leave the ACLU to launch a new independent organization whose sole focus would be to advance reproductive freedom and work not just in the US but internationally, which wasn't possible if we stayed as a project of the ACLU. I agreed to cofound the organization with her and others from the ACLU.

We dubbed our new organization the Center for Reproductive Law and Policy—now known as the Center for Reproductive Rights—and developed secret plans to leave en masse. We agreed that I would become the Center's vice president and take responsibility for all domestic litigation, policy advocacy in Congress and the states, and the organization's communications shop. My only condition was that the separation from the ACLU had to wait until after the *Casey* oral argument.

While I was enmeshed with *Casey*, Benshoof, with quiet support from Warren and Susan Buffet, found office space in a high-rise at the bottom of Wall Street and worked to assemble the furniture and equipment we would need to make a seamless transition to the new organization. As soon as the *Casey* argument was complete, we surreptitiously began moving books, files, and personal items out of the ACLU. At the beginning of June 1992, the Center was born.

Needless to say, the ACLU was not pleased to lose their largest litigation unit, our numerous clients, and Benshoof, one of its most accomplished lawyers and prodigious fundraisers. Joann and I were moving to a new house near Philadelphia the week my colleagues and I left the ACLU, and as soon as we arrived with the moving van, I received a FedEx package from the ACLU with a formal notice of my firing. Too late.

For the next several days there was a mad scramble as our clients decided whether they wanted to stay at the ACLU or be represented by Center attorneys. All of my clients, including the Pennsylvania clinics, stayed with me. As planned, when *Casey* was decided, I would be identified as an attorney for the new Center.

IT IS RARE that you know when a Supreme Court case will be decided. But June 29 was the last day for the Court to issue opinions that term, and *Casey* had not yet been handed down. I went to DC and was greeted by an amazing spectacle: dozens of trucks with large satellite discs surrounded the Court, as media from across the world prepared to broadcast the decision live from the courthouse steps. There were hundreds of activists from both ends of the political spectrum carrying signs and chanting slogans as they awaited the Court's ruling.

A standard maxim among Supreme Court advocates is that you can lose a case at oral argument but never win one. I never expected to win; indeed, my entire strategy was predicated on the view that I would lose. I had expected the Court to overrule *Roe* and allow states to ban abortion and that at least ten states would do so almost immediately. So when the Court upheld the hallmarks of *Roe*, I was perhaps more surprised by the high five from the Supreme Court than anyone in the courtroom.

Usually, only one Justice writes an opinion, which other members of the Court join. If there are five votes, it is called a majority opinion. If the Court is more fractured and there are four or fewer votes for what is written, it is called a plurality opinion. And if Justices agree on the outcome but not the reasoning, they can file a concurring opinion. If they disagree with the majority and concurring opinions, they can file a dissent, which recognizes their dissatisfaction with the result and some or all of its reasoning.

But in *Casey*, Justices O'Connor, Anthony M. Kennedy, and David H. Souter jointly wrote one opinion. In the five decades before *Casey* was decided, the Court had issued only five joint opinions. The issuance of a joint opinion highlighted the significance of the Justices bucking what everyone had expected them to do.

In cases where the Justices want to emphasize their opinions, they read excerpts from the bench. That morning, four of the Justices spoke for thirty minutes, which seemed like an eternity.

Justice O'Connor went first, and in her reedy, slightly quavering voice she reaffirmed what she considered the essential finding of *Roe*: that a woman has the right to choose an abortion until fetal viability, and thereafter when her life or health is endangered. But then Justice O'Connor went on to recognize that the state has a "legitimate interest from the outset of pregnancy in protecting the health of the mother and the life of the fetus that may become a child . . . so long as it does not unduly burden the woman's right to choose."

Justice Kennedy then spoke, reading more quickly from the joint opinion, and in exalted language recognized the physical pains and anxieties that a woman faces during pregnancy. He noted that "the destiny of the woman must be shaped to a large extent on her own conception of her spiritual imperatives and her place in society." But Justice Kennedy did not stop there, shifting his focus to emphasize what he found as the competing interests that the state possesses:

> Yet it must be remembered that *Roe v. Wade* speaks with clarity in establishing not only the woman's liberty but also the State's important and legitimate interest in potential life. . . . Though the woman has a right to choose, to terminate or continue her pregnancy before viability, it does not at all follow that the State is prohibited from taking steps to ensure that her choice is thoughtful and informed. . . . Throughout the woman's pregnancy the State may enact measures designed to persuade the women to choose childbirth over abortion.

Justice Souter continued in his slower cadence, explaining that even if the conclusion in *Roe* was wrong, preserving precedent was more important. He argued that "[a] decision to overrule *Roe*'s essential holding under the existing circumstances" would come "at the cost of both profound and unnecessary damage to the Court's legitimacy and to the Nation's commitment to the rule of law." *Roe* had created a workable solution that people had relied on for their most intimate decision making for nearly two decades.

By this time, I was reeling from the heady talk, historic nature, and surprising result of the ruling. I wondered what it would mean for my clients and the women they served. Except for the husband notification requirement, the joint opinion had upheld the majority of the Pennsylvania law, four of the five challenged provisions. Importantly, it chiseled away at *Roe*'s legal standard, adopting a new, less protective "undue burden test" to judge the constitutionality of abortion restrictions going forward. A law would be invalid only when its "purpose or effect" was to place a "substantial obstacle" in the path of a woman seeking an abortion before viability. An anti-abortion law could make women jump over hurdles or go through hoops, but not to excess and only if there were at least some minimal justification from the state. But my clients' worst nightmare, a complete ban on abortion, was not allowed.

The reading did not stop with the troika who authored the joint opinion. In a powerful, assertive tone, Chief Justice Rehnquist took the majority to task for continuing to uphold the hallmarks of *Roe*, which he and three other Justices would overrule. Clearly the joint opinion had been a result of a slew of negotiations and alliances among the Justices, meant to preserve the essential elements of *Roe*.

In contrast, Justice Stevens agreed with much of the joint opinion but took issue with its abandonment of *Roe*'s trimester framework. He further noted that even under the new undue burden standard, he would find most of the provisions unconstitutional. He recognized that the state had some interest in making sure that a woman has the full information needed to make a "thoughtful and informed" choice but that

> [d]ecisional autonomy must limit the State's power to inject into a woman's most personal deliberations its own views of what is best. The State may promote its preferences by funding childbirth, by creating and maintaining alternatives to abortion, and by espousing the virtues of family; but it must respect the individual's freedom to make such judgments.

The state could favor propagation as part of a pro-family bias but must do it in supportive ways, not by restricting access to abortion.

Justice Blackmun was more emphatic in his opinion. He cautioned about the fragility of his *Roe* legacy:

> I remain steadfast in my belief that the right to reproductive choice is entitled to the full protection afforded by this Court . . . and I fear for the darkness as four Justices anxiously await the single vote necessary to extinguish the light.

As the Justices disappeared behind the curtains, the Supreme Court's clerk pulled me aside and handed me a precious copy of the lengthy opinion. This gave me a few minutes to skim the multipart 169-page

decision before most members of the press corps. I walked into the hallway and stood at the top of the steps while I read portions of the opinion over the phone to my colleagues back in New York and to Wharton
in Philadelphia.

By the time I walked down to the scrum of reporters at the base of the
steps, I knew I would focus on the loss of *Roe*'s heightened protections
and the unleashing of the Court's new undue burden standard. My immediate response—that the Court had driven a Mack truck through *Roe
v. Wade*—became more tempered later in the day, as it finally sunk in
that the Court had not taken the opportunity to give states the chance
to ban abortion altogether. *Casey*'s upholding of the central hallmarks of
Roe was a significant victory, and a big relief—but far from perfect. As
the Court became more conservative in the following years, it would use
Casey's vague language to uphold more and more restrictions, allowing
anti-abortion forces to move abortion out of reach for far too many.

Years later, I learned that I had been correct in assuming the worst:
at the time of the oral argument in *Casey* there had been five votes on the
Court to overrule *Roe* outright. According to Justice John Paul Stevens's
memoir, immediately following the argument, the Court had adjourned
to their conference room and taken a preliminary vote. Chief Justice
Rehnquist, joined by Justices White, Scalia, Kennedy, and Thomas, had
agreed that the Court of Appeals had been correct in upholding most
of the law. The Chief assigned himself the job of writing the opinion.

The story goes that before the opinion was filed, Justice Kennedy
had a change of heart that ultimately would change the lives of many
women for decades to come. Working secretly with Justices Souter and
O'Connor, the three sought a more tempered approach and together,
with only the help of one clerk from each of their chambers, began
crafting the joint opinion.

On May 29, 1992, only two days after the Chief circulated his draft,
which would have ended *Roe*'s protection outright, Justice Kennedy
sent a note to Justice Blackmun saying, "I need to see you as soon as you
have a few free moments. I want to tell you about some developments in
Planned Parenthood v. Casey and at least part of what I say should come
as welcome news."

On June 3, Justices O'Connor, Kennedy, and Souter circulated a draft joint opinion among the other Justices that supported the Third Circuit's conclusion about each provision but contained a long and persuasive explanation of why "the essential holding of *Roe v. Wade* once again should be endorsed, continued, and reaffirmed." Justice Stevens and Blackmun made suggestions about how to rework the opinion so that they could join the first three sections. The majority "adopted most of my suggestions," noted Stevens, and with five Justices on board for the first three sections of the joint opinion, those holdings became binding precedent going forward. It was all about counting to five.

Despite all that has been written about *Casey*, I still can't be sure what it was that led to Justice Kennedy's changed thinking and his willingness to join the other Justices in a compromise that preserved access to abortion for the following three decades. It may well have been a shared concern that the Court was increasingly being seen as a political body. Rather than having the law turn on settled principles and respected reasoning, Justice Kennedy may have been fearful of having it look like the law turned willy-nilly on the individual political views of the Justices, who in turn largely reflected the views of the president who appointed them. That perception threatened to undermine the legitimacy of the Court as a neutral body. The enormous negative attention to the Court during the Anita Hill hearings just before *Casey*, and the public outcry over the loss of *Roe*, had only exacerbated those fears, as they would years later during the raucous Senate confirmation hearings of Justice Brett Kavanaugh and the highly controversial full-speed-ahead nomination of Justice Barrett during the 2020 presidential election.

Perhaps Solicitor General Starr admitting during oral argument before the Court that a return to a rational basis test would permit states to ban all but lifesaving abortions was just too extreme a step for Justice Kennedy to take. Or maybe he had greater empathy for an individual's procreative and sexual rights than he had previously revealed. Subsequent to *Casey*, Justice Kennedy would author four major Supreme Court opinions in support of rights for LGBTQ+ people, including his 2015 landmark opinion in *Obergefell v. Hodges*, which for the first time held that the Fourteenth Amendment requires states to recognize the marriage of two people of the same sex.

Nevertheless, when some today say that the Court would never permit states to ban abortion, I point out how wrong that is. Justice Rehnquist, joined by four Justices, did so in 1992, and only a late change of heart saved that opinion from becoming law. And now at least five Justices on today's conservative Court are likely to do so again.

CHAPTER 4

A *ROE*-SHAPED PIÑATA
FIVE DECADES OF ABORTION LITIGATION IN THE US

Assault on *Roe*'s legal framework should begin by enacting carefully drafted statutes which prompt the judiciary to consider expansion of an interest in the unborn, to include all stages of gestation, and limit the definitional scope of abortions allegedly performed for maternal health.

VICTOR ROSENBLUM AND THOMAS MARZEN,
ANTI-ABORTION LEGAL STRATEGISTS

IN 1987, A widely overlooked book, *Abortion and the Constitution: Reversing* Roe v. Wade *Through the Courts*, laid out the primary legal strategy abortion opponents would pursue for decades. These fervent anti-abortion attorneys, brought together by Americans United for Life, the leading anti-abortion legal group, recognized that the reversal of *Roe* would take careful planning and a long-term strategy. There were several prongs. First, hack away at *Roe*'s foundations by discrediting the origins of the constitutional right to privacy, and expand the recognized justifications for restrictions. In this way they would gradually develop a new theory of constitutional jurisprudence that could subsume *Roe*'s entire rationale. Next, target restrictions to particular types of vulnerable women—indigent women or young women, for example—and once upheld, apply the limits to a wider group.

These challenges would need to be heard by federal courts packed with conservative judges who would be willing to upend the law. Ultimately, conservative Supreme Court Justices would be key to *Roe*'s demise. Arguing that "nothing can be a substitute for patient deliberation, exhaustive research, and a grand design," this group of almost entirely male lawyers committed to working for the reversal of *Roe* until the job was done.

Combatting these relentless tactics developed by a well-funded and politically connected opponent, abortion rights advocates were kept busy on all fronts, overwhelmed by the swarm of anti-abortion laws that poured out of a hive of states dominated by conservative legislators and governors. Too often we were consigned to playing defense, with the rules of the game and the playing field largely controlled by our opponents. Along the way, the movement had some significant wins—increased access to new technologies and contraception, safer abortion, and the expansion of women's health care under the Affordable Care Act—but in the main, our end goal and priority was to save *Roe*. The landmark case had become a piñata that kept taking hits.

UNDER *ROE*, ONCE a plaintiff alleges that a law infringes on a woman's privacy, the state must come forward with a *compelling* reason that supports the intrusion. The Supreme Court in *Roe* had found two compelling justifications for limiting abortion access: the protection of women's health starting at the beginning of the second trimester of pregnancy and the protection of fetal life starting at viability. Thus the anti-abortion strategy, pushed by Americans United for Life, focused on enacting carefully drafted statutes that enable courts to undermine both of these justifications.

To ramp up the Court's recognition of fetal life before viability, their plan was to emphasize the "biological human character of the fetus" and argue, as Justice O'Connor had suggested in a 1983 case, that fetal viability occurs much earlier than the twenty-four to twenty-eight weeks of pregnancy recognized in *Roe*. The focus turned toward such scientifically nebulous concepts as fetal pain and early "heartbeat" sounds to justify bans on abortion earlier and earlier in pregnancy. Anti-abortion legislators additionally enacted bans on late abortion, naming them "partial birth" abortions that are performed both before and after viability.

Abortion opponents also were eager to undo the importance *Roe* had placed on protecting women's health as a justification for abortion. Recognizing that the public believed protection of women's health was more important than protecting fetal life, particularly early in pregnancy, abortion opponents began to claim that they were "pro-woman" and committed to women's health. They created groups with officious names like the Center for Medical Progress or the Center for Bio-Ethical Reform and used them to disseminate specious medical information and unsupported assertions about the physical and mental health risks of abortion—that abortion causes breast cancer, damages future fertility, and increases women's risk of suicide or depression. Such alleged risks are completely unsupported by the scientific literature and have been rejected by mainstream medical organizations such as the American College of Obstetrics and Gynecologists and the American Psychological Association. Nonetheless, state legislators and some courts relied on these erroneous claims to support burdensome health restrictions such as mandatory waiting period laws, state-sponsored misinformation on the risks associated with abortion, and the implementation of excessive, unnecessary clinic regulations known as Targeted Regulation of Abortion Providers, or TRAP laws.

In addition, anti-abortion lawyers would ask the courts to rely on legislative findings rather than medical judgments or the prevailing views of the medical community to determine whether the restrictions actually furthered this purported interest in protecting women's health. Finally, they sought to narrow the protection of women's health to allow postviability abortion only in cases where denying access would create "severe and long-lasting" risks to the woman's physical health. Mental health harm was deemed irrelevant, or bogus, as were physical conditions such as preeclampsia, inevitable abortion, and premature ruptured membranes, which might or might not be "severe" enough to meet this standard.

The last element of the legal strategy was focused on filling vacancies on the lower federal courts and the Supreme Court with judges who believed that *Roe* was wrongly decided and who were willing to forsake the traditional doctrine of precedent that would normally require them to give great deference to the decision.

Beginning in the 1980s, with the political power of the Moral Majority and President Ronald Reagan as a strong and savvy ally, the anti-abortion movement launched its strategy. Its high-ranking supporters in the Senate confirmed a pipeline of ultra-conservative anti-abortion judges onto the lower courts nationwide, who were then short-listed for a Supreme Court nomination. One by one, they added anti-abortion conservative judges from this group onto the Supreme Court, beginning with Justice Thomas and followed by Chief Justice Roberts and Justices Alito, Gorsuch, Kavanaugh, and Barrett. With a 6–3 majority in place by 2020, they now have surpassed the magic number five necessary to overturn *Roe*. The appointment of Justice Barrett positioned them to do so even without demonstrating the respect for precedent and procedural restraint previously needed to bring along Chief Justice Roberts, who prefers chiseling away at *Roe* rather than an outright reversal.

THE ANTI-ABORTION MOVEMENT became even more politically powerful by forging an alliance with the Republican Party. Outside the beltway in the states where Republican legislators held power, they passed a host of abortion restrictions at a fast and furious rate throughout the 1980s and '90s and on into the new millennium. Unfortunately, it took the Democrats almost a decade to publicly support abortion, as party leaders (mostly white men) were fearful of losing working-class Catholics who had long been a part of their base. The political battles waged in state legislatures were key to anti-abortion success. In the four decades after *Roe*, the anti-abortion movement's state-level strategy resulted in over one thousand abortion restrictions being passed into law.

The pace of restrictive laws varied over the decades, but was most pronounced when legislators believed that the appointment of new Supreme Court Justices would increase the likelihood that *Roe* was toast and their law could make that happen. The redrawing of state legislative district lines following the 2010 census swept abortion opponents into power in state capitals nationwide. An avalanche of restrictive laws soon flowed from these states. Between 2011 and 2016, over four hundred laws restricting abortion had been enacted and countless more introduced, which according to the Guttmacher Institute, gives that period the "dubious distinction" of accounting for more abortion restrictions than any other single five-year period since *Roe*. As a result, abortion access was whittled away state by state, clinic by clinic, and doctor by doctor, leaving significant hurdles that made abortion rights simply a shell for many.

The attacks combined to make abortion expensive, risky, and often unavailable. The more vulnerable and disempowered a woman was, the further out of her reach abortion was. Those seeking the reversal of *Roe* urged legislators to target restrictions on particular types of women, primarily poor women, women of color, and young women, who had less political power to defeat the measures legislatively. Once these restrictions were upheld in court, other states were quick to adopt broader versions. Laws that cruelly denied Medicaid funds for low-income women to pay for abortions later served as a rationale for banning all abortion funding in government health insurance programs.

WHEN IN 1992 the Supreme Court did not reverse *Roe* in *Planned Parenthood v. Casey*, many abortion rights supporters mistakenly believed that they had won the war and that *Roe* was safe from further attack. Progressives focused on expanding civil rights and liberties in other areas. Legalizing LGBTQ+ marriage and equality, funding initiatives through the Violence Against Women Act, seeking equal pay for women through the Lilly Ledbetter Act, and advancing similar state-level laws brought much-needed victories. The extraordinary outpouring of support for the Women's March following President Trump's election as well as the #MeToo movement galvanized supporters and demonstrated a new energy for political engagement. Although many abortion organizations and their members participated, and abortion rights were certainly on the to-do list, this new activism had far wider reach than decades of relentless battles for abortion rights.

During the Trump years, a host of unimaginable restrictions on immigrants, a loosening of environmental rules, and repeat attacks on the

Affordable Care Act required an all-hands-on-deck defense to protect many of the key gains made over preceding decades. Rightfully, racial justice came to the forefront, as brutal policing practices were exposed and mass protests demanded reforms nationwide. The reproductive justice movement has grown significantly in the past twenty years and linked systemic racism to the denial of reproductive freedom for women of color who had been left behind by the traditional pro-choice movement. Many national abortion rights organizations had to scramble to modernize their mission and leadership to reflect this need but are making significant progress.

Despite fierce opposition, however, in the last decade, a number of legislative advances for women's equality and reproductive justice have been made. Perhaps the most significant improvements arrived with the passage of the Affordable Care Act, which increased the availability of health care, including birth control, preventive services, and reproductive health care to over twenty million Americans, although it excluded undocumented immigrants from coverage.

The availability of more effective and safer contraceptive methods and the morning-after pill, now over the counter, also dramatically decreased the rate of unintended pregnancy and thereby decreased the need for abortion. And a widening availability of medication abortion and telemedicine has the potential to increase access to safe abortion in areas of the country that lack providers. While quality sex education is still not available in many schools across the nation, today any young person with internet access can find accurate information about sex, sexuality, and abortion from the privacy of their bedroom, laptop, or library cubicle.

Throughout history, Americans have had a tendency to take their rights for granted and have not been prepared to fight back until the last minute when less can be done. Decades of watching dark clouds roll in over *Roe* and crying that the sky is falling, however true, rendered that message powerless to spur action. The subtle actions that succeeded in making abortion out of reach for many gave a false sense of security that *Roe*, and with it abortion rights, remained strong.

As we write, the Trump-reconfigured Supreme Court is poised to take away the constitutional right to abortion or erode its protections so significantly as to make it meaningless to the majority of American women. When it succeeds (it is not *if* any longer), we know this will not be the end of abortion rights in the US; rather it is the beginning of a new stage of the fight.

It is well within the power of abortion rights supporters to reverse these trends. However, doing so requires that we commit to a long-range, multipronged strategy, just as the anti-abortion movement has done. It is time to acknowledge that "saving *Roe*" is no longer the ideal goal. Rather, we have an opportunity to redefine our big asks, expand our demands to include a broader concept of reproductive freedom and justice for all, and set in motion affirmative, human rights–based strategies that will unify abortion rights supporters, and the broader women's and LGBTQ+ movements to guarantee equality in a range of arenas. We have an opportunity to ensure that *everyone*, not just the most elite or those who live in majority-Democratic states, has access to essential reproductive health care.

Decades of battles to protect reproductive freedom have taught us much about why abortion matters. As we now face some of the biggest threats to the future of our rights and freedoms, we consider in these pages how we got to this precarious place and then propose an audacious, effective plan to safeguard the rights we hold dear.

CHAPTER 5

DR. JEKYLL AND REPRESENTATIVE HYDE
THE BATTLE OVER
GOVERNMENT FUNDING FOR ABORTION

> There is something drastically wrong with a conception
> of reproductive freedom that allows this wholesale ex-
> clusion of the most disadvantaged from its reach. We
> need a way of rethinking the meaning of liberty so that
> it protects all citizens equally.
>
> DOROTHY ROBERTS, AUTHOR AND LAW PROFESSOR

REPUBLICAN CONGRESSMAN HENRY HYDE, a white-haired Pillsbury
Doughboy doppelganger from the Chicago suburbs, was vehemently
anti-abortion and very effective in implementing his agenda. During his
first year in the House of Representatives, he led the effort to successfully pass a budgetary amendment with a singular focus: ending federal
funding of abortion for Medicaid recipients. Enacted in 1976, the Hyde
Amendment has been renewed every year since and has survived a Supreme Court challenge. It remains in effect today as the most destructive abortion restriction ever passed.

Over his thirty-two years in office, Representative Hyde held sway
with many members of Congress and never shied away from advancing
his views. Even if you support a woman's right to choose abortion, he'd
argue, taxpayers should not have to pay for it. Members on both sides
of the aisle agreed, thinking that they were adopting a reasonable middle ground on an issue that divided their constituencies. They closed

their eyes to its bias and the devastating effects that the funding ban had on millions of low-income women, particularly women of color. Hyde's amendment was the first step in his ultimate goal of ending all abortions. "I would certainly like to prevent, if I could legally, anybody having an abortion, a rich woman, a middle-class woman, or a poor woman. Unfortunately, the only vehicle available is the . . . Medicaid bill," he said, during the floor debate on his amendment.

Currently federal funding for abortion is prohibited under Medicaid, the Children's Health Insurance Program (CHIP), and Medicare, resulting in low-income women and women with disabilities being denied coverage. Over the years, the Hyde Amendment has included a variety of (very narrow) exceptions to the ban on funding—today it pays for abortion only in cases of rape, incest, and life-endangering pregnancy. As a result, nearly all women dependent on these programs are prohibited from obtaining funding.

The impact of the Hyde Amendment is enormous. As the Guttmacher Institute notes, abortion is prohibitively expensive for those with low incomes. A first-trimester abortion costs an average of $500, almost a third of the monthly income for a Medicaid-eligible family of three. A woman who lives in an area without an abortion provider or who has to make multiple trips to a clinic to comply with waiting period laws incurs additional expenses for transportation, food, overnight accommodations, and child care. Low-wage workers who often lack paid sick leave additionally lose wages and tips for the lost work time.

Without funds to pay for an abortion, women must divert limited resources from their families' other critical needs like rent or food, and may fall into a downward spiral. In the time it takes to raise the funds to have an abortion, the procedure can move to later in pregnancy and therefore be more expensive as well as more medically complicated and harder to obtain. For a woman who has progressed to the second trimester of pregnancy, the median cost rises considerably, averaging $1,195 for an abortion in the second trimester and $3,000 or more if past that.

Still other women, desperate to terminate a pregnancy, will attempt to self-induce or turn to illegal providers. In fact, just two months after the Hyde Amendment was implemented, Rosie Jimenez, a twenty-seven-year-old woman from McAllen, Texas, tragically died from an illegal abortion. A Mexican American daughter of migrant farmworkers, Jimenez was raising her five-year-old daughter as a single mother while studying to become a teacher. Because it was half the cost of a legal abortion, Jimenez obtained an unsafe, illegal one and contracted a bacterial infection in her uterus. She died less than two weeks later, leaving her daughter to be raised by relatives. As the first woman to die after the passage of the Hyde Amendment, Jimenez's death received national attention. The National Latina Institute for Reproductive Justice continues to keep her memory alive and spotlights how so many low-income Latinx people of reproductive age rely on Medicaid for their health care coverage and disproportionately bear the brunt of the Hyde Amendment.

For the government to use the power of the purse to influence or impede a woman's decision making is odious and unfair. The Hyde Amendment in particular sticks in our craw and has been something we have fought against for decades. A lack of funding puts abortion entirely out of reach for some, while women with means or access to funds may have an entirely different set of options. According to the Guttmacher Institute, approximately one-quarter of women who would have Medicaid-funded abortions instead give birth when this funding is unavailable.

Of the millions of people affected by the funding ban, a disproportionate number are women of color: 31 percent of Black women and 27 percent of Hispanic women of reproductive age were enrolled in Medicaid in 2015, compared with just 15 percent of white women. For these women, forced childbearing coupled with systemic racism in their communities causes a parade of negative social and economic effects, including reduced lifetime income and decreased educational opportunities, unwanted marriages, and overall negative health outcomes. Data on unintended children born from forced childbearing show a higher rate of infant mortality and morbidity, behavioral problems, and chronic medical conditions. While some women choose to carry an un-planned pregnancy to term with positive outcomes, forced childbearing because of a lack of affordable abortion services is a far more unfair scenario that perpetuates racial disparities and inequities for women and their families.

From its inception, the harmful and unjust effects of denying funding for abortion services were obvious to lawyers working to protect the rights of low-income people. The first cases that challenged state-level Medicaid funding restrictions at the Supreme Court, *Beal v. Doe* and *Maher v. Roe*, came out of work done by welfare rights advocates and neighborhood legal services lawyers. These two cases challenged the constitutionality of requirements in Pennsylvania and Connecticut that gave full funding for childbirth but provided no financial support for abortions unless doctors could certify they were medically necessary.

Unfortunately, there was no victory for poor women. The majority of the (wealthy, old, white, male) Justices failed to grasp what it was like to be a woman unable to afford an abortion and rejected all the statutory and constitutional claims in *Beal* and *Maher*. In 6–3 opinions, the Court found that neither the Medicaid statute nor the Constitution required states to fund all medical services. The Court emphasized what it viewed as a significant difference between a government policy that placed restrictions *directly* on abortion versus a policy that simply denied necessary funding in order to encourage (we would say coerce) women to select childbirth over abortion.

In 1976 when the Hyde Amendment was first enacted, a group of creative, committed lawyers from the Center for Constitutional Rights joined forces with the ACLU and Planned Parenthood of New York City to try again to shatter Medicaid funding restrictions. They brought a class action lawsuit against the secretary of Health and Human Services with a range of plaintiffs that included among others Cora McRae, a low-income pregnant New Yorker on Medicaid, hospitals and doctors that provided abortion services, and the Women's Division of the United Methodist Church. Rhonda Copelon, a fiery and compassionate human rights lawyer, made a strong Supreme Court argument in

Harris v. McRae. Over the next thirty years, she would work against gender-based violence and racial discrimination worldwide, and become a close friend and mentor to both of us.

Copelon and her colleagues in *Harris* asserted Fifth Amendment equal protection and due process arguments. The lawyers conceded that the federal government was not obligated to fund abortions; however, once it decided to fund all other medically necessary health services under Medicaid, the government could not single out abortion to be treated differently and worse. The extensive trial record demonstrated the harms wrought by the law, including that a legal abortion cost more than the entire monthly stipend for a family on welfare at the time, and that as a result some women would be forced to carry their pregnancies to term.

In a 5–4 decision, the Supreme Court again dropped the ball. It ignored the district court's factual findings, instead working to distinguish when a government actively blocked a woman's path to abortion as opposed to when it simply ignored her desperate need:

> Although government may not place obstacles in the path of a woman's exercise of her freedom of choice, it need not remove those not of its own creation, and indigency falls within the latter category.

In other words: *we didn't make her pregnant, we didn't make her poor, and we don't have to help her.* The majority was fine with the fact that the Hyde Amendment left an indigent woman with the same range of "choice" as she would have had if Congress had decided not to provide any health care aid at all.

In addition, the Court acknowledged that the impact of the amendment fell on indigent women but asserted that it did not itself render the funding restrictions constitutionally invalid, because poverty alone does not entitle a person to any shelter from the Equal Protection Clause. Nor would the Court recognize that the Hyde Amendment had a disproportionate impact on Medicaid recipients on the basis of race or sex despite the fact that it affected women who were disproportionately people of color. The law was considered rationally related to the legitimate governmental objective of protecting potential life and therefore was upheld.

The four dissenting Justices in *McRae* were incensed by the harsh and discriminatory effect of the Hyde Amendment. They focused on the fact that the denial of funding for "the poor and powerless" was tantamount to the denial of access to abortion altogether. Although the dissenters acknowledged that as a general rule the government can impose conditions on its funding, it cannot require the relinquishment of constitutional rights.

Medicaid is structured as a jointly funded state and federal program to provide health care for low-income people. Since the Supreme Court's *McRae* decision applies only to the federal funds in Medicaid, states may use their own funds to pay for abortion services if they so choose.

But in Pennsylvania, anti-abortion legislators had other plans. Following *Harris v. McRae*, in 1982, they passed a law cutting off state Medicaid funding for abortion. Pennsylvania would pay for an abortion only when a woman's life was endangered or in a case of rape or incest. The state added an additional requirement that the woman must promptly report the assault to the police before seeking an abortion. Because the Supreme Court had closed off the federal route, Kitty challenged the funding ban in state court, arguing that it violated the Equal Rights Amendment and equal protection clause of Pennsylvania's Constitution.

Each state has its own constitution. These unique documents, some of which predate the federal document, may contain rights more protective than those in the federal Constitution. The federal Constitution serves as the floor for rights; any state can offer more but cannot go lower.

Although the litigation was successful at delaying the cutoff of funding for five years, ultimately Kitty's arguments failed to convince the court. The case, *Fischer v. Department of Public Welfare*, wound its way to the Pennsylvania Supreme Court, which opted to interpret its own Constitution as providing the same rights as the US Constitution, despite the differing language in the two documents. The Court ruled that the "mere fact that only women are affected by this statute does not necessarily mean that women are being discriminated against on the basis of sex." It instead held that the state's funding decision was based on the fact that one class of women chose abortion while the other women chose to give birth, "a voluntary choice made by the women."

Fortunately, by 1986, legal challenges in state courts in California, Connecticut, Massachusetts, New Jersey, Oregon, and Vermont reached different and better results, finding that the cutoff of Medicaid funding violated their state constitutions or other state laws.

Abortion rights attorneys continue to believe in the power of state constitutions to provide greater recognition of women's rights to abortion. From the early days of the Center, Kitty spearheaded a concerted campaign that used state constitutional claims to expand the number of states that provided funding. These cases presented an opportunity to play offense, expanding abortion rights and effectively rendering void a particularly egregious Supreme Court ruling.

The goal of the campaign was to ensure coverage for at least half of Medicaid-eligible women in the US. Over the years, the Center filed seven such lawsuits in states nationwide. Attorneys from allied organizations, including the ACLU and Planned Parenthood, joined the Center in some of these cases or pursued similar litigation on their own. This litigation successfully expanded Medicaid funding in Alaska, Arizona, Minnesota, Montana, New Mexico, and West Virginia, although the hard-fought victory in West Virginia would later be scuttled by an amendment to the state constitution, and currently Arizona officials are refusing to abide by the positive ruling there.

In the decades following these initial cases, strong legislative advocacy by reproductive justice activists and allied organizations persuaded an additional seven states to fund abortion under their state Medicaid programs. Today sixteen states, either through court order or legislation, have bucked the Supreme Court and enable their Medicaid-eligible residents to obtain abortion funding for all or most abortions. Another seven pay for abortions in some limited circumstances that go beyond the Hyde limits. A lawsuit Julie launched challenging Indiana's abortion funding ban, which her Center colleague Bebe Anderson took to the

Indiana Supreme Court, gained some limited coverage for instances in which a Hoosier's pregnancy posed "a serious and irreversible risk to her health." Several other states pay where there are fetal anomalies. But the remaining thirty-three states still conform to the severe federal Hyde standards.

THERE IS A certain ferociousness about how low-income women and their families are targeted on those rare occasions when they do seek Medicaid funding for abortion services—for example, when their life is in danger or they are survivors of rape and incest. Not only do women have to jump hurdles of bureaucracy, but in some cases government officials have openly harassed or retaliated against them.

One particularly egregious example was the case of a rape survivor whom the Center defended when she faced criminal charges in 1997. In the only criminal case in her career, Julie, along with the Center's talented litigation director, Simon Heller, rushed to Crawford, a small town in Nebraska's panhandle that calls itself "an integral part of the Old West's folklore." A young woman, Michelle Hanig, had become pregnant after being violently raped by a man she knew. She was on Medicaid and had driven eight hours to a clinic near Omaha, where Dr. LeRoy Carhart performed an abortion without charging her, because he knew Medicaid would pay in a case of rape.

Carhart, a dedicated physician, provides some of the country's only abortions later in pregnancy. He has a warm demeanor and unwavering dedication to women. Shortly after helping Hanig, he became a plaintiff in the Center's challenges to both Nebraska's and the federal ban on so-called partial birth abortion, each of which went all the way to the Supreme Court.

But after Hanig returned home from the clinic, the local county attorney Vance Haug, in a two-paragraph criminal complaint riddled with mistakes and typos, charged her with Medicaid fraud and false reporting because she had not pressed criminal charges against the man who had allegedly raped her. Hanig herself had been brought into the local police station twice for questioning, which she found completely traumatizing, but she maintained that she did not want to press charges, because, as she told Julie and Heller, she feared for her safety and that of her two young children. That the man who raped her was well connected in her small town, she said, was the likely reason for the police harassment.

County Attorney Haug perpetuated an old-time western sheriff stereotype that Julie struggled to fight off whenever she looked at him. He seemed surprised to see Heller and Julie arrive to represent Hanig, displeased by the weighty reply brief they filed to dismiss the charges, and downright intimidated by the *New York Times* reporter they had tipped off to the case. Now no longer bullied by the legal system, Hanig rejected the state's plea offer. The charges against her were dropped in less time than it took her attorneys to find a vegetarian meal before heading back to New York. Haug, however, remains in power today.

Nebraska is by no means the only state that refused to fund those rare abortions permitted by the Hyde Amendment. Reproductive rights legal groups won a number of such cases in Pennsylvania, Kentucky, Illinois, and elsewhere to ensure states funded those abortions required by federal law. But many individual women are unaware of their rights or, like Hanig, fear being harassed about reporting the rape or incest, and consequently are denied coverage.

ANOTHER PARTICULARLY BRUTAL aspect of the denial of federal funding for abortion is that it lacks an exception when there is a severe fetal anomaly. The denial of funding in such cases is especially punishing because fetal anomaly is diagnosed later in pregnancy, involving more expensive medical procedures. The Center decided to challenge this policy on behalf of a woman from Massachusetts who was insured through a federal plan for military families, which included a Hyde-like ban on abortion funding.

Maureen Britell was a lively redhead who would go on to become a charming and fierce advocate for abortion rights and a delightful colleague. Sadly, Britell's fetus had suffered from anencephaly, a rare condition that results in certain death in utero or almost immediately upon birth. After Britell and her husband had consulted "their family, doctors, grief counselors, psychiatrists, and their parish priest," all of whom agreed with Britell's decision, she had an abortion at the New England Medical Center. The procedure was difficult, including thirteen hours of painful labor and delivery. When the Britells' military health insurance denied coverage, the Medical Center sued them in state court for the cost of the procedure; the case settled when they paid $4,000. The Center attorneys then sued the federal government in federal court for refusing to pay for the abortion.

An initial ruling in the Britells' favor was overturned on appeal by the Federal Circuit Court of Appeals, which found that despite the severe fetal anomaly, the government interest in the protection of fetal life was legitimate and sufficient to justify the denial of funds. The court found that the ban was rationally related to the state's legitimate interest in potential human life, even in cases of anencephaly where there is no chance of survival. The Britells decided not to appeal the case to a Supreme Court that would likely be similarly unreceptive.

The Britells' case demonstrates how the Hyde Amendment was a way for anti-abortion forces to rehearse restrictions on the most vulnerable populations, the poor, before applying them to an even broader group—military families. Today, Hyde-like restrictions are mimicked in federal insurance programs relied upon by more than two million women. Congress has enacted restrictions on abortion funding in plans covering current and retired civilian federal employees, as well as their family members who are enrolled in the Federal Employees Health Benefit Plan, the largest employer-sponsored insurance program in the world. Similarly, all active-duty military and their dependents covered through TRICARE and veterans who receive health care from the Veterans Health Administration have no insurance coverage for abortion.

Not only do these laws severely restrict the availability of abortion funding; they prohibit the performance of abortions at military bases or in VA health centers, even if a woman pays for the service with her own private funds. A servicewoman forced to travel for abortion care will experience financial and logistical demands that can put abortion out of reach, damage her career prospects when she must request unexpected time off, or expose her private decisions to others in her chain of command. For those stationed in such countries as Iraq or Afghanistan where abortion is inaccessible or illegal, deployed to remote areas or stationed at sea, it may be impossible to secure an abortion.

Likewise, women of reproductive age who receive their health care via special federal programs are denied access to essential health care by harmful Hyde-like restrictions that have wormed their way into federal appropriations bills. Native American women and Alaskan natives who receive their care through the Indian Health Service (IHS) are among the poorest women in the nation and frequently live in remote areas far from abortion providers, with limited or no public transportation. The denial of abortion funding can push access completely out of reach. Even in those rare cases of rape and incest in which the Hyde Amendment would permit funding, Native American women are often unable to obtain abortions or other appropriate reproductive health services. Despite higher rates of sexual assault among indigenous women, the IHS is appallingly under-resourced, and fails to administer rape kits and the morning-after pill.

The list of affected women seems endless. Peace Corps volunteers, who are denied federal support for abortion, are often stationed in remote areas or in countries that ban abortion. Women who are incarcerated in federal prisons, Immigration and Customs Enforcement (ICE) facilities, or other immigration detention centers, have little access to outside care and are entirely dependent on authorities for health services. In 2018, the Trump administration blocked a seventeen-year-old undocumented immigrant held in ICE custody in Texas from obtaining an abortion, despite a court order permitting her to obtain one. Federal authorities prohibited her from leaving the facility and subjected her to anti-abortion counseling and a sonogram against her will. With the tenacious assistance of ACLU attorneys, the teen ultimately obtained an abortion, and the policy was put on hold.

FOR DECADES AFTER *Harris v. McRae*, many pro-choice leaders, particularly those in DC, recognized that there were not enough votes in Congress to defeat the Hyde Amendment. Rooted in the appropriations bill, the Hyde Amendment had to be reintroduced each year, and anti-abortion lawmakers gleefully did so without much resistance. Even those legislators who strongly supported abortion rights viewed Hyde as the "third rail": nobody wanted to touch it.

Some women's rights organizations were slow to rally around attempts to eradicate Hyde at the federal level, partly because of the lack of political interest and an unfortunate reflection of systemic racism and classism within the movement. In the main, believing that they did not have the votes to defeat Hyde and unwilling to push the question, they concentrated on expanding the exceptions for a small number of sympathetic women and gave legislators cover if they supported legal abortion but not funding for it.

Reproductive justice advocates responding to the damaging effects of the Hyde Amendment are leading efforts to loudly and effectively call for its permanent repeal. They have built a coalition, All* Above All, that includes well over a hundred partners at the state and national levels pushing to enact the Equal Access to Abortion Coverage in Health Insurance Act (EACH Woman Act). The proposed law would ensure abortion coverage for every woman who receives care or insurance through the federal government and prohibits political interference with abortion coverage in private insurance, including that available in the Affordable Care Act marketplaces. By 2019, the bill had support in both the House and the Senate, with Democratic congresswoman Barbara Lee of California and Senator Tammy Duckworth of Illinois leading the way.

As more progressive women, including more women of color, have been elected to Congress, the repeal of funding restrictions thankfully has gained more support among Democrats. Almost all of the twenty-two Democrats running for president in 2020 supported the repeal of abortion funding restrictions, including Joe Biden, who had voted for Hyde and other abortion funding restrictions throughout his tenure in the Senate. Most Democratic members of Congress are now on board in support of funding as well.

In addition to the growing movement to overturn Hyde at the federal level, activists in many states and localities are advocating for funding for abortion services or related expenses and other neglected areas of

reproductive health care. New York City and Austin, Texas, have allocated city dollars to help women obtain abortions by paying for either
the service or their travel and other related expenses.

Private philanthropic and nonprofit organizations have increasingly
stepped up with resources. The National Network of Abortion Funds
(NNAF), a robust group of almost seventy local funds staffed primarily
by volunteers, helps women overcome financial and logistical barriers
by paying clinic fees and providing transportation and child care, trans-
lation services, and overnight lodging when needed. A youth-led group
that claims to "put the fun in abortion funding," NNAF is known for
lively events like bowl-a-thons and taco nights to provide direct support
to impoverished women in their states or cities. Individual clinics or
physicians will often provide services on a sliding scale that enable access when other funding sources fail. In addition, private foundations
and major donors have subsidized abortions at Planned Parenthood and
independent clinics across the country.

Yet despite the significant amount of charitable monies that have
been raised privately and the prevalence of sliding scale fees, the need
outweighs the available resources. Whether a woman can obtain state-
based or philanthropic support depends solely on where she lives or
which clinic she chooses, unlike Medicaid, which is available for all eligible women. A woman's ability to exercise her right to choose should
not be a matter of luck or dependent on her zip code or whether she is
able to obtain charitable gifts or a fee waiver.

FOR OVER FORTY years now, Congressman Hyde's punitive amendment
has inspired a host of policies that have denied abortion coverage in a
wide range of government health programs and have also spread like a
fungus through state regulation of private insurance coverage. The Hyde
Amendment has made it politically acceptable for states to carve out abortion in state employee insurance plans and even in insurance coverage
provided by private employers. Eleven states restrict abortion coverage in
these private employer-sponsored plans, and twenty-two others restrict
it in coverage provided to state employees. On the flip side, six states actually mandate abortion coverage in their health insurance marketplaces

and in private health plans. These leading states—California, Illinois, Maine, New York, Oregon, and Washington—can serve as a model for other states once there is the political will.

The passage of the Patient Protection and Affordable Care Act—commonly known as Obamacare, the Affordable Care Act, or the ACA—was a monumental step forward that greatly expanded the availability of health insurance for uninsured people in the US. The ACA gives states the option to expand Medicaid coverage to people with a higher income level than were previously eligible, now up to 138 percent of the poverty line. By 2020, thirty-eight states and the District of Columbia had chosen to expand their Medicaid programs. Even some Republican-controlled states that generally oppose government-supported health care were persuaded to expand coverage. Federal subsidies reduced state expenditures while more residents obtained coverage—a win-win. Those low- and moderate-income Americans not poor enough to qualify for Medicaid may still receive subsidies if they buy their health insurance through the federal or state insurance exchanges that the ACA launched. Under the ACA, twenty million additional Americans now have health coverage, and overall the rate of uninsured Americans dropped significantly over the first ten years of the program.

The ACA's mandate that certain services be included in all marketplace plans has vastly improved the availability of women's reproductive health care. Eighteen forms of FDA-approved contraception are provided at no cost to the insured. As a result, about sixty-one million women can obtain contraception without cost, saving consumers at least $1.4 billion on birth control pills alone. A woman can get an intrauterine device (IUD)—previously costing up to $1,000—at a reduced price or free through her health insurance. A round of applause for the ACA for also mandating maternity care services, wellness visits, and breastfeeding support. Screenings of all sorts are now standard operating procedure to better protect people from breast or cervical cancer, HIV/AIDS, and domestic violence.

Another big bonus the ACA brings to women is that it prohibits insurance companies from denying coverage for "pre-existing conditions." Insurance companies were notorious for banning health coverage to women who had a prior Caesarean section or had been survivors of domestic violence, claiming that these conditions were likely to be predictors of higher medical expenses in the future. As House Speaker Nancy Pelosi declared upon passage of the ACA, "Being a woman is no longer a pre-existing condition."

While the ACA particularly has helped women obtain much-needed reproductive health care, not surprisingly, it has severe restrictions on abortion coverage. The Affordable Care Act initially did not contain specific restrictions on abortion. However, shortly after its passage, President Obama issued an executive order that prohibited inclusion of abortion in the federally established mandatory benefits with only narrow exceptions. The order was a result of a deal made to secure the votes of Bart Stupak, an anti-abortion Democratic congressman from northern Michigan, and several of his colleagues, who had threatened to vote against the full health care bill. Once again, abortion rights were horse-traded away.

Additional provisions in the ACA explicitly permit states to prohibit abortion coverage in health care plans sold in state marketplaces—and so far, twenty-six states have leaped at the opportunity. Even those small number of private insurance plans that cover abortion face additional administrative rules to ensure that federal funds are not spent for abortions beyond the Hyde exceptions in cases of rape, incest, or life endangerment.

In the past decade, conservative forces and many mainstream Republicans have become further aligned with anti-abortion advocates, joining together to oppose expanded health coverage for all Americans. In contrast, the Democratic Party has embraced a call for greater access to health insurance for all, expanded women's reproductive health care coverage, and (finally) began to support repeal of Hyde and Hyde-like restrictions on abortion funding. The election of President Biden has brought this health care expansion to the fore but is not a magic nor permanent solution.

As new proposals for health care coverage are debated and considered, we must take heed of the history of Hyde and its copycats. A full range of reproductive health services including abortion must be firmly and securely part of any health care reforms. We will only be able to preserve reproductive freedoms when *all* women have not just the right but the means to obtain an abortion, regardless of their age or financial status. Too often the government has been allowed to use the nation's checkbook to paternalistically dictate women and teens' most private health care decisions. Directly denying funding as well as putting onerous and costly restrictions on abortion harms all women but in particular, women of color, low-income women, and teenagers who are often less able to overcome these hurdles.

CHAPTER 6

THE KIDS ARE NOT ALL RIGHT
STATES LIMIT TEEN ACCESS TO SEX EDUCATION, BIRTH CONTROL, AND ABORTION

Let's talk about sex for now . . .
Don't be coy, avoid, or make void the topic
Cuz that ain't gonna stop it

SALT-N-PEPA,
"LET'S TALK ABOUT SEX"

KITTY WAS WORKING at her desk at the Center's eighteenth-floor office overlooking Manhattan's shimmering East River when she received a call about a woman in trouble. Rosa Hartford, a middle-aged everywoman living in Shunk, Pennsylvania, had been charged with child kidnapping for helping Crystal Lane, the girlfriend of her teenage son, obtain an abortion. The girl was thirteen and had no way to get to the clinic from their rural town, so Hartford had asked her neighbor to drive them. Now a zealous prosecutor was charging Hartford under a state law that prohibited "interfering with the custody of a minor."

The statute prohibited "enticing" a child away from her parents' custody and included a penalty of up to seven years in prison if convicted. It was 1995, and a creative and aggressive prosecution of this kind had never before been attempted in Pennsylvania. As far as anyone knew, it was the first of its kind in the nation—but would not be the last.

During the summer, Lane had dated Hartford's eighteen-year-old son, Michael Kilmer, had sex with him, and became pregnant. Lane's mother, Joyce Farley, had seen Lane with Kilmer on a few occasions and told them both that Kilmer was too old for Lane and that she didn't want Kilmer to come to the house or call her daughter. Before deciding to obtain the abortion Lane consulted with her older sister, several friends, Hartford's stepdaughter, Kilmer, and Hartford. Yet Lane did not want her mother to know about her pregnancy or abortion decision.

Shunk was more of a small crossroads in a wooded area than a town. The closest abortion clinic was ninety miles north in Binghamton, New York. Hartford's stepdaughter made an appointment for Lane and had planned to drive her and a friend to the clinic but was sidelined by a migraine the morning of the appointment. When Hartford heard the girls were now planning to go without an adult, she stepped in to assist.

If Lane had gone to a clinic in Pennsylvania, she would have been required either to notify one of her parents or to obtain a court order allowing her to have the abortion and then wait twenty-four hours between the time she received counseling and when she had the procedure. In practice, this law, which had been upheld in *Casey*, meant that Lane would need to make two separate trips to a clinic—about a three-hour journey each way. Fortunately, New York was nearby and had no such impediments, so Lane was able to obtain the abortion at her appointment without making repeat trips to court or to the clinic.

When Lane's school called to report her absence that day, her mother notified the police. The local officer sent the matter to the county prosecutor after Hartford's role in helping Lane travel to the clinic was revealed.

Kitty and a team of attorneys from the Center filed a motion to dismiss the criminal charges, believing that the child custody charge was ill-fitting and motivated by anti-abortion animus. District Attorney Max Little claimed that his office had "never considered this case to be a challenge to abortion rights" and insisted that his prosecution of Hartford was solely "about the rights of a parent." However, he undermined his assertion before the trial by saying, "They are arguing that this is a terrible blow to abortion rights, but that's not true at all unless we're talking about abortion rights for children under thirteen."

The local common pleas judge was a thin, dark-haired man with a serious "stick to business" demeanor. He quickly rejected Kitty's constitutional arguments and set the case to be tried before a jury that fall. Kitty's top pick to be cocounsel was Janet Crepps, an attorney she had recruited to work at the ACLU and then to join the Center, where she worked for over twenty-five years. Crepps had been a public defender in Alaska early in her career and was a crack litigator with a hearty laugh who operated as a one-woman outpost of the Center in Denver. Next to join the defense team was David Gans, Kitty's paralegal in *Casey*, who had circled back to the Center after attending law school. They packed Kitty's white sedan with three-ring trial binders, snacks, and a cutting-edge fax machine, and headed to Pennsylvania a few days before the trial.

As a civil litigator, Kitty had never represented anyone in a criminal case. Nor had she presented a case to a jury. In fact, most lawyers never see a jury other than on television. The vast majority of civil and criminal cases settle before trial, but the principles at stake in this case, like many of the Center's cases, were ones that made compromise highly unlikely. Kitty was nervous and pessimistic as she considered how unlikely it was that potential jurors from this extremely conservative area would be sympathetic to Hartford's plight.

Over the course of a two-day trial, Kitty emphasized to the jury the unfairness of prosecuting Hartford for helping Lane, a teen unwilling to go to her own mother for help. In response, the prosecution introduced evidence that Hartford had misled the state police and had falsely told the clinic that she was Lane's stepmother.

Not unexpectedly, the jury returned a verdict of guilty. Perhaps it was a result of the strong anti-abortion sentiment in the area and resentment of big-city lawyers getting involved. Maybe it was in reaction to the pressure of national media attention on their small town and an understandable uneasiness about a thirteen-year-old being sexually active. Whatever their motivation, the jury convicted Hartford of a third-degree felony, and the judge sentenced her to twelve months of probation and 150 hours of community service, recognizing that sending her to prison would not serve any purpose.

Kitty passed the case to the Juvenile Law Center, a public interest center in Philadelphia, to bring an appeal. Thankfully Hartford's conviction was reversed, and she was diverted into a program for first-time offenders so that she would not have to face a retrial. In addition to the prosecution of Hartford, her son Kilmer was convicted of two counts of statutory rape and served several months in prison.

THE KIDS ARE not all right. The Hartford case is a striking example of how states wrongly adopt a shut-it-down approach toward teenage sexuality and unintended pregnancy. It's a three-step approach to failure: first, deny the fact that many teens are going to be sexually active and that many are unable to discuss sexuality with their parents; next, fail to address the lack of reproductive health education and reproductive health services for teens; and finally, penalize the teens who face an unintended pregnancy and any sympathetic adult like Hartford who is willing to help.

The Hartford case was part of a wider problematic trend that continues today in which prosecutors distort criminal statutes in order to charge women or girls criminally for disfavored behavior during pregnancy. Prosecutors have charged pregnant women with child endangerment or attempted murder for drug or alcohol abuse or attempts to self-abort. Allowing such misapplication of criminal laws, like the child custody law at issue here, gives prosecutors unfettered discretion to push their own political views and often perpetuates racial bias. District Attorney Little's assertion that Hartford's case was about parental rights and not abortion seemed laughable. Little never would have brought charges against Hartford had she taken Lane to get a tattoo or to have her wisdom teeth extracted.

A few years later, anti-abortion members of Congress sought to make it a federal crime for an adult to take a minor to another state for an abortion if the teen's home state had a parental involvement law. The National Right to Life Committee as well as Farley and Lane invoked Hartford's case when testifying before Chairman Henry Hyde's Judiciary Committee in support of the Child Custody Protection Act. The proposed law would force a girl to carry the parental involvement law from her home state like an unwanted backpack: if she traveled to a neighboring state for an abortion, even when that was the closest clinic to her, she would have to go through her home state's hoops. The proposed law was reintroduced as recently as 2019 but has never passed.

Meanwhile the US has some of the highest rates of adolescent pregnancy, birth, and abortion in the developed world, with the exception of former Soviet Bloc countries. The US teen pregnancy rate is over four times that of the Netherlands and exceeds by high margins those in Norway, Israel, and France. Similarly, the US teen birth rate is eight times higher than in the Netherlands.

The pregnancy rate has declined considerably in recent decades, according to the Guttmacher Institute. By the most recent survey, in 2016, the pregnancy rate among teens ages fifteen to nineteen was the lowest it had been since *Roe* and has fallen in all fifty states. Many attribute the decline to better access to more effective and longer-lasting contraceptives such as a new type of IUD, the birth control shot (Depo-Provera), and long-lasting implants as well as legalization of the morning-after pill. Nevertheless, almost half a million older teens became pregnant. Twice as many teens carried their pregnancies to term as had abortions.

Even as the US is showing rapid declines in teen birth rates across all major racial and ethnic groups, racial disparities still hang on. According to the Pew Research Center, data from 2018 showed that the birth rate for Hispanic and Black teens ages fifteen to nineteen was almost double the rate among white teens and more than five times as high as the rate among Asian and Pacific Islander teens.

Girls like Lane who become pregnant at age thirteen are rare. Data provided by the Guttmacher Institute found that adolescent pregnancies were concentrated among eighteen- to nineteen-year-olds, accounting for almost three-quarters of all pregnancies among young women ages fifteen to nineteen.

Teen pregnancy and childbearing may pose challenges for young women. Systemic inequities exacerbate these challenges. Teenage parents are more likely to live in poverty, with low-paying jobs and limited advancement opportunities. They often lack access to affordable housing and, as minors, may be excluded from some government housing subsidies or face discrimination from landlords. High school–age parents are at greater risk for dropping out, being pushed out of school, or being steered toward low-achieving schools. As a result, a high school diploma is out of reach for almost half of teen mothers; in contrast, 90 percent of women who did not give birth during adolescence received a high school diploma. Teen fathers also face a lower probability of graduating from high school than teenage boys who are not fathers. For a variety of reasons—including inequities in health care—children born to young mothers experience higher rates of infant mortality and morbidity and demonstrate disproportionate rates of behavioral problems and chronic medical conditions.

Historically, the US has framed teen pregnancy as the *cause* of a variety of social problems, particularly when it comes to teens of color. While statistics regarding school dropout rates or increased rates of poverty for young people who become parents cause concern, these statistics too frequently are used to simply stigmatize young women, depicting their motherhood itself as problematic. Public service announcements, television shows such as *16 & Pregnant* and *The Secret Life of the American Teenager*, and other embellished accounts of teen pregnancies in the media denounce teen mothers and employ scare tactics or ridiculous stereotypes. In 2013, a teen pregnancy prevention campaign by the Candie's Foundation, for example, used star-studded ads to admonish teens that "you're supposed to be changing the world . . . not changing diapers."

Slogans such as "enjoy your youth by being a kid, not raising one" derive from a class-based view of adolescence as a time to go to college and enjoy and enrich oneself through socializing, travel, and sports before even considering marriage and then parenthood. This model presumes an extended adolescent stage of life that is out of reach or undesirable for many.

The reproductive justice movement brings a greater nuance and understanding of teen pregnancy to the conversation by rejecting a blame-and-shame approach that defines all young parenthood as a mistake. Bold Futures, a grassroots youth-led reproductive justice group based in New Mexico, notes that the US approach toward teen pregnancy derives from a long history of racist policies, including forced sterilization and mandatory contraception, designed to control the reproductive autonomy of women and girls of color. Being truly pro-choice, reproductive justice advocates contend, means working to make reproductive health care more affordable and accessible for young women, while also accepting and respecting the varied choices that all women make regardless of their age.

While for some young women, parenting may mean they must postpone their educational goals, for others motherhood comes as a deliberate choice that is more accessible and less elusive than higher education. The aim is not solely pregnancy prevention but how to build support for young teens who choose to be sexually active, help ensure pregnancy is planned, and support teens who opt to become parents. We need initiatives that effectively provide sexual and reproductive health, affordable education, and services—not campaigns that bring shame, stigma, or even worse, criminal charges.

HISTORICALLY, MANY STATES have classified sex with a teenage girl as statutory rape, even if the sex is consensual. Age disparity between the two is all the evidence needed. These laws were originally intended to preserve the premarital chastity of white women and the sanctity of marriage.

While undercurrents of race and class bias still run through statutory rape laws, feminists in the 1970s began to turn to these laws to address the fact that all too often sex between older men and teenagers could be coercive or involuntary. They advocated for changes to the law to require greater age disparities between the parties and to apply the laws equally regardless of gender. Still, statutory rape charges are sometimes used to assert state or parental control in a situation where in reality there is no victim.

When it comes to minors obtaining abortions, most states, including very blue ones, have adopted stringent requirements that make abortion more difficult to obtain. Anti-abortion legislatures have created laws to force parental involvement in a teen's decision making when there might otherwise be no involvement. In reality, most teenagers already involve at least one parent in their abortion decision. As the ACLU notes,

Based on a national survey of more than 1,500 unmarried minors having abortions in states without parental involvement laws, 61% of young women discussed the decision to have an abortion with at least one of their parents. The younger the teen, the more likely she was to have voluntarily discussed the abortion with her parent. In fact, 90% of minors under fifteen involved a parent in their decision to have an abortion.

Clinics take particular pains to support teens and encourage them to discuss the abortion with their parents. But when teens decide not to communicate their reproductive health decisions with their parents, there is often good reason. The pregnancy might be a result of rape or incest by a parent or stepparent. A parent may be absent from a teen's life—may be incarcerated or suffering from mental health problems or substance abuse, for example—or a teen may legitimately fear that telling a parent could result in abuse. Teens who are unable or unwilling to discuss their pregnancy with their parents often turn to older siblings or other trusted adults.

Beginning immediately after *Roe*, in 1974, states sought to pass measures mandating that teens obtain parental consent in order to obtain an abortion. One of the first laws that came out of Missouri made its way to the Supreme Court in *Planned Parenthood of Central Missouri v. Danforth*. The *Danforth* Court noted that minors do have some constitutional rights—rights do not "magically" come into being at the age of majority. However, the Court remarked, states also have significant interest in regulating the activities of a minor that are "not present in the case of an adult." The Court realized that allowing a nonconsenting parent to veto the teen's abortion decision would not likely do much for family harmony, particularly in situations where the very existence of the pregnancy already has fractured the family structure. Ultimately the Court found unconstitutional the parental consent provision because it enabled the state to place an "absolute, and possibly arbitrary, veto over the decision of the physician and his patient to terminate the patient's pregnancy." Once again a (presumably white, male) physician's opinion was key to a woman's or teen's abortion decision.

Over the next two decades, the Supreme Court heard challenges to a variety of abortion laws that mandated either parental consent or notification prior to an abortion. Through a series of cases from Massachusetts, Minnesota, Missouri, Ohio, and Pennsylvania, the Court ultimately allowed states to require a teen to give notice or obtain consent from a parent prior to obtaining an abortion. But if the teen is unable or unwilling to get parental permission, the law must afford the opportunity to obtain consent from a judge or through an alternate, less formal procedure. Commonly referred to as a "judicial bypass" provision, this route had to be available within twenty-four to forty-eight hours to avoid delaying the abortion. The judge or other decision maker must consider the teen's intelligence, emotional stability, and understanding of the consequences of an abortion in order to determine whether she is mature enough to make the abortion decision independently, and, if so, the abortion must be permitted without parental involvement.

Unfortunately, in many locations, teens who enter a complicated legal system to obtain a bypass order can face intimidation, bias, and exposure. Yet in practice, few judges hearing bypass cases reject the teenager's request. To do so, the judge would have to find that the minor is too immature to make the abortion decision on her own, yet mature enough to raise a child.

On the flip side, clinics report a disturbing unintended consequence of parental involvement laws: not infrequently, a parent attempts to coerce a teen into an abortion when the teen wants to carry the pregnancy to term. As a check on this type of coercion, clinic counselors commonly separate the parent or adult accompanying the adolescent to ensure that the teen's decision is truly voluntary and respected.

TODAY THIRTY-SEVEN STATES require some compulsory parental involvement in a minor's decision to have an abortion. The majority require either the consent or notification of one parent, although four require *both* parents to be involved—Kansas, Mississippi, North Dakota, and Minnesota. A few states allow a grandparent or other adult relative to be involved instead of a parent. Most provide a judicial bypass procedure, although some states allow a medical professional to waive parental involvement in some limited circumstances. In 2020, Massachusetts amended its notification law so that it applies only to teens under age sixteen.

These laws stand in sharp contrast to how states treat minors who opt to carry their pregnancies to term. The ACLU data shows that *no* state requires parental consent for a minor to obtain a test for pregnancy or a sexually transmitted infection. For those teens who receive prenatal care and delivery services, no parental consent is needed. A teen who is putting a child up for adoption can do so without parental involvement in all but five states.

The burdens teens face in accessing abortion are now more onerous than ever. The logistics of traveling long distances to an abortion clinic have become grueling as fewer and fewer clinics exist in the US. In Crystal Lane's case, she had no license or car to drive to the Binghamton clinic, nor was there any public transit. She had to rely on adults. The fact that she had to leave so early in the morning, would be back late, and would miss school inevitably led to her mother discovering that she was having an abortion. For teens, the difference between making a ninety-mile trip, as Lane did, versus a four-hundred-mile one (the average distance that many teens must now travel for a confidential abortion) is significant. The farther a teen needs to travel, the greater the likelihood she will be unable to have an abortion.

For the young women living in rural areas or those seeking confidentiality, the need to travel long distances and the lack of transportation are just two of many daunting obstacles. The lack of Medicaid coverage may leave teens without funds for the procedure. Waiting periods cause additional delays and in some cases make two or more trips to a clinic necessary. A teen who needs to obtain permission from a judge often will need to navigate complicated court procedures, confront disapproving judges, or risk loss of confidentiality. As the ACLU notes,

> in Massachusetts a young woman's intention to obtain an abortion was exposed when her sister's civics class came through the courthouse; another teen ran into a neighbor in the courthouse; another encountered her godmother who worked in the court. In Minnesota,

anti-abortion activists sat in the court hallways and used yearbooks from the local high schools to identify the teens who came in for judicial waivers and expose their decisions to have abortions.

Teens are more likely to have erratic menstrual periods that make it difficult to recognize the signs of pregnancy, and so it often takes them longer to recognize that they are pregnant. If a teen is in or near the second trimester of pregnancy, any additional delay will make it harder to find a provider and make the abortion more expensive. Since 1992, laws requiring parental involvement have resulted in half a million teen births. Nevertheless, the vast majority of teens facing these punitive laws find ways to have an abortion.

Because of these factors, parental involvement laws are opposed by all of the major medical organizations including the American Medical Association, the American Academy of Pediatrics, the Society for Adolescent Medicine, the American College of Obstetricians and Gynecologists, and the American Public Health Association. The question for us all is: how can we do better for the thousands of American teens who experience unplanned pregnancies each year?

IN THE SAME way that most children don't want to think about their parents having sex, most parents don't want to imagine their children being sexually active. Parental attitudes still vary based on the gender of both the parents and the teen. As a society we tend to praise boys' sexuality as a rite of passage and either ignore or spurn girls' sexuality.

Heterosexuality is normalized and encouraged, while any conversation about the feelings or needs of LGBTQ+ teens is often stigmatized or shunned. Non-binary teens—those who do not identify as exclusively male or female—and transgender teens are often overlooked or rejected by their families or communities.

Frequently parents' awkwardness or avoidance of "The Talk" means that sexuality education falls to schools and is controlled by local school boards or classroom teachers who too frequently are ill-equipped or under-resourced to provide the necessary information. By the mid-1990s, schools nationwide were providing little by way of sexuality

education, and there was a growing trend to emphasize "abstinence before marriage."

While Congress has used its power of the purse to fund programs
that encourage the use of contraception among teens, most notably Title X monies for family planning, it has also supported the proliferation
of abstinence-only or abstinence-based sex education programs that are
grounded in ideology, not science, and whose heteronormativity results
in misinformation and bias. Between 1986 and 2018, over $2 *billion*
of federal assistance was allocated to programs that exclusively promote
abstinence. Such programs do not advocate contraceptive use or even
discuss contraceptive methods, other than to emphasize or exaggerate
contraceptive failure rates. Although evidence shows that abstinence
programs are ineffective and, in some cases, harmful to teens, they remain a favorite for political reasons. They are also a lucrative funding
stream for so-called crisis pregnancy centers and anti-abortion groups
that promote and sell these programs.

As part of an effort to spotlight the bias and harms of abstinence
programs, in 2008 while at Legal Momentum, formerly the NOW Legal Defense and Education Fund, Julie convened a group of experts
to document the harms wrought by these ideological, religious-based
programs. With the help of Representative Henry Waxman, the chair
of the House Committee on Oversight and Reform, she presented this
evidence at a congressional briefing.

With a team of experts from the leading sexuality education non-
profits, Julie traveled to college campuses to let students know what
their elected officials thought about sex before marriage, bridging the
gap between DC politics and the students' reality. The team exposed
how abstinence programs that censor truthful and pragmatic information about sexuality, contraception, and abortion put young people's
sexual health and well-being at risk and reinforce gender stereotypes
that negatively affect relationships during adolescence and beyond.

One abstinence education program equated a young woman's sexuality with a piece of chewing gum: once you've been "chewed," nobody else
is going to want you. Programs dangerously featured incomplete or misleading information on preventing HIV/AIDS and STIs and exaggerated

condom failure rates. When young people ultimately do become sexually active, they may be discouraged from using condoms or birth control because the programs have given them such sparse, misleading, or even negative information about contraception, HIV/AIDS prevention, and the morning-after pill.

The disconnect between their lived experience as young people and the curricula was enormous and infuriating to the college students in the audience. They reacted with a combination of horror and humor to slides of abstinence-only programs that encouraged young people to "just say no" to sex. Eventually tolerance for these programs grew thin in DC as well. When the Obama administration arrived in 2008, federal funding for sexual health programming began to noticeably shift toward more comprehensive, science-based, and age-appropriate curricula. Two small funding streams were a step in the right direction to promote sexual health overall, even though they were designed foremost as teen pregnancy prevention programs: the Personal Responsibility Education Program and the Teen Pregnancy Prevention Program.

Unfortunately for America's teens, the pendulum swung rightward again when the Trump administration entered office in 2016 and set to work redirecting funds to programs that promote abstinence. These efforts were stopped by a number of lawsuits that found the redirection had unlawfully violated congressional intent or had terminated grants illegally.

The larger question is how as a nation we can move to the point where teen sexuality is not seen as a taboo topic but part of adolescent development that requires education and conversation. While there has been progress in recent years, there is still a long way to go to fully recognize that sexuality does not begin and end with procreative sex within heterosexual marriage. Adolescents in the US continue to face unacceptably high risks of sexual abuse, homophobia, forced pregnancy, sexually transmitted infections including HIV/AIDS, and dating violence from which they are woefully unprepared to protect themselves. We need to address the social conditions that negatively impact teenagers, instead of simply stigmatizing teen sexuality.

The prosecution of Rosa Hartford and shaming of Crystal Lane raise a range of difficult and uncomfortable issues about teenage sexuality and abortion. Rather than litigating whether Rosa Hartford was a criminal for helping Lane, our energies would be better spent ensuring that teens like Lane have access to accurate, effective sexuality and health education free from bias and political or religious ideology as well as the health and social services that respect young women and help them make healthy and safe choices.

CHAPTER 7

DEATH BY A THOUSAND PINPRICKS
ATTACKS ON CLINICS AND DOCTORS MOVE ABORTION FURTHER OUT OF REACH

No person seeking medical care, no physician providing that care, should have to endure harassments
or threats or obstruction or intimidation or even murder from vigilantes who take the law into their own
hands because they think they know what the law
ought to be.

PRESIDENT BILL CLINTON,
ON SIGNING THE FREEDOM OF
ACCESS TO CLINIC ENTRANCES ACT

WALKING INTO THE FBI headquarters alongside the leaders of major
women's organizations brought an ironic smile to Kitty's face. For
many of these women, the J. Edgar Hoover building, a brutalist concrete structure with rows of browned windows stretching the length of
the block, represented an FBI that had frequently spied on civil rights
leaders and harassed political activists. It was an untrustworthy adver-
sary, not an organization that would be protective of abortion providers. But here they all were, headed into the bastion of law and order
to discuss much-needed security for clinics facing significant increases
in domestic terrorism. Throughout the 1990s the murders, bombings,
and arson against clinics and their staff skyrocketed. Because local police departments often turned their backs on these providers, Kitty and

her colleagues beseeched the federal government for remedies to protect dwindling access to abortion services.

The extreme violence and intimidation deliberately aimed at doctors, clinic staff, and patients, along with the massive destruction of property, instilled fear in medical professionals and their allies, dissuaded younger doctors from becoming abortion providers, and drove a wedge between abortion providers and mainstream medicine.

The violence took many forms. On one end of the continuum was domestic terrorism, including assassinations of doctors, arson, bombings, acid attacks on clinics, and letters threatening anthrax poisoning. On the other end were aggressive actions by more mainstream abortion opponents, which fueled the extremists—clinic blockades, harassment of patients, protests at doctors' homes. Both groups regularly used dramatic, uncompromising language to talk about providers as "murderers," while calling for divine intervention to "save babies" and "stop the genocide." Too often, anti-abortion organizations and politicians were slow to condemn the violence, further stoking the extremism. There was often shockingly little daylight between the two wings of the movement.

These strategies succeeded in dramatically decreasing the number of abortion providers nationwide. Today, 89 percent of US counties do not have a single abortion provider. Thirteen states have fewer than six providers statewide; six of these have only one. Many under-resourced states are clustered together, creating "abortion-provider deserts" over wide areas such as North and South Dakota and Wyoming. These three states have a combined total of five providers for a land mass of nearly 250,000 square miles—an area almost ten times the size of Ireland. Gains in the number of providers have been slight and are concentrated in urban areas, forcing women to travel more than fifty, a hundred, or even two hundred miles to reach services.

Clinic violence restricts access to a wide range of reproductive health care, including screening and treatment of sexually transmitted infections and reproductive cancers, and access to contraceptives. The impact is particularly felt by women of color, as Michelle Batchelor, deputy director of In Our Own Voice notes:

No one is more affected by clinic violence than the poor, young, and women of color, and with Black women 55 percent more likely to be uninsured than white women, we need the services that are being provided by these very clinics that are being targeted for violence.

One group of anti-abortion activists, Operation Rescue, first called for widespread hard-hitting tactics against clinics in the summer of 1991, bragging that its activities were on the "cutting edge of the abortion issue." In what came to be known as the "Summer of Mercy," the group targeted three clinics in Wichita, Kansas, including one run by Dr. George Tiller, a courageous and committed physician who was one of only a handful of doctors performing abortions later in pregnancy. The group's leader, Randall Terry, was a charismatic used car salesman who was not shy about being arrested for his illegal maneuvers.

Terry became the public face of a confrontational brigade who chained themselves to clinics, put Super Glue in the door locks, and mounted enormous blockades. In defiance of a federal court order, the protestors' siege closed the clinics for over three weeks and resulted in sixteen hundred arrests. Operation Rescue members were "flinging themselves under cars, sitting by the hundreds at clinic doorways, and blocking women from entering as they read them Scripture." Local police carried away protestors who went limp, and officers on mounted horses tried to dispel the large crowds.

Two years later in 1993, an increasingly emboldened Operation Rescue expanded its campaign with similarly destructive tactics in an action it called "Cities of Refuge." It targeted providers from San Jose to Philadelphia with blockades and posted threatening "Wanted" posters with clinic staff's names and photographs around town.

Kitty had met the media-savvy Terry when they appeared on TV talk shows that were eager to show "both sides" of the issue, but she had not seen the group's intimidating tactics firsthand until that summer, when Linda Wharton, her *Casey* cocounsel, sought her advice on preventing Operation Rescue from shutting down the Women's Suburban Clinic outside Philadelphia. On an uncommonly hot and humid afternoon over the July Fourth holiday, Kitty watched the mass of shouting, angry white men waving gruesome and inflammatory signs and chaining themselves at the entrance of the clinic. It left an indelible impression of testosterone-driven rage aimed at women who dared exercise their constitutional rights and the doctors who sought to help them.

The National Abortion Federation (NAF), an organization representing independent abortion providers, began keeping track of abortion-related violence in 1977, only a few years after *Roe*. Their data showed a marked escalation in both number and intensity of violent incidents following the Operation Rescue Summer of Mercy shutdowns, including the murder of Dr. David Gunn in the parking lot of his Pensacola, Florida, clinic in March 1993. The national director of Rescue America commented, "While Gunn's death is unfortunate, it's also true that quite a number of babies' lives will be saved."

It's alarming and appalling to list all the doctors and clinic staff whose lives were lost or forever changed as a result of anti-abortion extremists. These acts of terrorism sent sadness and shockwaves through the abortion rights community and beyond. One day of horrific violence took place in 1994 at two clinics less than two miles apart in Julie's hometown of Brookline, Massachusetts, where many of her childhood friends sought reproductive health care. Two office workers, Shannon Lowney and Leanne Nichols, were assassinated, and five other people were injured, shattering the stereotype that more liberal states were immune from the violence.

Those attacks were part of a national effort that claimed the lives of too many of those committed to protecting access to abortion and their allies. Dr. John Bayard Britton and his bodyguard, retired Air Force Lieutenant Colonel James H. Barrett, were gunned down at point-blank range in an attack that also injured his wife outside the same Pensacola, Florida, clinic where Dr. Gunn was murdered. Dr. George Tiller was injured by gunfire at his Wichita, Kansas, clinic in 1993 and later murdered in a brazen assassination while he was serving as an usher at his church in 2009. In 1998, Dr. Barnett Slepian was executed in his kitchen by a sniper's bullet shot through the window of his family home outside Buffalo, New York. His executioner was found three years later, having fled to Dublin, Ireland, where he made a home with an extremist anti-abortion religious sect. In Birmingham, Alabama, in 1998, a bomb placed in the New Woman All Women clinic—one of Julie's clients— killed police officer Robert Sanderson, who was moonlighting as a clinic security guard, and severely injured Emily Lyons, a nurse at the clinic.

NAF reported that overall violence climbed again after an anti-abortion organization, inaptly named the Center for Medical Progress, released "highly edited, and incendiary videos" in its campaign against Planned Parenthood in July 2015. In November of that year at a Colorado Springs Planned Parenthood, police officer Garrett Swasey and clinic visitors Jennifer Markovsky and Ke'Arre Stewart were killed by an anti-abortion extremist who "dreamed he'll be met in Heaven by aborted fetuses wanting to thank him for saving unborn babies."

The Army of God, a clandestine group of domestic terrorists, claimed responsibility for some of the murders, as well as attempted murders, clinic bombings, fake anthrax attacks, and a death threat against Supreme Court Justice Henry Blackmun following his retirement from the bench. Shelley Shannon, who was convicted of the attempted murder of Dr. Tiller in 1993, and Eric Robert Rudolph, the Atlanta Olympic Park bomber who also bombed abortion clinics in Atlanta and Birmingham and a lesbian bar in Atlanta, were among its best-known members. Law enforcement officials found buried in Shannon's yard an Army of God manual that included detailed instructions for how to mount chemical attacks and clinic invasions, commit arson, and build bombs.

Assassination of abortion providers was only one form of the violence, intimidation, and terrorism that incapacitated clinics. Between the mid-1970s and 2000, over two hundred incidents of arson and bombing caused numerous injuries and hundreds of thousands of dollars of property damage. Attacks with butyric acid, a clear liquid with a rancid, vomit-like odor that forced clinics to replace all interior carpeting and furniture, were common. And if that weren't enough, over seven hundred letters threatening anthrax poisoning were sent to clinics that forced temporary closures and cancellation of appointments. There have been thirty-one damaging bombings and arson incidents of clinics and another twenty-four attempts since 2000 alone.

Anti-abortion extremists sought not only to push existing providers out of business but to scare medical students away from even thinking about providing abortion as a part of a reproductive health care practice. One anti-abortion group in Texas mailed thousands of medical students "The Abortionists' Jokebook" filled with veiled threats, including this joke: "Q: What would you do if you found yourself in a room with Hitler, Mussolini, and an abortionist, and you had a gun with only two bullets? A: Shoot the abortionist twice." The result of this campaign of threats and stigmatization meant that fewer new providers entered the field and the population of providers continued to age.

While it was up to law enforcement to stop the terrorists, the clinics engaged in a variety of strategies to discourage the relentless harassment on their doorsteps. Clinics organized volunteer escorts to surround patients and walk them safely through throngs of protestors. They scheduled appointments in the very early morning before protestors arrived. They hired attorneys to get injunctions, seek damages under civil rights statutes and racketeering laws, and negotiate with landlords who refused to rent to them because of clinic protests or violence. Doctors and clinic staff took elaborate steps to stay safe, with security protocols, bullet-proof cars, and armed guards at home and the office.

NOW brought suit, charging that the violence violated the federal Racketeer Influenced and Corrupt Organizations Act (RICO), a law that had been designed to prosecute members of organized crime. While initially successful at obtaining a unanimous Supreme Court ruling that RICO could apply to anti-abortion protestors, years later, after two trips to the Supreme Court, NOW's claims were dismissed.

Similarly, lawyers from the NOW Legal Defense and Education Fund attempted to use the Reconstruction Era Civil Rights Act of 1871, known as the Ku Klux Klan Act, to stop Operation Rescue from trespassing and obstructing clinic access. By a 6–3 vote in *Bray v. Alexandria Women's Health Clinic*, the Supreme Court dismissed the civil rights lawsuit because the clinics could not prove that the obstructions were motivated by hatred of women or another class of persons, a requirement of the law. The Court held that "there were common and respectable reasons for opposing abortion other than a derogatory view of women."

With no help coming from the Supreme Court and extreme violence by "pro-life" groups on the rise, abortion supporters turned to
their allies in DC for help. A new federal tool became available when,
in the spring of 1994, Congress passed the Freedom of Access to Clinic
Entrances Act (FACE), making it a federal crime to use force, threats,
or physical obstruction against abortion doctors or clinics such as arson,
massive blockades, shootings, or other actions that prevent a patient
from obtaining an abortion. In addition to protecting abortion clinics,
the law also prohibited threats to churches, since arson and violence
against Black churches were on the rise. Defendants charged with FACE
violations unsuccessfully challenged its constitutionality, arguing that
the law violated their First Amendment right to free speech or was unconstitutionally vague, but the law stood strong.

The federal criminal charges FACE provided were a more effective
deterrent, and especially helpful in locations where local law enforcement was reluctant to prosecute offenders for political reasons. Civil
FACE remedies, including injunctions and monetary damages, meant
an organization or individual's office, home, or bank accounts could be
seized to satisfy a judgment. Overall FACE was far better tailored to
protect reproductive health care access than earlier RICO or Ku Klux
Klan Act lawsuits had been.

As a result, blockades like Operation Rescue's Summer of Mercy
thankfully were squelched before they were scaled up further, although
protestors continue to harass and intimidate women outside of individual clinics today. During the Clinton White House years, there was
a strong response to clinic violence that included use of FACE, civil
lawsuits, and Attorney General Janet Reno's National Task Force on
Violence Against Reproductive Health Care Providers. Leaders of the
FBI invited Kitty and other women's rights activists into their bastions
to respond to the concerns of the clinics and provide better protection.
As a result, the violence decreased. Ultimately hundreds of Operation
Rescue affiliates were closed or struggled to change their tactics.

But FACE enforcement efforts and the level of violence seesawed
during subsequent Republican and Democratic administrations. Fewer
prosecutions were brought and violence increased during President

George W. Bush's administration. The pendulum swung again during President Obama's tenure as enforcement was stepped up following Dr. Tiller's murder in 2009.

As would be expected, violence against clinics and doctors rose dramatically during President Trump's term, accompanied by increases in racist, homophobic, and xenophobic violence and harassment egged on by the president. NAF reports that in 2019 there was "a disturbing escalation of intimidation tactics, clinic invasions, and other activities aimed at disrupting services, harassing providers, and blocking women's access to abortion care." The six thousand incidents of anti-abortion picketing at clinics in 2010 rose to more than one hundred twenty-three thousand incidents in 2019. In an unclassified report issued in January 2020, the FBI anticipated that "violent threats and FACE Act violations would likely remain elevated through the next twelve to twenty-four months in the midst of . . . the 2020 election."

While not formally affiliated, there is a history of deep connection and ideological alignment between anti-abortion terrorists and the racist, xenophobic, anti-Semitic, homophobic, and transphobic ideologies of the extreme right. One early and public display of this alliance occurred when the Florida branch of the KKK celebrated the murder of Dr. Britton, rallying in support of his assassin in the mid-1990s. More recently, these ties became apparent when, as NARAL Pro-Choice America documented, anti-abortion extremists promoted and participated in the insurrection at the US capital in 2021, including the founder of "Baby Lives Matter," Tayler Hansen, who posted on Twitter that he had been inside the Capitol and next to an insurrectionist shot by police.

The anti-abortion and white supremacist groups diverge where, as Professor Aaron Winter notes, white supremacist organizations decry abortions obtained by white women but applaud those obtained by Black women, because it aligns with their racist support for eugenics. However, the two movements join hands again in their shared anti-Semitic, homophobic, and transphobic ideologies. White supremacists believe that by encouraging white women to abort their fetuses, Jews are conspiring to destroy the white race and rob white male Americans of their rightful power. Anti-abortion groups describe abortion as a "holocaust" larger and more problematic than that perpetrated by the Nazis during World War II. Similarly, anti-abortion extremists, white supremacists, and patriot movement anti-government groups align with abortion opponents in vehemently opposing same-sex marriage and LGBTQ+ protections. All gained followers and legitimacy as a result of President Trump's inflammatory, hate-filled rhetoric, his consistent support of far-right nationalists, and his unwavering backing of the anti-abortion movement.

As a result of the shifting tides at the federal level even before the Trump administration, some states passed their own clinic protection acts, as well as a range of anti-noise and loitering restrictions, limitations on picketing in residential neighborhoods, and "buffer zone" laws that protected clinic entrances and created zones around patients who were harassed while trying to enter clinics. In recent years, the Supreme Court has been more amenable to anti-abortion protestors' free speech claims, particularly when protests take place on public sidewalks or roads, such as in 2014, when it found unconstitutional the Massachusetts law that created a fixed thirty-five-foot buffer around clinics.

THE VIOLENCE AGAINST clinics and doctors certainly sent a chilling and sustained message that providing abortion services was a dangerous career choice, but brutality was not the only tactic used to make sure that abortion access was pushed out of reach for many women. Opponents utilized many legal maneuvers—death by a thousand pinpricks—to ensure that abortion as a medical treatment was siloed, stigmatized, and overall diminished, and drove down the number of abortion providers.

In the years immediately following *Roe*, doctors who had performed abortions in legal hospital settings along with reproductive health activists opened independent clinics in order to increase patient access to abortion services. Freestanding clinics such as Reproductive Health Services in St. Louis, Philadelphia's Elizabeth Blackwell Health Center, and the Women's Health Center in Duluth, Minnesota, opened their doors with a deep commitment to providing reproductive health care, including abortion. Planned Parenthood clinics that already offered contraception now began offering abortion services and soon grew to become the largest provider of abortions in the nation. Just three years after *Roe*, the majority of abortions (61 percent) were being performed in clinics, not hospitals, and by 2008 that number had risen to 95 percent of abortions.

Because not all Planned Parenthood clinics provided abortion services, and some only provided them early in pregnancy, independent abortion providers played, and continue to play, a vital role. These providers are often more vulnerable to legislative and terrorist attacks since they are the ones offering abortion services later in pregnancy. Today, the majority of abortion-seeking patients (58 percent) "receive care at independent clinics, compared to 37% percent who obtain care at Planned Parenthood and only 1% who go to a physician's office for an abortion."

In the first several decades, this shift from hospitals to nonhospital clinics was a boon to women, reducing the cost of service and ensuring that counselors, nurses, and doctors were sensitive to the needs of women facing an unintended pregnancy. Nevertheless, when nearly all abortions are provided in specialized clinics, there are several downsides. Clinics and doctors are easier to target with violence when they are in their own buildings, separate from other types of medical providers or businesses. Because only a small number of abortions are performed in hospitals, including teaching hospitals, most medical students have no exposure to or training in abortion care. By the early 1990s, approximately 12 percent of obstetrics and gynecology (OB/GYN) programs offered training in abortion care. Students interested in gaining this practical experience had to arrange to do so outside of the standard educational path. As a result, there were fewer younger abortion doctors to supplement or replace those providers who were aging out of their practices.

To address this shortage in 1993, Jody Steinauer, an enterprising medical student at the University of California, San Francisco, created Medical Students for Choice, which today thrives at medical schools nationwide. Steinauer had received the threatening "comic book" sent to medical students and was motivated to address the lack of abortion training opportunities. The organization's advocacy has been primarily responsible for the restoration of abortion training and clinical opportunities at numerous medical schools and for doctors in a wider range of specialties—from obstetrics and gynecology to pediatrics, internal medicine, and emergency medicine—now providing surgical and medication abortions to their patients.

Steinauer herself now leads UCSF's Bixby Global Center for Reproductive Health, where she trains medical students and doctors to perform abortions and has created free curricula and teaching tools about sexual and reproductive health. A 2018 study of OB/GYN residency training programs showed that 64 percent of programs now routinely dedicate time to abortion training, a marked improvement, although we hope to someday see 100 percent. The Reproductive Health Access Project also offers intensive training for family medicine clinicians, so they can provide, teach, and advocate for abortion as part of comprehensive reproductive health care.

But a dearth of providers remains. Unfortunately, some medical schools and many clinical placements are in facilities controlled by religious institutions opposed to abortion. The largest group of nonprofit health care providers in the nation is the Catholic Church, and ongoing mergers and consolidation have led to its continued dominance. With more than 650 Catholic hospitals, each day more than one in seven patients in the US receives care from a Catholic hospital. These hospitals refuse to see abortion patients or treat those seeking contraception or sterilization, including tubal ligations and vasectomies. Medical schools run by the Catholic, Mormon, and Seventh-Day Adventist Churches are not likely to be friendly to those students interested in learning about how to perform abortions.

The less frequently abortion providers interact with their peers, particularly with OB/GYNs who do not perform abortions, the more marginalized they become within the medical community. Anti-abortion rhetoric that labels providers as murderers makes it easier for peers to consider them pariahs and inferior practitioners, all the while depending on them to provide necessary treatment to their own patients. When violence escalates, physicians step further away from their colleagues who provide abortions, in order to avoid being targeted themselves.

Overall, independent clinics in abortion-hostile states have an incredibly difficult time finding doctors to employ. Many of these clinics have had to rely on itinerant doctors who fly state-to-state to perform abortions on differing days of the week. For years Dr. Susan Wicklund was one such doctor who traveled to provide abortion care throughout the Midwest at clinics in Wisconsin, Minnesota, and North Dakota. "My schedule required daily flights or drives of two hundred miles or more. At least three nights a week, I was in a motel room," Wicklund recalls. Adding to her exhaustion was the "almost constant presence of anti-abortion protesters intent on persuading—or coercing—doctors to stop providing abortions in the far-flung locales." Wicklund's weekly circuit running a "gauntlet" of protestors at every airport caused her to don outlandish disguises to pass unrecognized, wear a bulletproof vest, and carry a .38-caliber revolver. Wicklund subsequently opened her own clinics in Montana, but several other doctors still follow a similar path traveling to clinics far from their homes, committed to providing abortion services where they are sorely lacking.

ONE OF THE most promising strategies to ameliorate the shortage of doctors is to allow qualified mid-level medical providers, including physician assistants, nurse midwives, and nurse practitioners to provide routine surgical and medication abortions. Mid-level providers are empowered by states to provide a range of medical care, either under a doctor's supervision or independently, and they are particularly helpful in rural states where there are significant shortages of physicians. Today mid-level professionals perform routine primary care as well as more complicated and dangerous medical procedures, including delivering babies and prescribing a range of controlled substances.

The exclusion of mid-level providers from abortion services is grounded in *Roe*'s over-reliance on doctors as decision makers. *Roe* presumed that a doctor would be involved in a woman's abortion decision. Currently, only a physician may provide both surgical and medication abortions in thirty-two states. Other states and the District of Columbia allow mid-levels to prescribe medication abortion consistent with the recommendations of the World Health Organization and practices worldwide. But these states still require a doctor for surgical procedures despite recent studies, which verify that first-trimester surgical abortions provided by mid-level practitioners are as safe as when performed by physicians.

Susan Cahill was one such physician assistant who began performing abortions immediately after *Roe*. Cahill was tough, with a steely core, and had followed her heart from New York to Montana. Since then she had been delivering abortion services as a part of a primary care and family planning practice in rural northwest Montana. One day in 1995, Cahill was suddenly barred from performing abortions. A new Montana law that limited the performance of abortions only to physicians threatened to close her down. Center lawyers represented Cahill and a group of doctors in a federal court challenge, *Armstrong v. Mazurek*, that found Montana's doctor-only provision unconstitutional because it imposed an undue burden on women's right to choose abortion. But the case was appealed to the Supreme Court, which went the other way in 1997, summarily upholding the law on appeal without oral argument or full briefing.

Julie joined Janet Benshoof and Simon Heller as they tried another path by filing a lawsuit on Cahill's behalf in state court, arguing that the law violated the Montana Constitution. This lawsuit was part of the Center's work to strategically use state constitutional law to guarantee broader rights than those available under the US Constitution. This time, Cahill won and again began to offer abortions. Julie was struck by Cahill's dedication to providing her patients with a full range of services and impressed by her can-do approach and her ability to tolerate the freezing weather, which Cahill downplayed, saying, "It's a dry cold."

Despite the legal victory, however, Cahill was cruelly put out of business after her clinic, All Families Healthcare, was vandalized in 2014. Anti-abortion zealot Zachary Klundt broke into Cahill's clinic and poured iodine on the floor, damaged the heating and plumbing systems, and took a hammer to Cahill's personal photos. Klundt's mother had served on the board of directors of a nearby anti-abortion crisis pregnancy center, Hope Pregnancy Ministries.

The destruction of Cahill's clinic sent a strong warning to others as well. Samantha Avery, who had trained under Cahill, told National Public Radio around the time of Klundt's trial in 2015, "I know that she wanted me to be the one to take over her clinic, [and] even before all of this, I told her, 'I just don't know if I could do that to my family—my future family. I can't be the [next] Susan Cahill. I'm not that brave of a person.'" In 2018, Helen Weems moved to Montana and reopened All Families Healthcare, crediting Cahill as its "pioneering foremother."

However, Weems was a nurse practitioner, not a physician assistant. The Center and the ACLU successfully returned to state court to ensure that nurse practitioners and nurse midwives could provide abortions. Weems now provides a wide range of inclusive health care services, including first-trimester abortions.

Over the last several years, additional successful lawsuits have allowed qualified mid-level practitioners to perform abortions, increasing the number of abortion providers in several states. State-level activists have also succeeded in repealing some states' physician-only laws. A federal district judge in Virginia found the state's doctor-only provision unconstitutional in 2019, and the legislature recently repealed it. Similarly, the Massachusetts legislature passed a new law that allowed mid-level clinicians to provide abortion care if they have received appropriate training. As a result of these efforts, thirteen states and Washington, DC, now permit mid-level practitioners to perform both surgical and medication abortions, and five others permit them to dispense medication abortions, significantly expanding the availability of early abortion. Progress, yet not enough.

DOCTOR-ONLY LAWS ARE not the sole rules that deter doctors as well as mid-level providers from providing abortions. Unfortunately, FDA rules—called Risk Evaluation and Mitigation Strategies (REMS)—also discourage practitioners from prescribing medication abortion and adversely affect its availability.

Beginning in 2000, with FDA approval of the abortion pill mifepristone (also known as RU-486), women have had the option to choose medication abortion. Under the most common regimen, women first take a mifepristone pill to stop the pregnancy from progressing, followed by a second pill, misoprostol, twenty-four to forty-eight hours later, which causes cramping and bleeding and thus empties the uterus. Medication abortion is safe and effective up to ten weeks of pregnancy and today comprises over a third of abortions at eight weeks' or less gestation. Some women prefer medication abortion even when the surgical method is available because it can be used very early in pregnancy, and may provide greater privacy or feel more natural than surgery.

Misoprostol, which has been approved for ending a pregnancy when used on its own, is less effective than the two-drug regimen but easier to obtain. In many countries, misoprostol is commonly available over the counter either alone or as an abortion kit with mifepristone. In the US it is available by prescription at any pharmacy.

In contrast, the FDA has treated mifepristone as the redheaded stepchild of the pharmaceutical world, prohibiting retail pharmacies from dispensing it. FDA REMS require that clinicians obtain a unique certification prior to prescribing it and that patients pick up the medication in person from their medical provider's clinic, medical office, or hospital. The good news is that the patient can then choose where to swallow the medication, and most decide to do so at home.

The bad news is that these medically unnecessary REMS, which force doctors to jump through extra hoops, dissuade them from offering the drug. As a result, fewer medical professionals have stepped up to provide medication abortions as had been hoped when this modern method first arrived on the scene. For the most part, those who already provide surgical abortions are the ones providing the medication.

The REMS also construct hurdles for patients who are forced to travel, miss work or school, face increased costs, and risk harassment by protestors outside of clinics in order to pick up the drug. The ACLU has filed lawsuits challenging these restrictions. Although they were temporarily suspended for some months during the pandemic, in January 2021 the Supreme Court left the REMS in place until the appeal in the case is concluded. Chief Justice Roberts made clear that he was not ruling on whether the rules are an undue burden; rather he deferred to FDA expertise on whether to lift them. Justice Sonia Sotomayor, joined by Justice Kagan, filed a passionate dissent, arguing that the rules unfairly prevent women from obtaining abortions and unnecessarily risk their health during the pandemic. Fortunately, in 2021, the FDA pivoted and suspended the REMS through the duration of the COVID-19 public heath emergency. In our view, they should banish them forever.

At the end of the day, even if we preserve some formulation of *Roe* and *Casey,* abortion rights are a hollow shell if there are too few abortion providers. The extreme violence against providers, coupled with limitations on the performance and teaching of abortion in hospitals and medical schools, plus doctor-only laws that prevent mid-level medical personnel from providing both surgical and medication abortion, and FDA requirements that discourage providers from prescribing medication abortion, add up to create a dramatic shortage of abortion providers in vast areas of the country. The resulting dearth falls far too inequitably on women of color and far too harshly on rural women and those who cannot afford their way around restrictions.

While these overlapping barriers at times combined to place abortion almost entirely out of reach, it was a preview to what came next from abortion opponents. Ultimately, women's health, lives, and dignity would be even more jeopardized by barefaced attempts to ban abortion outright.

CHAPTER 8

IN-YOUR-FACE POLITICS
ABORTION BANS INFLAME THE DEBATE

Sometimes you just have to put on lip gloss and pretend to be psyched.

MINDY KALING, ACTOR, WRITER, AND PRODUCER

JANET BENSHOOF ALWAYS had a flair for the dramatic. When she and Kitty were at the ACLU's Reproductive Freedom Project in 1990, the island of Guam boldly outlawed all abortions with very few exceptions, and Benshoof sprang into action. After Anita Arriola, an attorney and the defiant daughter of the bill's chief legislative sponsor, phoned the ACLU for help, Benshoof threw some warm weather clothes into a suitcase, hopped on a plane, and headed to Guam. Because Guam is a US territory and thus subject to constitutional law, the plan had been to seek an injunction in the federal court on the island. But before she had time to file, Benshoof was in court facing criminal charges herself.

To draw attention to how radical Guam's new law was, particularly the portion of the law that prohibited even the "soliciting" of abortion, Benshoof announced at the Guam Press Club that abortions could be obtained in Hawaii. Then, in her usual spirited way and with a hint of a smile, she encouraged women to go there and gave out the telephone number for Planned Parenthood in Honolulu. Three hours later the Guam attorney general prosecuted her for solicitation. She faced a year in prison if convicted. She hadn't even had time for a dip in the ocean.

The ACLU team, now including Arriola as local counsel challenging her mother's law, scrambled to obtain a federal court order that the law was unconstitutional. Attorneys for Guam, working with attorneys from Americans United for Life, tried several different legal arguments to squirm out of being bound by *Roe*. Fortunately, the Court held that "[t]he bits and pieces assembled by Guam fall short of compelling us to do that which the Supreme Court itself has declined to do—overrule *Roe v. Wade*." The law was struck as unconstitutional, and the criminal charges against Benshoof were dropped. She left the palm trees behind to return to her day job back east.

Guam was not the only place that year that demonstrated such utter contempt for existing law. Legislators in Idaho, Utah, and Louisiana also adopted clearly unconstitutional bans on abortions. It was an in-your-face strategy. Anti-abortion forces were confident that by the time any lawsuit challenging the ban arrived at the Supreme Court, there would be a fifth Supreme Court Justice delighted to overrule *Roe*. State legislators opposing abortion had votes to gain and nothing to lose, other than the taxpayer money required to defend these blatantly unconstitutional laws in extensive litigation.

While the bans enacted in Guam, Idaho, Louisiana, and Utah included some varying exceptions for rape or incest or severe and physical health risks, they all competed to be the most inhospitable in the nation. Each of the laws would prohibit nearly all abortions if not struck down by the courts.

Within a few days of Benshoof's arrest in Guam, Kitty headed to Idaho to lobby against a similarly extreme abortion ban. Idaho's version of the legislation permitted abortion only in cases of a rape that was reported to police within seven days, incest if the victim was younger than eighteen, severe fetal deformity, or threat to the physical health of the woman.

Idaho is better known as the nation's top producer of potatoes than as an anti-abortion hotbed. The state produces more than ten billion pounds of potatoes a year, a third of the nation's supply. So feminists decided to hit Idaho with a national tater boycott proposed by the president of NOW, Molly Yard. Word spread quickly across the country as women, who did most of the family grocery shopping, were looking for a way to send a strong message of support for abortion rights. Abortion supporters capped their protest of the bill by dropping ten thousand pounds of spuds on the capitol steps.

Anti-abortion Democratic governor Cecil D. Andrus, who had wavered on whether to sign the ban bill into law, politely declined to schedule an appointment with Kitty. However, during her meeting with his general counsel, much to her surprise, the governor himself popped in to "borrow a book" and listened in as Kitty pointed out the bill's constitutional flaws. Thankfully he vetoed the measure soon thereafter.

Next up was Louisiana, and Kitty headed to New Orleans to await the passage of an even stricter bill banning nearly all abortions. Wandering the French Quarter, she saw Louisiana's racism and extremism firsthand as David Duke, the former grand wizard of the Ku Klux Klan, was in a runoff election for governor against Edwin Edwards, a powerful former governor dogged by charges of corruption and later convicted of federal racketeering charges. Bumper stickers blatantly proclaimed "Vote for the Lizard, not the Wizard" and "Vote for the Crook: It's Important."

The law was passed by a wide margin, but then-Governor Buddy Roemer vetoed the measure because it did not allow abortion in cases of rape or incest. Yet with only three women in the entire Louisiana legislature and a strong anti-abortion majority, the bill was quickly passed over the governor's veto. The only opposition came from Black legislators, including Representative Alphonse Jackson, Democrat of Shreveport, who wisely noted, "Who are we—males for the most part—to make a decision about what happens to a woman's body? We do not have that right."

Kitty and her cocounsel, Bill Rittenberg, who was one of the few Louisiana lawyers willing to publicly align with abortion rights, headed to federal court for an emergency order to stop the law from taking effect. The case was assigned to District Court Judge Adrian G. Duplantier, a Carter appointee who made no secret of his opposition to abortion. But it was his overt misogyny and anti-Semitism that shocked

Kitty and served as a poignant reminder of how David Duke could have a chance at being elected governor. Kitty had purchased a red skirt suit—the power color of the era—to wear to court. During a meeting of all attorneys in the judge's private chambers, Judge Duplantier kept snidely referring to Kitty as "that lady in red," a reference to New Orleans's sex workers. At the end of the meeting, he cordially bid goodbye to Louisiana's attorney general, William Guste. Turning to Rittenberg and Kitty, who are both Jewish, he added with a sneer, "Or should I say, 'Shalom'?"

Ultimately, despite his personal distaste, Judge Duplantier granted Kitty's request for relief, noting that he was bound by *Roe* to invalidate the statute despite his own views on abortion. But he sent a strong message to the Supreme Court that it was time to overrule *Roe* and permit Louisiana and other states to ban abortion. He "wholeheartedly agreed" with Justice White's dissenting opinion in *Roe*, that *Roe* had created "a new constitutional right for pregnant women . . . with scarcely any reason or authority for its action." Fortunately, Judge Duplantier and the Louisiana legislature's hope that the Supreme Court would use the state's ban to overrule *Roe* was short-circuited by the Supreme Court's decision in *Casey*.

Louisiana is particularly passionate about the sanctity of motherhood that fuels its anti-abortion beliefs—even the state flag displays a white pelican feeding her three young at her breast with her own blood. Indeed, since *Roe*, the state has adopted eighty-nine abortion restrictions, far more than any other state. One of the clients Kitty and Julie worked with in several cases was Robin Rothrock, the founder of Hope Medical Group for Women in Shreveport, Louisiana. Rothrock and her clinic were solid supporters of abortion rights, providing top quality care from behind windows boarded up to safeguard against anti-abortion violence. Years later, the Hope clinic, now run by Robin's son, would be one of the last remaining providers in the state and a plaintiff in *June Medical Services v. Russo*, the 2020 Supreme Court case on abortion discussed at the start of this book.

While these onerous abortion bans during the early 1990s were invalidated by the courts, today ten states have on their books what are known as "trigger laws"—bans on abortion that would immediately take effect at the moment *Roe* and *Casey* are overturned. An additional nine states still have abortion bans on their books from before *Roe* became the law of the land. It's a safe presumption that abortion opponents will seek to resuscitate them. Thus, when *Roe* is toppled, abortion may quickly become a criminal offense in nearly one-third of the United States.

AFTER *CASEY* ULTIMATELY foreclosed total bans in 1992, anti-abortion activists quickly resurrected an old strategy they had tried unsuccessfully once in Missouri: ban a singular method of abortion. This time they targeted what they christened "partial birth abortion," methods of abortion that were used in the second or third trimester of pregnancy. Their campaign took off like greased lightning. Legislators nationwide passed so many bans so quickly that within a decade, so-called partial birth abortion bans became the bulk of the Center's litigation docket.

"Partial birth abortion" was a fictitious medical term coined by the National Right to Life Committee (NRLC) in 1995. It portrayed an abortion technique as a barbaric practice that was both harmful to women and the unconscionable murder of a child "just two inches from birth." The concept was based upon a medical procedure called dilation and extraction (D&X) developed independently by two skilled doctors, Martin Haskell and James McMahon, as a safer way to perform those very few abortions that took place after the twentieth week of pregnancy.

The NRLC commissioned a grotesque cartoonlike drawing to illustrate the method and ran it as an advertisement in newspapers to build public opposition. The plan, according to NRLC lobbyist Douglas Johnson, was to spotlight an exaggerated image of one method of abortion in order to foster opposition to late abortion overall. The language of these laws was so vague and fabricated that it left open the possibility that they could prohibit abortion as early as thirteen weeks but certainly would apply later in pregnancy.

Dr. Haskell's home state of Ohio leaped to be the first in the nation to pass a partial birth ban. Recognizing the threat these laws imposed and the importance of Dr. Haskell's practice for the women who traveled long distances for his services later in pregnancy, Kitty quickly agreed to represent him. With the aid of Al Gerhardstein, a dedicated civil rights attorney from Cincinnati, and others, she successfully blocked Ohio's partial birth ban. But like a starfish growing back an arm, a few months later anti-abortion members in Congress introduced a bill modeled on the Ohio ban that would apply nationwide and subject doctors to a two-year prison sentence.

Lobbying against the federal bill, Kitty and her colleagues decided to provide a fuller picture of women with wanted pregnancies who needed later, postviability abortions because of severe fetal anomalies. Tammy Watts was one of several courageous women who stepped up to share their ordeals. In the late stages of a much-wanted pregnancy Watts's routine ultrasound had revealed that the fetus was afflicted with a lethal chromosomal abnormality. Knowing it would not survive and would probably suffer a great deal before dying, and because continuing the pregnancy posed grave risks to Watts's health and her future fertility, she had an abortion procedure that would have been banned by the Partial-Birth Abortion Ban Act Congress was considering. As Watts explained, "I would have given my life and traded places with my daughter, Mackenzie. And in fact, we tried desperately to find something that could cure her. You simply look for a magic wand and it's not there."

None of it was easy or pleasant to talk about, and that was exactly what the anti-abortion movement wanted. By focusing on the medical procedure, they erased women from the picture. In order to bring a human face to a political battle that was too often fraught with hyperbole and invective, Watts and another dedicated woman, Vicki Wilson, told their heart-wrenching stories in an episode of *60 Minutes* and testified before Congress. The women stressed that other abortion methods all posed greater health risks, including more blood loss or risk of lacerating the cervix and thus harming future fertility. But Congress passed the bill nonetheless. Watts, Wilson, and several other women appeared with President Clinton when thankfully he vetoed the measure.

There are downsides to highlighting women who are having late abortions because of fetal anomalies. While it was admittedly an effective political strategy here, it underplays the other reasons that women have late abortions and risks politicians and the public dividing women into categories of those who "deserve" access to abortion or not. More-over, focusing on women with fetal anomalies discounts the significant burdens erected by anti-abortion legislation like funding bans, waiting periods, and parental involvement laws that can delay any abortion into the second trimester.

Despite the defeat of the federal ban, some thirty states enacted laws banning partial birth abortion between 1997 and 2000 alone. The tidal wave of these measures nearly overwhelmed the Center's attor-neys. Ultimately the Center landed back before the Supreme Court in a challenge to Nebraska's partial birth abortion ban. Representing Dr. Carhart, who performed about ten D&X procedures a year for abortions after the twentieth week of pregnancy, Center attorney Simon Heller successfully persuaded the Court in *Stenberg v. Carhart* that under *Roe* and *Casey*'s strictures, the Nebraska law was unconstitutional because it banned abortion before viability, and postviability it failed to include an exception to preserve the woman's health.

Even with a Supreme Court decision finding these laws invalid, Congress was not deterred and passed a partial birth ban *again* in 2003, this time with President George W. Bush there to sign the measure into law. Back to Court came Dr. Carhart, represented by Center attorney Priscilla Smith and Planned Parenthood's Eve Gartner. But by now the Supreme Court had changed. *Casey*'s crucial swing vote, Justice San-dra Day O'Connor, had been replaced by President Bush's conservative pick, Justice Samuel Alito.

Justice Kennedy, who had earlier joined Justice O'Connor in *Casey*, now became the crucial swing vote and authored a 5–4 ruling that up-held the federal ban. Congress in passing the law had asserted that this method was never "medically necessary," allowing Justice Kennedy to find that there was no need for a health exception to the ban.

A powerful dissent from Justice Ginsburg stood up for science and rebuked the majority for allowing Congress to ban a procedure that medical experts from the American College of Obstetrics and Gyne-cologists (ACOG) had found the most appropriate and safe in some circumstances. In doing so, the majority was blurring the line between previability and postviability abortions and permitting a ban devoid of any safeguards for women's health.

The strategy outlined by anti-abortion lawyers back in 1986 had just borne fruit nearly two decades after its launch. Today, twenty-one states ban the provision of partial birth abortion, the majority of which are similar to the federal version that was upheld by the Supreme Court. While the federal law is currently in effect, as well as several state partial birth abortion bans, many contain health exceptions, are unenforceable under the Supreme Court's *Carhart* decision, or operate in states that lack any second-trimester abortion providers.

More recently, anti-abortion legislators have been seeking to expand this win as widely as possible by enacting bans on the commonly used D&E abortion. The real danger of these bills (and the anti-abortion movement's primary incentive in advocating for them) is that they provide yet another opportunity for the newly constituted Supreme Court to overrule *Roe* and *Casey* and strike at women's reproductive freedom.

Along the way, though, the partial birth strategy also enabled abortion opponents to control the public debate and put the Center and other attorneys on the defensive, spending years playing a nightmare version of whack-a-mole litigation. Rather than laboring for better access to contraception and early abortions, our legal work focused almost exclusively on abortions late in pregnancy, despite the fact that these procedures were less than 1 percent of all abortions performed. We both vastly prefer proactive litigation, using our creative skills to play offense. Ultimately the endless flow of partial birth bills and litigation was demoralizing and helped make it easier when each of us left the Center and moved on to other social justice work.

IN ADDITION TO the partial birth abortion bills, some of the most egregious bans on access to abortion happened when individual doctors or hospitals made up their own rules. When the Center attorneys learned of such cases unfairly denying an individual's constitutional access to abortion, we quickly responded. Julie found these cases to be the most gratifying because they often involved assisting families in the most desperate and unfair circumstances. These cases also demonstrated the chilling effect of the anti-abortion movement's success at stigmatizing abortion.

Michelle Lee, a twenty-six-year-old recently divorced mother of two young children in Monroe, Louisiana, fell victim to one such scenario in 1999. While pregnant with her second son, Lee developed a serious heart condition that required her doctors at Louisiana State University Medical Center (LSUMC) to put her on the list for a heart transplant and advised her not to get pregnant. She followed their advice, but unfortunately, birth control is not foolproof. Lee knew she could not safely carry the pregnancy to term and asked her doctors for an abortion. Louisiana law banned using any state hospital or other public funds for abortion services except in life-threatening circumstances or cases of rape or incest. A committee of five LSUMC doctors determined that the hospital would not provide her an abortion because *Lee did not have a greater than 50 percent chance of dying.* The committee had narrowed the criteria for eligibility for a life-threatening standard to the equivalent of one foot on a banana peel and the other foot in the grave.

Lee turned to Robin Rothrock of Hope Medical—yes, the same woman whose son would be at the Supreme Court twenty-two years later as a Center client—but Rothrock could not find a local doctor willing to do the procedure. Rothrock next called Maureen Britell of the National Abortion Federation—yes, the same woman whom the Center had represented when she had been denied federal insurance funding for an abortion after a rare fetal anomaly. Britell raised $10,000, arranged for Lee to be transferred by ambulance to a doctor in Houston, and called the Center for legal help. Once Lee returned home from Texas, she wanted restitution for how she had been treated, and she wanted to be sure no other woman went through that life-endangering experience.

Working closely with Janet Benshoof, Julie decided the best legal remedy was to sue the hospital and the doctors for a whole mix of constitutional and medical malpractice claims. Endless depositions of many LSUMC doctors revealed that they had not acted out of abortion animus but out of fear of reprisal by the hospital or the state if they performed an abortion.

Lee was a bright, lively young woman, and Julie enjoyed getting to know her, her sons, and Rothrock, as she spent many hours in Shreveport litigating the sprawling and costly case. Lee knew she would not live to see her sons grow up but wanted to enjoy her time with them, provide the best she could, and let them and the state know what was the right thing to do. Lee's case was extreme but typical of how the criminal sanctions and stigma attached to abortion results in doctors and hospitals denying women care to which they are legally entitled.

That same year, in the Center's own backyard, Julie wrangled with doctors at a prominent private, secular New York City hospital that was refusing to provide a pregnant comatose mother of two with a lifesaving abortion. The young woman was suffering from eclampsia, a rare and potentially fatal complication of pregnancy for which her doctors had recommended abortion after other treatments had failed. The woman's husband explained that their religion, Orthodox Judaism, counseled abortion when there was a risk to the pregnant woman's life or health, and that his rabbi and his wife's parents all supported the decision. Although the hospital had respected the husband's decision-making authority over all aspects of his wife's care, it refused to provide an abortion without a court order compelling it to do so.

When Julie arrived at the hospital, it quickly became clear that the woman's medical condition was too precarious to delay an abortion while waiting for a Court hearing and risk bringing unwanted attention from abortion opponents known to try to meddle on behalf of the fetus. A longtime Center ally, Dr. William Rashbaum, agreed to do the procedure. That evening, Julie arranged an ambulance to transfer her client to Manhattan's Beth Israel Medical Center, where he had surgical privileges.

Three weeks later, the couple showed up together unannounced at the Center's offices. Julie was overwhelmed as she was introduced to the client she had never seen awake or even outside of a hospital bed. It's not often that lawyers get to feel anything close to saving a life. And while it's not too often that doctors get cold feet and deny lifesaving abortions, it does happen in every corner of the world.

ABORTION OPPONENTS SEEK to limit not only the ways in which women can get abortions but also the reasons why. Starting in 2009, anti-abortion legislators turned to limiting the permissible reasons for abortion. After a decade of focusing on eliminating methods of abortion, fifteen states enacted legislation banning an abortion if a woman had based her decision on the sex of the fetus. Two other states enacted bans if the woman used race as a determining factor.

These bans parrot the language of anti-discrimination laws but twist them to portray themselves as protecting the rights of girls or Black babies. They sound reasonable in theory—who would want to support abortion on the basis of sex or race?—but in fact, there is just no evidence that this is a widespread practice needing legislative attention. Instead, these bans are an attempt to denigrate women seeking abortions and begin to narrow the justifications for abortion throughout pregnancy.

In Indiana, State Senator Liz Brown, the sponsor of a ban on abortions for sex selection, justified the law with offensive stereotypes that South Asian cultures "don't value women." The National Asian Pacific Women's Forum, a reproductive justice group and leading advocate for Asian American and Pacific Islander (AAPI) women and girls, notes that this stereotype "is not only ugly—it's dangerous" because it leads to AAPI women being singled out for unwanted scrutiny, racial profiling, or denial of care, all because of a law that tries to address a problem that likely does not exist.

Similarly, the ban on race-selective abortions "presumes that women choose to terminate pregnancies based on the race of the fetus, the race of the men that impregnated them, or a woman's own perception that her race is 'undesired.'" These bans are a variation on an anti-abortion trope that abortion is a "genocide of Black babies." But as the National Women's Law Center finds, the only cases cited to demonstrate that race selection occurs are the few instances in which racist white parents or grandparents want to force their relatives to have an abortion because of the race of the men who impregnated them.

These reason bans have not yet been directly before the Supreme Court. In 2019, the Court declined to review a case that had invalidated Indiana's ban on abortions performed solely because of race, sex, or other fetal characteristics. Even though the issue was not before the Court, Justice Thomas wrote a striking twenty-page concurring opinion arguing that prohibitions on abortion based on race selection are a necessary check on eugenics. Justice Thomas's opinion channeled the inflammatory rhetoric of anti-abortion groups that portray the Black community as victimized by aggressive marketing by abortion providers, particularly Planned Parenthood, which abortion opponents claim "aborts 360 Blacks every day." To vilify the organization, they also highlight some of the disturbing views of Margaret Sanger, the organization's founder, whose legacy unfortunately includes support for eugenics, a practice that both Planned Parenthood and other abortion rights organizations adamantly disavow.

JULIE'S AUNT ELLEN always said that if something comes back into fashion, you shouldn't wear what you have in your closet from the last time it was in vogue. The anti-abortion movement nonetheless has rejected this wise advice in recent years by bringing back abortion bans that affect women at early stages of pregnancy, refashioning them to restrict far more women.

States primarily in the South and Midwest have enacted new abortion bans based on the gestational age of the fetus, some shockingly early in pregnancy. Eight states—Arkansas, Georgia, Iowa, Kentucky, Louisiana, Mississippi, Ohio, and South Carolina—prohibit abortion from the moment a fetal heartbeat can be detected. Some of these laws could be interpreted to ban abortion as early as six weeks of pregnancy, a time when an ultrasound may be able to hear fetal noise, although a fetal heartbeat is generally not heard until nine to ten weeks of pregnancy through the more commonly used fetal Doppler. Importantly, many women are not even aware they are pregnant as early as six weeks.

Missouri drew a line in the sand by banning abortion at eight weeks, Arkansas at twelve, and Louisiana and Mississippi at fifteen. None of these bans are currently in effect, thanks to winning legal strategies mounted by reproductive rights lawyers. Unfortunately, even more are in the anti-abortion pipeline to the Supreme Court.

Anti-abortion politicians also leaped to exploit the coronavirus pandemic in 2020 to completely ban abortion, albeit temporarily. By defining abortion as "nonessential," governors in eleven states ordered clinics to shut their doors until the end of the emergency. With the support of ACOG and other medical organizations that reiterated that abortion is an essential and time-sensitive medical procedure, abortion rights lawyers successfully obtained emergency relief from the federal courts to enable providers in Alabama, Ohio, and Tennessee to perform abortions. After these initial rulings, eight states modified their orders and allowed other medical and surgical procedures, including abortion, to proceed.

In what is certainly a replay of the greatest hits of the '90s, a 2019 Alabama law subjects doctors to up to ninety-nine years in prison for performing an abortion at *any* stage of pregnancy unless a woman's life is endangered or there is a lethal fetal anomaly. While Alabama governor Kay Ivey concedes this law is likely unenforceable, it enables Alabama legislators to broadcast from the legislative floor their fervent views that life begins at conception. Moreover, a ban like this aims to be the rocket that lands *Roe* and *Casey* before the Supreme Court, providing an opportunity to further burden abortion or likely abolish it altogether. How many more whacks at the piñata before *Roe* falls?

All this should, by now, leave you asking the inevitable question: *How can legislators do this?* The answer: *They have the power to create laws that serve the abortion question to the Supreme Court on a plate.* And more importantly, who can stop them?

However stellar the abortion rights legal team, they have been dealt a weak hand. Thanks to decades of Republican focus on appointing judges, and recently Senator Mitch McConnell's dogged efforts as Senate majority leader, the road to the Supreme Court is now paved with over two hundred conservative federal court jurists who are cognizant of the sharp rightward tilt of the Supreme Court. President Trump's appointment of three vehemently anti-abortion Justices sends the strong message that the Supreme Court is likely to welcome bans enacted by Alabama or other states in order to present an opportunity to decimate *Roe* and *Casey*. Justice Barrett's appointment has brought the anti-abortion prophesy even nearer to completion.

And that is all that matters. Remember *Sesame Street*: five is the magic number, and now they have six. Within the near future, a case challenging *Roe* and *Casey* will land on the Court's regal steps.

CHAPTER 9

A WOLF AT THE DOOR
NEW SUPREME COURT MAJORITY PUTS PROCREATIVE AND SEXUAL FREEDOMS AT RISK

> The decision whether or not to bear a child is central
> to a woman's life, to her well-being and dignity. It is
> a decision she must make for herself. When the gov-
> ernment controls that decision for her, she is being
> treated as less than a full adult human responsible for
> her own choices.
>
> RUTH BADER GINSBURG,
> 1993 SUPREME COURT CONFIRMATION HEARINGS

WE WERE IN the midst of writing this book when feminist icon and human rights defender Justice Ruth Bader Ginsburg suddenly passed away. Little more than a month later, Justice Barrett, only forty-eight years old, was whisked onto the Supreme Court, where she can now stay for the rest of her life.

Julie was stunned, somehow expecting a knight in shining armor to sweep in and rescue RBG's seat from right-wing zealotry. Kitty, how-ever, had long ago given up on fairy tales. More significantly, we had started writing *Controlling Women* because we both knew the Supreme Court was not the place to go to protect, never mind expand, abor-tion rights. We were tired of our movement repeatedly banging its head against the Court's marble walls and sought to strategize an affirmative path forward.

The fact that there had not been a clear Supreme Court majority favoring unencumbered abortion rights in over four decades was painfully obvious. The Democrats took major steps to shore up these rights with the appointment of Justices Ginsburg, Stephen G. Breyer, Kagan, and Sotomayor. Nevertheless, when Justice Kennedy, the swing vote on abortion, retired in 2018, support for even limited abortion rights left the building.

The abortion rights movement has been accused of crying wolf about the demise of abortion rights. But the appointment of Justice Barrett tips the balance, putting abortion at risk along with a range of procreative and sexual freedoms that are at the heart of why abortion matters. The wolf is at the door.

We opened *Controlling Women* with a discussion of the Supreme Court case that Kitty and Julie went to hear in March 2020, *June Medical Services v. Russo*. That case is a good example of a dodged bullet for abortion rights and a harbinger of what's to come.

What is most significant about *June Medical* is that just four years earlier, the Supreme Court had heard arguments in a nearly identical challenge to a Texas Targeted Regulation of Abortion Providers or "TRAP" law, *Whole Woman's Health v. Hellerstedt*. In fact, Kitty and Joann had gone to listen to that argument, which had also been litigated by the Center's attorneys. The two laws were so similar that it was particularly ominous that the Court was considering the matter a second time.

The Texas law in *Whole Woman's Health*, like the subsequent Louisiana law in *June Medical*, sought to restrict the number of facilities that could perform abortions by imposing onerous, costly regulations on clinics. Abortion providers are already subject to strict regulations such as safety and licensing requirements, and medical and professional ethics that regulate the profession overall. TRAP laws like the ones in these court cases go well beyond that by needlessly applying standards of ambulatory surgical centers to abortion clinics, even though abortion is a much less invasive, low-risk procedure. Not only do the laws impose unnecessarily large room and corridor sizes, specialized equipment, and medical certifications, some, like the Texas and Louisiana laws, also require abortion doctors to have admitting privileges at a hospital within thirty miles of their clinics or offices—something most clinic doctors are unable to obtain. The rules are applied even to medication abortions, when no surgery is performed.

Although these rules masquerade as health regulations, they do little to further abortion patients' health and thus have been opposed by ACOG and the AMA. The real intent is to make the rules so burdensome and expensive that clinics are forced to shut their doors. The types of regulations vary considerably from state to state, but the most arduous—like those in Arizona, Arkansas, Texas, and Louisiana—have proven to be remarkably effective. When courts have stepped in to squelch the regulations, clinics have been able to reopen, as happened in Texas in 2014, while *Whole Woman's Health* wound its way to the Supreme Court.

The Texas law at issue in *Whole Woman's Health* was much more extreme than many of the other restrictions the Court had considered since *Casey*. Yet watching the *Whole Woman's Health* Supreme Court argument, Kitty was struck by how different the atmosphere was from her argument in *Casey*. The Court now had three female Justices—Ginsburg, Sotomayor, and Kagan—who strongly supported abortion rights. The *Casey* Court's lone female Justice, Reagan-appointee Sandra Day O'Connor, had shown only tepid support. The Court's changed composition dramatically improved the tenor of the argument in *Whole Woman's Health*. Justice Kagan emphasized how if the law took effect, three-quarters of a million women would be further than two hundred miles from a clinic. Justice Ginsburg pressed the state to justify why a doctor who was only providing medication abortions would ever need to have hospital admitting privileges, since complications were so rare. Justice Sotomayor questioned whether there ever "was a medical benefit to having a medication abortion at a . . . multimillion-dollar surgical facility." Music to Kitty's ears.

A few months later, the Court's opinion reflected that new tune. Written by feminist ally Justice Breyer and joined by Justices Kennedy, Ginsburg, Sotomayor, and Kagan, the majority opinion applied the

Casey standards and held unconstitutional the provisions of the Texas law. The Court found that on balance, the statute lacked a sufficient medical benefit to justify the undue burden it imposed in violation of the Constitution.

The Court recognized that the hospital admitting privileges requirement would have resulted in a drop in the number of licensed abortion facilities in Texas by more than half. Allowing the law's smothering building code requirements—estimated to cost between $1 to $1.5 million per facility—would leave fewer than ten clinics to serve over five million Texan women of reproductive age. Significantly, the Court acknowledged that the bulk of closures would occur in southern and western Texas, causing the greatest harm to poor, rural, and disadvantaged women who are disproportionately Latina. Thankfully, *Casey* lived to fight another day.

Following the oral argument in *Whole Woman's Health,* there was cause for optimism. With President Obama on the verge of nominating a new Justice favoring abortion rights, plus the likelihood that former secretary of state Hillary Clinton would become president the following November, the future of abortion rights looked bright. The wolves could huff and puff, but at that moment in early 2016, it looked as if the *Casey* standard was a house made out of brick, not straw.

The optimism quickly crumbled. Several weeks following the argument, President Obama nominated Merrick Garland to the Supreme Court following the death of Justice Scalia. Garland was by all accounts a moderate and one likely to be a reliable supporter of abortion rights. But Senate Majority Leader McConnell, flagrantly politicizing the confirmation process, refused to allow Senate consideration of Judge Garland's nomination. McConnell prioritized his personal goal of creating "seismic change" at the Supreme Court "that will stay with the nation for generations to come" above his obligation to oversee a fair, constitutionally mandated confirmation process.

McConnell's judicial power grab was not limited to the Supreme Court. He was determined to ensure that all levels of the federal judiciary would be filled with conservative judges, one of the anti-abortion movement's key strategic goals. With McConnell leading the charge,

Republican senators blocked a total of 105 of President Obama's federal judicial nominees—more than at any other time in recent history, and thus these seats remained empty for President Trump to fill upon taking office. As a result, during the Trump era, Republicans installed over two hundred conservative district court and courts of appeals judges, mostly white men, with the potential to radically alter the law as we know it. He was shameless—and successful.

The ultra-conservative sea change at the Supreme Court began with the appointment of two new strongly anti-abortion Justices in the first years of Trump's presidency. Justice Neil Gorsuch took Justice Scalia's seat in April 2017 after Senator McConnell derailed the Democrats' Garland nomination. The following year, Justice Kennedy, one of the architects of *Casey*, resigned from the Court, and President Trump nominated Brett Kavanaugh, a conservative judge on the Court of Appeals for the DC Circuit.

The Kavanaugh proceedings were a remake of the Justice Thomas hearings decades earlier. Where Thomas's confirmation hearings had exploded around Anita Hill's accusations of sexual harassment, during Kavanaugh's confirmation hearings Dr. Christine Blasey Ford accused the nominee of sexually assaulting her when they were in high school. The two women's claims were similarly incendiary and similarly disregarded. In both cases, additional women who had credible accusations of sexual misconduct by the nominee were not given an opportunity to testify. A contentious hearing in the Senate brought about nationwide protests and divisiveness that further damaged the Court's credibility. Nonetheless, the Senate approved Kavanaugh's nomination by a razor-thin, two-vote margin.

The ascendency of Justices Gorsuch and Kavanaugh to the Court was not accidental. Each had clerked on the Supreme Court, each had been appointed to a Court of Appeals at a young age, and both had been groomed by right-wing organizations to be on a Supreme Court short list, all part of the Republicans' concerted effort to pack the lower federal courts and the Supreme Court with ultra-conservatives. It was an orchestrated push that aligned well with the plan to decimate *Roe*.

The opinions that Justices Kavanaugh and Gorsuch had each written as Court of Appeals judges did not reveal their views of *Roe* or *Casey*. Nor did either judge show his hand at his confirmation hearing. Nonetheless, court watchers, including the two of us, believed that both judges would provide solid anti-abortion votes. Both men had been vetted by the Federalist Society—the leading conservative legal organization pushing for a more conservative court—garnered support from a wide range of anti-abortion groups, and were being appointed by a president who had vowed to stack the Court with "pro-life" judges. Not only would their opposition to abortion align with Trump's promise, it was a natural outcome of their judicial philosophy and religiously influenced personal ideology. Presumptions about the Justices' strong anti-abortion views were validated just a few years later in 2018, when the Court considered the Louisiana TRAP law in *June Medical*.

After a six-day trial, the federal District Court had concluded that under *Casey* and in line with *Whole Woman's Health*, the law in *June Medical* was clearly unconstitutional. On appeal, however, the conservative-dominated Fifth Circuit Court of Appeals bucked its responsibility to defer to the trial court. Astonishingly, it reversed the lower court's ruling by disagreeing with nearly every one of the District Court's factual findings and then upheld the Louisiana law.

The Center and its clinic clients were between a rock and a hard place that echoed *Casey*, just as the anti-abortion movement had planned. Should they appeal to the Supreme Court, they risked a loss with nationwide impact. If they let the law stand, not only could it shutter more clinics in Louisiana, but it could inspire copycat laws in other states around the country. Ultimately the doctors and clinics decided to appeal, and the Supreme Court accepted the case for review in 2019.

As we walked into the Court for the *June Medical* argument in March 2020, it was clear that our colossal apprehension was warranted. An ultra-conservative, anti-abortion majority was now firmly in the driver's seat. Watching the proceedings from less than ten feet away, Julie fixated on how Justice Kavanaugh's hulking figure dwarfed Justice Ginsburg's petite frame. Would this be the case in which *Roe* was

overpowered? At the end of the day, we jumped on a train back to Philadelphia and New York, fearing that the demise of *Roe* was imminent
notwithstanding a strong argument by the Center's attorneys.

But late in June, despite the addition of two new anti-abortion Justices, the Court surprised Kitty, Julie, and nearly all court watchers by
rejecting the Louisiana law. Exhale. By a 5–4 vote, the Supreme Court
found the Louisiana law unconstitutional, just as it had in the Texas
case. A plurality opinion, authored by Justice Breyer, joined by Justices
Ginsburg, Sotomayor, and Kagan, respected precedent and relied on
Casey and *Whole Woman's Health* to hold that the burdens of Louisiana's "unnecessary health regulations" outweighed its benefits and thus
were an unconstitutional, undue burden on women. A doctor's ability
to represent a patient's interest was upheld as well.

Chief Justice Roberts had saved the day—for now. He recognized
that the Louisiana law created a burden on women that was as severe as
what the Court had invalidated earlier in *Whole Woman's Health*. Consistent with the Court's precedent, he sent the Louisiana law to join its
Texas twin in the dustbin.

But ominously, Chief Justice Roberts rejected the cost-benefit reasoning of the four liberal Justices, who had found that the benefits did
not outweigh the burdens the law imposed. Instead Roberts asserted that
the Court should be asking *only* whether the law imposed a substantial
obstacle in the path of a woman seeking an abortion, the original undue
burden standard from *Casey*. In Justice Roberts's view, a pointless law
could stand so long as it did not make it *too* difficult to access abortion.

The anti-abortion groups were extremely upset that the Chief Justice
had sided with the more liberal Justices, particularly because he had
voted to uphold the equivalent Texas law when it was before the Court
in 2016. And while abortion rights advocates were thrilled, many were
quick to point out that Chief Justice Roberts might not come to the
same favorable conclusion applying the traditional *Casey* standard in
future cases.

Dissenting opinions by Justices Kavanaugh, Alito, Gorsuch, and
Thomas gave us an early warning sign about how the new conservative

Justices would rule on these issues if they were able to convince Justice Roberts to fully join their team.

Justice Alito asserted that he would give legislatures "wide discretion" in assessing whether a regulation serves a legitimate medical need, essentially allowing anti-abortion lawmakers to create "health regulations" no matter how specious or unnecessary actual medical professionals believe them to be. Justice Kavanaugh agreed with Justice Roberts that the *Casey* standard should apply and also agreed with Justice Alito that the law safeguards women's health but said the case should be sent back to the lower courts to decide.

Like the other dissenters, Justice Gorsuch found that doctors have no standing to represent their patients' interests because they have "no close relationship" with them and their interests may be in conflict. Kitty and Julie thought about all the doctors who dedicated their lives and safety to providing women with abortion services and wondered if Justice Gorsuch had ever had a conversation with a single abortion provider.

In all likelihood, Justice Roberts, as the Chief Justice, was seeking to preserve public faith in the neutrality of what would be forever known as the Roberts Court. His ruling had blocked the Court from switching directions on an identical statute within a short time frame. Perhaps he was waiting for a calmer, less volatile moment, allowing time for the deep-seated ill will surrounding Justice Kavanaugh's confirmation— reflected in protestors' signs that had declared "Kava-Nope" and "Save Roe, Stop Kavanaugh"—to fade from view. Nevertheless, he left open the possibility that he could vote to uphold other abortion restrictions as he had once done under the *Casey* standard.

While the four dissenting Justices did not share one voice about why they would uphold the Louisiana law, they were all singing the same song. It's a safe bet that when they have the votes to do so, they will uphold the next abortion restriction to come before them and go much further to eradicate *Roe* and *Casey* altogether. While Justice Roberts might not have joined their choir this time, Justice Barrett is very likely to do so.

THE DEATH OF Justice Ginsburg in September 2020, only forty-five days before the presidential election, turned up the flame under the simmering pot of national politics. Justice Ginsburg was the first woman and first Jewish person to lie in state. Only hours after a memorial service was held for her in the Capitol's Statuary Hall, President Trump nominated Amy Coney Barrett to fill her seat, in a Rose Garden celebration that became a COVID-19 super-spreader event. McConnell now rushed to proceed with Barrett's nomination even though voting in the national election had already begun, flouting Justice Ginsburg's deathbed wish that her successor's nomination be delayed until the next president was sworn in. It was an act of astounding hypocrisy from the senator who had blocked Merrick Garland's Supreme Court nomination a full eight months before the last presidential election by claiming that voters should be able to weigh in on who would select the next Justice.

Eight days before the election, on October 27, 2020, Amy Coney Barrett was confirmed as an Associate Justice by a fifty-two to forty-eight vote. Only one Republican, Senator Susan Collins, joined the unanimous Democratic delegation to oppose the confirmation—the first time in 151 years that a Justice was confirmed without a single vote from the minority party. A few hours after the Senate vote, Justice Barrett was given the Constitutional Oath by Justice Thomas at a televised nighttime White House ceremony, and she began her duties the following day.

Despite the fact that Justice Barrett remained mum about her views on several key cases during her lightning-round confirmation process, it is possible to divine the impact her ascension to the Court will have on the new majority's rulings on procreative and sexual rights.

According to people on both sides of the aisle, Justice Barrett is a brilliant and affable lawyer, two qualities that will make her an extremely effective Justice. Unfortunately, she is likely to be most effective at reducing civil rights and liberties, particularly those that preserve reproductive freedom and decision making. Barrett's long marriage and seven children (four biological and three adopted, including a child with Down syndrome) became a focal point during her confirmation process. So many male senators praised her role as a mother that some critics joked this was her "mominee process," in which motherhood was a theme, not a footnote, to the questions posed to the constitutional scholar. Rather than focus on her views of case law or precedent, Senator Ted Cruz of Texas "casually asked Barrett for tips on managing children during the lockdown," while Louisiana Senator John Kennedy seemed befuddled that Barrett could combine a career and motherhood: "I'm genuinely curious," he said. "Who does laundry in your house?"

Barrett's worldview is influenced by her membership in an insular religious group called People of Praise, which prescribes traditional gender norms, with men in almost all positions of power. During the confirmation hearings, Judge Barrett was adamant that her religious views would not influence specific votes in the cases she considers. But notably, a law review article she cowrote early in her career argued that when judges are obliged to adhere to church teachings, recusal is required. Her Catholic religion's opposition to the death penalty, she wrote, would mean that "Catholic judges (if they are faithful to the teaching of their church) are morally precluded from enforcing the death penalty." Yet in one of the first cases she considered after joining the Court, it appears that she permitted an execution to proceed—neither recusing herself nor staying faithful to the tenets of her religion.

At the Rose Garden event announcing her nomination, Justice Barrett declared fealty to her mentor, Justice Scalia, for whom she served as a law clerk in 1998. Barrett highlighted his "incalculable influence" on her and espoused that "his judicial philosophy is mine." This means that she is a textualist—a judge who interprets statutes based solely on the language within them, rather than the context in which they are passed. On matters of constitutional law, she is an originalist—one who believes that constitutional text means what it did at the time it was ratified.

In contrast, many Supreme Court Justices over the last century have viewed the Constitution as a living document, one that stands the test of time by evolving with cultural changes. Not only is the historical meaning and intention of the framers often difficult to discern, critics note, but many issues before the Court present questions that the framers could never have envisioned, such as modern birth control, the morning-after pill, medication abortion, and in vitro fertilization. These jurists espouse that the framers intentionally left the document's language vague and indistinct to allow it to adapt to new circumstances. In the First Amendment, freedom of speech or the press was not delineated, nor was the Fourth Amendment's proscription on unreasonable search and seizures. Similarly, words like "liberty," "equality," and "due process" found in the Fourteenth Amendment were deliberately wide-open concepts—houses framed but waiting to be given walls and changeable decor to keep up with the times. These broad terms permit Justices to weigh contemporary evidence and circumstances when determining the Constitution's meaning.

Moreover, critics note, our founding framers' viewpoints must be viewed with a skeptical eye because some are so repugnant to modern society—enslavement being the most outstanding example. As Benjamin Franklin said just days before delegates to the Constitutional Convention voted to adopt the document after months of wrangling in 1787, "When you assemble a number of men to have the advantage of their joint wisdom, you inevitably assemble with those men, all their prejudices, their passions, their errors of opinion, their local interests, and their selfish views."

At her debut before the Senate Judiciary Committee, Barrett danced around many substantive issues, just as she had three years earlier when being considered for the Court of Appeals for the Seventh Circuit. Following the lead of recent Supreme Court nominees, she refused to answer even the simplest of questions: Did the Constitution or federal law give the president the authority to delay an election unilaterally? Is it illegal to intimidate voters at the polls? But when pressed by a visibly exasperated Senator Amy Klobuchar about whether she considered *Roe* to be a "super-precedent," Barrett stiffly noted that legal scholarship defines super-precedents as "cases that are so well settled that no political actors and no people seriously push for their overruling," and proposed that because "I'm answering a lot of questions about *Roe*," that indicated to her that *Roe* did not fall into the super-precedent category.

Similarly, Barrett dodged answering whether she agreed with Justice Scalia that the Supreme Court's 1965 ruling legalizing birth control for married couples, *Griswold v. Connecticut*, was wrongly decided and that states should be able to make it illegal to use contraceptives if they so choose. Artfully, Barrett said she found it unlikely that the decision would ever be overturned because it seemed unthinkable that any legislature would pass a law taking away the right to buy or use contraception. This was not reassuring to millions of people, given the anti-abortion movement's general opposition to many forms of contraception.

Justice Barrett's allegiance to Justice Scalia's judicial philosophy presumably would include support for his explicit view that the liberty clause of the Fourteenth Amendment afforded only procedural protections—limits on *how* the law operates, like providing the right to a hearing before the government deprives individuals of their liberty or property. In contrast, substantive rights provide the foundation of constitutional protections that Americans have relied on over the last century, including the right to privacy and liberty. These substantive rights empower Americans to decide how to structure their life and family and protect decisions about sex and sexuality, marriage, contraception, pregnancy, assisted reproductive technologies, end-of-life care, and abortion—decisions that go to the heart of life's most intimate choices. Justice Scalia believed that these substantive protections should not be recognized under the Fourteenth Amendment.

Despite her refusal to answer the senators' questions about *Roe*, Barrett's vehement opposition to abortion and reproductive technologies is well documented. The *Guardian* reported that in 2006, Barrett had signed on to an anti-abortion ad in the *South Bend Tribune* that called *Roe* "an exercise of raw judicial power" and urged overturning its "barbaric legacy." The ad also argued that life begins at fertilization and that the discarding of unused or frozen embryos created in the in vitro fertilization process ought to be criminalized. Yes, you read that right: couples who discard unused embryos because they already have the number of children they want should be held criminally liable.

Similarly, Justice Barrett has a freewheeling view of precedent that would essentially give the Justices carte blanche to reverse important decisions like *Griswold*, *Roe*, and *Casey*. In a 2003 law review article, she wrote—in direct contravention of existing Supreme Court holdings—that respect for precedent ought to be flexible and not pre-clude either the Supreme Court or lower federal courts from revisiting legal or factual questions if the underlying case law is wrongly decided.

For decades the Court has chosen a route that whittles away at *Roe* by exploiting the opportunity to burden rights that *Casey* provided. That has resulted in preserving the appearance of *Roe* for all while in re-ality carving out the insides like a Halloween pumpkin, leaving the most marginalized women with scarily little access to abortion. Chief Justice Roberts's opinion in *June Medical Services* indicated he would continue that approach, avoiding a large political backlash and preserving the in-stitutional integrity of the Court that bears his name. Justice Barrett, on the other hand, is much more likely to upend both *Roe* and *Casey* and give states free rein to prohibit abortion.

As we've seen, it can take years for a case to work its way to the Su-preme Court. However, there are a number of abortion cases currently on the runway that could give the Court the opportunity to revisit *Roe* and *Casey* and decide whether to diminish abortion rights bit by bit, or take them out with one big whack. It is hard to predict which case will be the first to be accepted for review. It could be a challenge to a TRAP law that threatens to shutter clinics. Or a state law that prohibits all early abortion and its more subtle cousin: a law that bans abortion after a "fetal heartbeat" is detected, which has been trendy in conservative-dominated states. Such bans are certainly the most dramatic and wide-sweeping of the anti-abortion legislation right now but are by no means the only possible route for overturning *Roe*. A ban on the D&E procedure commonly used in the second trimester of pregnancy or even a more limited ban on abortion based on sex or race selection could be the first to make it to the High Court. For years these laws have been eagerly circling the airport, waiting to land.

Make no mistake: with Justice Barrett on board, the ultra-conservative Justices could go well beyond revisiting and undermining *Roe* and *Ca-sey*. They could dismantle precedent on a host of issues that affect sexual and procreative freedoms and women's equality. The ultra-conservative quintet is likely to give the government great latitude to limit funding for Planned Parenthood, family planning, and sexual health programs or otherwise proscribe the type of information these organizations must give patients about their health care options.

Despite Justice Barrett's reassurance about contraception during her hearings, with her vote, the Court is likely to diminish contraceptive access overall. Her judicial views align with the majority decision in a 2014 case, *Burwell v. Hobby Lobby Stores*, which allowed an employer to assert religious justifications to exclude contraception from its employee health plan. She would also likely hop on board with a 2020 Supreme Court decision that allowed the federal government to exclude contraception from insurance plans bought through the ACA marketplaces when employers have religious objections, which has resulted in over 125,000 women losing access to no-cost contraceptive services.

Justice Barrett's expansive view of religious freedom will affect more than reproductive freedoms. In one of her first decisions on the Supreme Court bench, she joined an unsigned order in *Roman Catholic Diocese of Brooklyn v. Cuomo* to invalidate New York's public health emergency order limiting the number of persons who could worship together during the pandemic as a violation of the Free Exercise Clause. She is also undoubtedly likely to join the Court's conservatives who used religious freedom to undercut anti-discrimination laws in *Masterpiece Cakeshop, Ltd. v. Colorado Civil Rights Commission*. There the Court allowed a baker to refuse to sell a wedding cake to a gay couple because it offended his religious views, despite state laws prohibiting discrimination against LGBTQ+ people.

If given the opportunity, Justice Barrett might provide the majority vote to further withdraw constitutional protection for LGBTQ+ Americans by overruling *Lawrence v. Texas*, which decriminalized homosexuality, or *Obergefell v. Hodges*, which legalized same-sex marriage. Indeed in 1986, her mentor Justice Scalia thought it entirely appropriate for the government to criminalize homosexual sodomy and chastised the Court for "eliminating the moral opprobrium that has traditionally attached to homosexual conduct." He also took issue with the Court's support of same-sex marriage, which he viewed as a threat to American democracy.

Justice Gorsuch is likely the only one of these five ultra-conservative Justices who could take a more conciliatory view of LGBTQ+ rights cases. In 2020 in *Bostock v. Clayton County*, Justice Gorsuch, joined by Chief Justice Roberts and Justices Ginsburg, Breyer, Sotomayor, and Kagan, interpreted prohibitions on sex discrimination in Title VII, a federal anti-discrimination law, to prohibit discrimination against LGBTQ+ workers by their employers. He used a textualist's analysis to find that Title VII's language "because of sex" included a prohibition on discrimination against LGBTQ+ people as well as women, a welcome and surprising finding given his conservative mien.

But his like-minded bench mates—Justices Alito and Thomas— chastised his reading of the statute and expressed how much they missed Scalia's influence, testily noting that

> The Court's opinion is like a pirate ship. It sails under a textualist flag, but what it actually represents is a theory of statutory interpretation that Justice Scalia excoriated—the theory that courts should "update" old statutes so that they better reflect the current values of society. If the Court finds it appropriate to adopt this theory, it should own up to what it is doing.

Justice Kavanaugh also found that reading "because of sex" to include LGBTQ+ people was a step too far. He gave a tip of the hat to the "[m]illions of gay and lesbian Americans who have worked hard for many decades to achieve equal treatment in fact and in law," but then closed the courthouse doors to them, claiming that it was the job of Congress to protect against LGBTQ+ discrimination, not the Courts.

Justice Barrett joining the conservative cabal could lead the Court to alter basic notions of women's equality as well. During his time on the Court Justice Scalia espoused the view that it was permissible for the Virginia Military Academy to remain an all-male bastion, as it had been part of a "long tradition of open, widespread, and unchallenged use" in education. It's the way it's always been done; ergo it's constitutional. Justice Barrett's adoption of similar positions would be an affront to Justice Ginsburg's life work and the women's rights cases that are her legacy as an advocate and jurist.

With Barrett now in the 6–3 majority of ultra-conservatives, this is perhaps the most right-leaning Supreme Court in contemporary US history. Its views are far afield from those of a majority of Americans. Chief Justice Roberts's concern for the legitimacy of the Court and his unwillingness to regress too far from the modern views of the American people shaped his votes upholding the Affordable Care Act and finding the Louisiana abortion law unconstitutional. But his foot on the brake is now largely irrelevant because on most issues, there will be five ultra-conservative votes driving the majority without him.

It is crystal clear that those of us who believe that everyone should be free to make the personal and private decisions that affect our lives and well-being without government interference or bias can no longer depend on the federal courts to preserve our liberties. New approaches and strategies will be necessary. As we push for reforms, we can find not just inspiration but a road map in those nations where women's rights are human rights and government has an affirmative duty to safeguard them for all. Rhonda Copelon, the attorney who challenged the Hyde Amendment, wrote of a possible future in which reproductive rights were recognized as positive rights: "My hope for the next phase of the movement for procreative and sexual rights is that we not limit ourselves simply to winning back what we have lost, but rather set our sights on winning what we need: recognition of an affirmative right of self-determination."

CHAPTER 10

MEANWHILE, ACROSS THE POND
A HUMAN RIGHTS APPROACH
TO ABORTION

Human rights are inscribed in the hearts of people; they were there long before lawmakers drafted their first proclamation.

MARY ROBINSON, FIRST WOMAN PRESIDENT
OF IRELAND, FORMER UNITED NATIONS
HIGH COMMISSIONER FOR HUMAN RIGHTS

JULIE'S STORY:

If you used one of those fifth-grade line graphs to chart a comparison of abortion rights in Ireland versus the US, it would look like a giant X. Reproductive freedom in the US plummets downward for decades, despite significant medical advances and an increased commitment to racial equity. Rights in Ireland, meanwhile, have skyrocketed.

Kitty and I are always looking for new models of affirmative campaigns. What I saw and did and learned about human rights during my years working to liberalize abortion laws in Ireland informs the innovative view of expanding rights that we espouse.

I arrived in Dublin in 2000 to discover that abortion was completely illegal. Leaving behind my job as a staff attorney at the Center was the downside of heading off to live in Ireland, but I was intrigued by the idea of being abroad and seeing more of the world. Once I married Tom, my Irish-American boyfriend of many years, I could legally work there and would eventually become a citizen. As it turned out, my waitressing experience would translate better than my American law degree, since Ireland's insular legal system required that I spend a year of unpaid "devilling" for a "master" before being able to practice as a barrister. No thanks.

Curious to learn more about Ireland's abortion laws, I cold-called a few top activists who generously briefed me on Ireland's complete ban on abortion. "The jewel in the crown of the pro-life movement," as I later christened it, was enshrined in the Irish Constitution: "The State acknowledges the right to life of the unborn and, with due regard to the equal right to life of the mother, guarantees in its laws to respect, and, as far as practicable, by its laws to defend and vindicate that right." This meant that even lifesaving abortion was unavailable in practice. Complementary constitutional provisions prohibited doctors or other counselors from providing information on how to obtain abortion abroad. In modern, secular Dublin, women had zero access to legal abortion.

The Irish constitutional ban had been inspired by the ripple effects of *Roe*. In 1973, relying on privacy rights similar to those invoked in *Roe*, the Irish Supreme Court had legalized prescription contraceptives for married people in *McGee v. The Attorney General*. In doing so it created a (legitimate) fear that the Irish Supreme Court might also liberalize abortion. By 1983, an increasingly powerful anti-abortion lobby persuaded the government to introduce a referendum allowing voters to endorse a constitutional amendment banning all abortion. At the time, the anti-abortion referendum was a gift to allies in the powerful Catholic Church hierarchy and a much-needed diversion from the government's own scandals, the political troubles in the North, and a failing economy.

The amendment was all Irish, but there were clear signs of an American influence. Modeled on the Human Life Amendment that was pending in the US Congress, its aim was to grant full legal rights to an egg from the moment of fertilization. The provision would not just ban all abortions but would force several forms of contraception off the market and imperil in vitro fertilization and stem cell research as well. An alliance of the Catholic hierarchy and a conservative Irish government succeeded in implementing a law the likes of which the American anti-abortion forces had only dreamed.

JUST AS DUBLIN'S dank winter was arriving, an innovative former colleague of mine from the Center, Viviana Waisman, called from Spain asking me to join an exciting new legal rights organization she was designing, called Women's Link Worldwide. Funded by a grant from the European Union (EU), Viviana was looking to hire lawyers to analyze the domestic laws and international treaties that ruled women's lives in Ireland and other European nations. I would be working with the Irish Family Planning Association (IFPA), a small, feisty organization affiliated with the International Planned Parenthood Federation that provided reproductive health services and advocated for reproductive rights. Abortion was specifically excluded from the research because it was considered too controversial to be eligible for EU funding. Yet the consultancy only funded part-time work, leaving me plenty of time to research abortion rights as a free bonus project.

Coming from the high-rise Wall Street offices of the Center, where I was one of a team of staff lawyers, supported by junior attorneys and my own paralegal as well as fundraising and administrative staff support, I joined this scrappy DIY team with a belated appreciation for the comparatively enormous resources—tech support! travel allowance! bagels on Wednesdays!—I had been privileged to have before.

Evenings I worked my way into the epicenter of the abortion rights movement in Ireland. It was a devoted and often clandestine group of veteran Irish advocates meeting occasionally in the IFPA's offices under the banner "Abortion Reform." This group of a dozen volunteers included barristers, academics, a postal worker, an official at the Department of Foreign Affairs, some tradeswomen, and an office worker or two. Because criminal restrictions tightly governed access to abortion and restricted people from providing information about abortion services abroad, a shadow of illicitness hung over the group's organizing. Many members made sure their families and employers remained unaware of their participation. Abortion rights allies in government were few, none of whom were eager to put their heads above the parapet and be stigmatized for advocating for liberal access to abortion. Significantly, they were dwarfed by abortion opponents, since a conservative government entwined with religious leaders had successfully enacted draconian anti-abortion laws that imposed severe criminal penalties for providing abortion services or information.

The tide briefly turned in the summer of 2001, when the group Women on Waves planned a maiden voyage of its abortion ship in collaboration with Irish activists. The ship, flying under the Dutch flag, would bring Irish women twelve miles out to sea, where, in international waters, legal medication abortions would be provided by an onboard medical staff. It was a bold and clever plan that Dutch doctor Rebecca Gomperts had devised. I was committed to making sure the ship stayed within legal bounds whether at sea or in harbor.

Unfortunately, at the last moment while the ship was already at sea, the Dutch authorities, allegedly at the request of the Irish government, forestalled granting the ship a permit for its onboard clinic. Although the Dutch crew insisted the permit was an unnecessary piece of bureaucracy, this was a deal breaker for the Irish allies. My deep friendship with Gomperts and my experience as a child of divorce were incredibly helpful in negotiating a settlement whereby the ship's crew would agree to provide family planning services but not abortions and the Irish group would continue to participate. For the nearly three hundred women who called seeking abortion services, the ship's doctor provided referrals to England and the Netherlands, prescribed contraceptives, and inserted IUDs on board the ship during its two-week voyage to Ireland.

Ultimately the project succeeded in bringing much-needed worldwide attention to Ireland's harsh abortion ban, putting the government on the spot and, for the first time, the anti-abortion movement on the defensive. Most importantly the ship provided an extraordinary opportunity for organizing groups of Irish politicians, doctors, lawyers, artists, and more, and opened up a much-needed dialogue about legalizing abortion.

As the ship pulled out of the harbor, I went back indoors to stare down the Irish Constitution.

THE IRISH CONSTITUTION has never been particularly friendly to gender equity. After recognizing "the family as the natural primary and fundamental unit group of Society, and as a moral institution possessing inalienable and imprescriptible rights," the Constitution relegated Irish women to their place in the home and specified that their primary role was caregiving: "The State shall, therefore, endeavour to ensure that mothers shall not be obliged by economic necessity to engage in labour to the neglect of their duties in the home." Trust me: there are no similar provisions regarding men's role as fathers.

Marriage, family, and women's special role in the home and at the hearth are enshrined in the Irish Constitution to this day. As a result, divorce was illegal in Ireland until 1996, and all abortion was banned until 2018.

The abortion ban seemed like a thatched-roof relic for a country with a high rate of employment for women, a thriving international tech industry, and close ties to Western Europe. After centuries of painful mass emigration, by 1990 Ireland's population had increased as employment opportunities enabled college-educated young people to remain in the country and provided new opportunities for immigrants arriving from other EU nations. An increasingly secular population resented the powerful Catholic Church imposing its religious values through political ties. Even the most pious were dismayed by scandals of church cover-ups of sexual abuse and malicious treatment of "unwed mothers" and "wayward girls" imprisoned in brutal state-sponsored religious institutions.

Moreover, as a member of the EU and a signatory to many human rights treaties, Ireland had long since adopted human rights values. Ireland had even ratified my hero treaty, the Convention on the Elimination of All Forms of Discrimination Against Women (CEDAW)—nicknamed "the international bill of rights for women"—which the US still has failed to ratify.

The total ban on abortion survived in such a progressive society because of the Irish solution to the Irish problem: send women to England or elsewhere in Europe to obtain abortions. The so-called Irish Journey created a steam valve to release the pressure and avoid some of the most negative consequences of a constitutional ban on abortion. At that time there were very few illegal abortions available in Ireland. By relying on the silent strength of women and girls who clandestinely traveled abroad for abortion services, Ireland avoided the high rate of death the US had experienced pre-*Roe* and allowed the medical profession and politicians to downplay the injuries and other harms caused by banning abortion.

Evidence showed that Ireland's abortion rate when accurately calculated remained similar to that of countries with legal abortion. The ban did not prevent the majority of women from obtaining abortion; it just made it more difficult, risky, and shameful. For anyone with a high-risk pregnancy, with medical complications, or needing a procedure later in pregnancy for severe fetal anomalies or other reasons, it was a particularly cruel journey and one that could put their life at greater risk. For those in state care, refugees and asylum seekers with limited travel visas, teens, rural women, survivors of domestic abuse, and those who lacked funds or were unable to travel, it often was not a solution at all.

Despite a 1992 ruling by the Supreme Court of Ireland in *Attorney General v. X*, which carved out an exception to allow abortion necessary to preserve a pregnant woman's life, abortion was almost entirely unavailable within Ireland. X, a fourteen-year-old teenager pregnant as a result of rape by a so-called family friend, had headed to London to obtain an abortion. Prior to leaving, her parents contacted the local police to ask about preserving the fetal tissue as forensic evidence to assist in the prosecution of the rape. The question was ultimately sent to Irish Attorney General Harry Whelehan, who leaped at his chance to protect the rights of the unborn under the still-untested constitutional provision. He obtained an interim injunction from the High Court, a mid-level trial court, that prohibited X from leaving Ireland for nine months and restricted her parents from helping her travel or obtain an abortion.

The family received word only after they had already landed in England and immediately returned home to contest the injunction. By this point, their daughter's life was endangered because she had become a suicide risk. The High Court upheld the injunction against the family after it found the substantial risk that X might take her own life was "of a different order of magnitude than the certainty that the life of the unborn will be terminated if the order is not made."

The family appealed to the Irish Supreme Court, who showed some mercy and common sense. The Court allowed abortion when necessary to preserve a pregnant woman's life, but only "if it can be established as a matter of probability that there is a real and substantial risk to the life, as distinct from the health, of the mother which can only be avoided by the termination of her pregnancy." X returned to England with her family, at which point she miscarried, ending her personal ordeal but launching a political one.

The X case brought out massive demonstrations in Dublin on both sides of the debate. By the end of the year, the government put forward a referendum proposing three possible revisions to the Constitution. The first took aim at the X case and sought to exclude risk of suicide as a justification for lifesaving abortion. The other two would liberalize the law by making it clear that women were free to travel abroad to obtain abortions and that with some limitations people in Ireland were free to give or receive information on abortion. The voters selected the options that most supported abortion rights. They maintained suicide as a reason for abortion access within Ireland, liberalized access to abortion information, and reaffirmed the freedom to travel for abortion services.

Despite the fact that the Irish Supreme Court in X had ordered the Irish parliament to create legislation to enable abortion in lifesaving circumstances, no such initiative was advanced over the next decade. Ireland continued to rely on women traveling abroad even for lifesaving abortions.

THIS WAS THE situation when I landed in 2000. After several years of aggressively litigating cases with the Center under the tutelage of Kitty, Janet Benshoof, and other mentors, I had developed a good sense of what it took to challenge abortion restrictions in America. But the Irish legal system was different. Was there a way to challenge the harsh Irish law?

At first glance, there seemed to be many impediments to a legal challenge. There was no reproductive rights legal organization in Ireland and

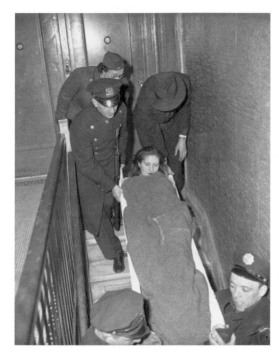

While the full circumstances behind this photo of a woman being carried out after police officers raided an illegal abortion in progress are not known, it chillingly represents the dangers of clandestine services when abortion is criminalized. (1944) *Bettmann*

A march organized by the National Organization for Women to show support for abortion rights drew over five hundred thousand people to Washington, DC, a few weeks before the *Planned Parenthood v. Casey* argument. (April 1992) *Mark Reinstein*

Kitty speaks to the press on the steps of the Supreme Court immediately following her argument in *Planned Parenthood v. Casey* while her son Sam peers out from behind her. (April 1992)

This 1992 cartoon of Kitty arguing *Planned Parenthood v. Casey* accurately depicts the attitude of some of the Supreme Court's conservative Justices when it came to preserving abortion rights. Nevertheless, she persisted. *Tim Menees, Pittsburgh Post-Gazette*

The Supreme Court roster that decided *Planned Parenthood v. Casey* in 1992 included a lone female Justice. From left: Justices Thomas, White, Souter, Scalia, Stevens, Blackmun, Kennedy, O'Connor, and Chief Justice Rehnquist. *Bettmann*

The Center for Reproductive Rights staff dresses up for a dinner honoring Justice Harry Blackmun. Kitty is in the front row, second from the right. (1994)

Michelle Lee, a Louisiana client who was refused a lifesaving abortion because her doctors claimed she did not face a greater than 50 percent chance of dying, is pictured here along with one of her sons, Julie (far left), and Janet Benshoof (far right). (1998) *Julie F. Kay*

The New Woman All Women clinic in Birmingham, Alabama—Julie's client in an abortion ban case—after a horrific bombing by an anti-abortion terrorist who killed police officer Robert Sanderson and severely injured Emily Lyons, a nurse at the clinic. *© 1998. The Birmingham News. All rights reserved. Reprinted with permission.*

Dutch doctor Rebecca Gomperts stands on the dock in Dublin outside the *Women on Waves* abortion ship on its first voyage to Ireland where they had planned to provide abortion services at sea in international waters. (June 2001)

After arguing against Ireland's ban on abortion in *ABC v. Ireland*, a very pregnant Julie leaves the European Court of Human Rights with the Irish Family Planning Association team. From left: Niall Behan, Rosie Toner, Anthea McTiernan, Julie, Carmel Stewart, and Mercedes Cavallo. (December 9, 2009) *Paul O'Driscoll*

Exhuberant abortion rights supporters at a rally in Dublin when a nationwide referendum repealed the Irish constitutional provision that had banned nearly all abortion. (May 26, 2018) *Paul Faith/AFP via Getty Images*

Abortion rights activists vehemently (although cheerfully here) protests the nomination of Brett Kavanaugh to the Supreme Court because of his severe anti-abortion views and testimony by Dr. Christine Blasey Ford that he and his friend had sexually assaulted her during high school. (September 2018) *Chris Goodwin/desrowVISUALS*

Margaret Atwood's dystopian feminist classic *The Handmaid's Tale* inspired abortion rights supporters from around the globe to don the vivid red robes and white bonnets seen here outside the Senate confirmation hearings for Justice Kavanaugh. (September 2018) *Win McNamee/Getty Images*

The festive and patriotic atmosphere of this march for women's abortion rights and liberty in Washington, DC, shines through in this photo Julie took for the *Harvard Crimson* while her classmates carried signs in the background. (April 1989) *Julie F. Kay*

Activists on the steps of the Supreme Court seeking to Save *Roe*! (July 2005) *Mike Theiler/ EPA/Shutterstock*

The original women of the Supremes—Justices Sandra Day O'Connor, Sonia Sotomayor, Ruth Bader Ginsberg, and Elena Kagan—together prior to Justice Kagan's Investiture Ceremony on October 1, 2010. *Steve Petteway, Collection of the Supreme Court of the United States*

Justice Clarence Thomas administers the Constitutional oath to Amy Coney Barrett at a nighttime White House ceremony while her husband, Jesse Barrett, and President Donald J. Trump look on. (October 26, 2020) *Official White House Photo by Andrea Hanks*

Participants in their pink pussy hats at the Women's March in Washington, DC, protesting the inauguration of President Donald J. Trump. (January 2017) *K. McGinley 2017*

Abortion rights supporters in Argentina rally behind a trademark green banner proclaiming "Not one more death due to clandestine abortions," just weeks before their successful campaign pushed the government to legalize abortion in 2020. *Ronaldo Schemidt/Contributor*

Kitty and Julie rally with abortion rights supporters (and hats) in front of the Supreme Court on the sunny morning of the argument in *June Medical Services v. Russo.* (March 4, 2020)

little public interest litigation overall. Ireland's loser-pays-all approach to litigation expenses largely squelched public interest challenges. Fear of paying an opponent's costs was not the only reason barristers were deterred from challenging the abortion ban. The constitutionally backed provision was bolstered by severe criminal penalties for having or assisting in an abortion in Ireland, possibly including life imprisonment. No attorney would put an individual doctor or woman at the center of such a maelstrom with so little chance of success and such a high risk of incarceration. Moreover, barristers were sole practitioners in Ireland. In addition to not having financial support for abortion rights legal work and limited ability to work for free, the stigma of advocating to legalize abortion could drive away paying clients regardless of their personal opinion on the issue.

Despite all these hurdles, Ireland's legal grass still seemed pretty green to me. My research had introduced me to the European Convention on Human Rights, a treaty enforced by the European Court of Human Rights (ECHR). Progressive rulings by the ECHR had led to decriminalization of homosexuality in Ireland in 1988 and set in motion the legalization of divorce. Based in Strasbourg, France, the ECHR houses judges from more than forty-five countries in a shiny glass and steel courthouse meant to reflect the transparency needed for true justice. These judges had the power to determine whether Ireland's abortion law was in violation of its obligations under the European Convention. It seemed like a glittering new world of rights to me, compared to what I had learned on the other side of the pond.

The US Constitution was drafted by newly independent former colonists reacting to a ruling monarchy in 1787. The founding framers were rejecting King George III while striving to create a new state that prioritized freedom *from* tyranny (at least for white men) and restraining government from restricting an individual's conduct, especially interfering with religious worship and belief (at least for some religions). The US still clings to its exceptionalism as a "newer" country and its traditional isolationism, remaining particularly hostile to the social and economic obligations a human rights approach mandates. Well before President Trump made a mockery of US foreign relations, the US still maintained a distance from human rights values embraced by most other developed nations. The fanged Don't Tread on Me approach embraced by Tea Party members and white nationalists resists government intervention even to support those most in need. Live free or die indeed.

In contrast to constitutional rights, which are granted by government, human rights are innate—they are those we are all entitled to simply by virtue of being born human. Human rights doctrine took off in the aftermath of World War II in reaction to the horrors of the Nazi persecution and the murder of more than six million Jews as well as countless LGBTQ+ people, persons with disabilities, Romani, Jehovah's Witnesses, and others. Worldwide support grew for a human rights approach as a way to set standards, help abolish crimes against humanity, detect early attempts at genocide, and address unjust denials of basic freedoms. President Franklin Delano Roosevelt's 1941 State of the Union address spoke of four essential freedoms: freedom of speech, freedom of religion, freedom from want, and freedom from fear. In 1948, three years after her husband's death, First Lady Eleanor Roosevelt's efforts led to the adoption of the Universal Declaration of Human Rights by the United Nations and spurred the recognition of the UN as a forum to promote human rights, peace, and better living standards. The European Convention on Human Rights, which I was relying upon to challenge the Irish abortion ban, was the first to give effect to many of the rights stated in the Universal Declaration of Human Rights and to make them binding in a judicial forum.

Human rights are broad and aspirational. Those in power—government institutions and individuals—are responsible for ensuring access to the key services and programs that *proactively* advance such values as dignity and full participation in society. The human rights approach focuses on protecting those who are most marginalized, excluded, or discriminated against, often requiring an investigation of gender stereotypes and then mandating government interventions to alleviate them. The human rights framework has intersectionality in its DNA.

For this reason, not only does a human rights approach have the potential to provide additional support for abortion access, but it prioritizes increased access to health care and socioeconomic benefits and seeks to make rights more accessible to those at the margins or who face multiple intersecting forms of discrimination.

Despite identifying a promising legal theory and potential forum to bring a challenge to Ireland's ban on abortion, I knew it would be an uphill battle to convince the European Court of Human Rights just to hear a case. The Court, like almost all international human rights bodies, considers itself a court of last resort. Only an applicant who has reasonably tried all other routes in the country at issue can seek review. As an arbiter of international human rights doctrine, the Court's role is to supplement, not supplant, a signatory's domestic legal system.

The Court's workload is immense, and as a result it is extremely difficult to get a case heard in a timely manner. A lawsuit can take five or more years to work its way through the process, making the US Supreme Court look speedy in comparison.

While the abortion issue had been before the European Court in a few cases starting in the early 1970s, it had deftly avoided addressing the scope of abortion rights under the European Convention. Fueled by cups of strong black Irish tea and wearing wooly slippers, I dove in to research the options. Reading the tea leaves, I was fairly certain that the Court would reject the idea that the Convention's Article 2 Right to Life clause—"Everyone's right to life shall be protected by law"—applied to a fetus. But the case law provided fewer clues as to whether the Court would say the privacy rights housed in Article 8 or, better yet, the equality rights enshrined in Article 14 would include protection for abortion.

I swapped my slippers for rain boots and began making the rounds, ninety-page legal memo in hand and seeking feedback, advice, and, most importantly, buy-in. The Irish Family Planning Association was on board. Its work assisting women traveling abroad gave it a deep commitment to advancing abortion access within Ireland.

By this time, I had been in the trenches (and pubs) with Ireland's pro-choice legal minds for three years—long enough to earn their trust. The first person I approached about the lawsuit was Ivana Bacik, a whip-smart youth activist turned Trinity law professor and later Irish senator who had literally written the book on the topic: *Abortion and the*

Law: An Irish Perspective. From when I'd first landed in Dublin, Ivana had been generous with her time, wisdom, and humor. Although some abortion rights supporters raised an eyebrow at this more aggressive, American model of litigation, Ivana agreed to join the legal team and publicly backed bringing a lawsuit to the European Court. Prominent barrister and longtime IFPA supporter Catherine Forde meanwhile quietly built support for us among her trepidatious colleagues in the hallowed hallways of Dublin's Four Courts building.

Predicting how a court will rule is always difficult in an area as controversial as abortion, and I was terrified at the possibility of setting a bad precedent that would apply to forty-five European countries. Tom listened to me brood over the possibilities and offered legal feedback and support while we walked and talked together around the small farm in County Mayo that had belonged to his grandparents. I continued to seek input and pushback from a range of lawyers in Ireland, the US, Canada, and England until I was confident about not "creating bad law" by bringing the case.

Next, it was important to find women to be at the heart of the case. The IFPA and I were adamant that the case would present the Court with a range of women who had a variety of reasons for seeking abortion. Mild-mannered Niall Behan, the CEO of the IFPA, was fiercely determined to help a large swath of the women who poured through the doors. I wanted to avoid giving the Court the ability to carve out exceptions to the ban only for those seen as "deserving" of access to abortion or in rare cases of fetal anomaly. It was important to ensure that the Court understood that abortion was a normal part of women's lives and health.

IFPA social workers asked some of the women seeking follow-up care upon returning from abortions abroad whether they were interested in participating in challenging the Irish ban on abortion. Surprisingly, many women expressed their commitment and felt that being forced to travel abroad was an injustice that should not happen to others.

An application to the European court must be filed within six months of the incident, and therefore any woman involved in the lawsuit would have to be within six months of having an abortion. Three of the women identified by IFPA ultimately became the applicants A, B, and C in *A, B, and C v. Ireland* (*ABC*). Anonymity was crucial. They had not revealed their abortions to some of their closest family and friends or to their doctors. The rabid tabloid press, eager to sensationalize abortion matters, tended to out unnamed applicants in Irish courts. I was later exposed in the *Irish Mail* in an article that, much to my delight, called me "the mastermind behind this week's European Court of Human Rights' ruling that threatens to reopen the country's most bitter moral issue." The "exposé" hangs on my office wall, and A, B, and C's identities remain secret.

The first woman, A, was a single mother of four young children, living in poverty, who had become pregnant because she (wrongly) believed her partner was infertile. Recently sober, A was working to regain custody of her children who were in foster care as a result of problems she had experienced as an alcoholic. She believed that another child would jeopardize her health and the successful reunification of her family. Unable to raise the funds, she borrowed €650 (over $850) from a local moneylender and traveled alone to England for an abortion. She made sure to return home the same day so she would not miss a visit scheduled with one of her children. Although A experienced pain, nausea, and bleeding for weeks thereafter, she did not want to risk seeking medical advice in her small town or taking any action that might alert her social worker to her situation.

Applicant B became pregnant when emergency contraception failed to work after unprotected sex with a man she later found out was not single as he claimed. B borrowed a friend's credit card and traveled alone to England. She gave a false address and left the "next of kin" line on the clinic form empty; even in an emergency nobody was to know she had traveled from Ireland. Of the three applicants she was the youngest and felt the most humiliated by her experience traveling for an abortion.

The third applicant, C, was a cancer survivor whose doctors refused to tell her whether carrying her pregnancy to term would present risks to her life or the fetus. C was from Lithuania and found it ridiculous that she would have to travel to England for the procedure.

Our approach here was more of a moon shot than your average litigation. It never hurts to assert more rights than the court is likely to grant. Often in such legal challenges a lawyer is more likely to get a win if there are ways to lose as well, making the judges feel positioned comfortably in the middle and giving advocates something more to fight for outside the courtroom.

The Article 8 right to privacy presented our best chance at a win, even though like many other abortion rights activists I believe that prohibitions on abortion are essentially about gender discrimination. But because case law around abortion, contraception, and LGBTQ+ rights has been firmly rooted in privacy law in the US and throughout human rights doctrine for several decades now, it was the strongest claim.

Knowing the legal process would take several years, I took a senior staff attorney position at Legal Momentum in New York, where I worked to oppose government funding for abstinence-only programs and support LGBTQ+ couples seeking legalization of marriage in several states.

Meanwhile, the IFPA pushed forward an abortion rights campaign in Ireland that centered around the lawsuit. Catherine Heaney, a communications wizard with years of experience in the Irish political arena, created a strategy to modernize a stale national abortion debate. No longer would abortion supporters be in a defensive crouch pummeled by inflammatory photos of fetuses waved around by the Society for the Protection of Unborn Children. During the years of waiting we would wave the human rights flag to call global attention to Irish women's hardships. Moreover, even if the Court turned out to be hostile to all our claims, we would have "success without victory," by reframing the public dialogue around abortion in Ireland to focus on women's human rights.

Four years after I'd filed with the Court, in July 2009, the call finally came: we had been granted a hearing of the case in front of the Grand Chamber, the highest level of the European Court. I was thrilled and panicked. The fact that the case was heading straight to the Grand Chamber boded well. The Court was taking this very seriously, pointedly bypassing a hearing by the three-judge committee or even a seven-judge panel. But I was pregnant with my second child, and oral argument before the Court had been scheduled for six weeks before I was due to give birth. Time to find a maternity business suit and also a cocounsel to pinch-hit if the baby came early, provide legal camaraderie in Strasbourg, and add an Irish accent to the case.

OUR OPPOSITION, IRELAND'S attorney general and his team of six senior government attorneys, focused their argument almost entirely on a "failure to exhaust domestic remedies" and the audacity of an American lawyer who had completely bypassed the Irish system. They relied on a case decided just a year before, *D v. Ireland*, in which the Court had closed the door on an Irish woman who had sought an abortion on the grounds of a fatal fetal anomaly. D's lawyers failed to persuade the Court that going through the Irish courts would be futile, and her case was thrown out. In the aftermath of *D*, I rushed to provide a detailed briefing about the hurdles and hardships that A, B, and C would face in Irish courts, frantically seeking to distinguish my clients from the *D* case, and it worked.

One month before the hearing, the IFPA team was still seeking an Irish attorney to partner with me. At last Carmel Stewart, an Irish barrister and constitutional law expert, was recruited to bravely stick her head above the parapet. We spent evenings around Forde's dinner table conducting a moot, planning my opening remarks, and strategizing about the questions the Court might ask from the bench. Daytimes I attended meetings with leaders of other Irish nonprofit organizations to try to enlist their support for the case, to no avail. Very tired and very pregnant, I grew frustrated as supporters would meet with me privately but decline to speak publicly about the *ABC* case. One director of a prominent rights organization summed it up well: *Good luck, and sure, we'll put out a statement of support if you win.*

Onward to Strasbourg for a few days of rehearsal, rest, and a quick crepe at the famous Strasbourg Christmas market. Mercedes Cavallo, a young Argentine lawyer interning at the IFPA, came along and helped with everything from stellar legal research to plugging in a laptop, since I was too pregnant now to crawl under the hotel room desk. Back home in Brooklyn with our second grader, Tom began to wonder if he'd have to travel to France for the birth of our second child.

For the morning of argument, the Court has a collegial tradition where the attorneys meet together with the president of the Court in his chambers before argument begins. On the elevator ride up, Stewart spoke about the weather with the Irish attorney general, while I extolled the virtues of Strasbourg crepes to fill the awkward silence. Nobody mentioned my pregnancy—the elephant in the elevator.

Back downstairs, oral argument went by in a blur. With seventeen judges, I was uncertain where to look and slowly rotated my head like an owl. Unlike in the US Supreme Court, the judges do not interrupt. Instead, at the end of opening arguments, the judges pile on questions for the attorneys, who rapidly jot notes and then have a ten-minute interlude to prepare their answers before responding orally. No laptops allowed. Stewart and I each responded to several of the judges' questions, none of which provided strong clues to the opinion the Court would release almost exactly a year later.

As we stepped out onto the Court's plaza afterward, the crisp December air alleviated my total fatigue. We took questions from the hordes of reporters asking how Ireland's abortion ban violated women's human rights. Bam. Our human rights framing had become the new norm. Years later I would hear an anti-abortion activist on *Midwest Radio Shannon* rant about the "human rights of the unborn." Imitation is the sincerest form of flattery. I flew home to wait, again covering my stomach with a briefcase as I had on the way over to avoid being caught violating Aerlingus's "expectant mothers" policy that gave the airline discretion to forbid pregnant women from travel.

A YEAR LATER, I left the new baby at home with Tom and rushed back to Dublin to gather with the IFPA team for the release of the Court's ruling. As our hastily rented and far too fancy Dublin hotel ballroom filled with reporters, we did not know if we were planning for a wedding or a wake. Heaney prepared public remarks that would allow us a quick pivot in either direction. Because the Court also had not yet ruled on the admissibility of our claims, normally the first step in any litigation, my big fear was that they would find that we had failed to exhaust our domestic remedies, the whole thing would be for naught, and I would look, as they say, like a "feckin' eejit" for bringing everyone down this path.

Fortunately the Court did admit our case, and the majority opinion expressed serious concern that Ireland's abortion laws violated women's human rights, but ultimately ruled in favor only of Applicant C. Initially it dismissed Applicant C's claim that her right to life under the Convention had been infringed. Because C had sufficiently taken matters into her own hands and found her way to abortion services in England, there was no risk to her life. Yet, as I had hoped, the Court put to rest the anti-abortion position that Article 2 could ever provide an absolute right to life for a fetus. The Court next turned its attention to Article 8, the right to respect for private and family life. We knew that this was always going to be a case that centered on privacy rights.

The preliminary part of the Court's analysis found that the abortion ban, pursuant to Irish law, had interfered with the women's right to respect for their private lives. But the question for the Court was whether, under the Convention, the state's interference could be considered proportionate to its asserted goal and thereby justified. The majority opinion that had been signed by eight of the seventeen judges, and joined by three others in two separate concurring opinions, started by acknowledging a "consensus amongst a substantial majority of the Contracting States of the Council of Europe toward allowing abortion." Only three states out of more than forty at the time had abortion restrictions equal to or greater than Ireland's. It acknowledged that traveling for abortion services had been "psychologically and physically arduous" for A and B, particularly given A's poverty. They considered that the ban was likely ineffective as well because so many women evaded it by traveling abroad.

But then the majority judges started backpedaling. Acknowledging Ireland's "lengthy, complex, and sensitive debate" on abortion, they caved to what they described as "the profound moral views of the Irish people as to the nature of life." In a stunning bit of hypocrisy, a majority of Justices decided that A and B's ability to obtain abortion abroad had meant that the law was not disproportionate; therefore, their rights under Article 8 of the Convention had not been violated. An Irish solution to a European problem.

Six judges vigorously dissented from the majority opinion regarding A and B. These judges from Greece, Belgium, Sweden, Finland, Switzerland, and Moldova noted that the "undeniably strong consensus among European States" was that a woman's health and well-being "are considered more valuable than the right to life of the fetus." In language that seemed almost radically feminist even for a dissenting opinion, they noted that

> [T]he values protected—the rights of the foetus and the rights of a living person—are, by their nature, unequal: on the one hand there are the rights of a person already participating, in an active manner, in social interaction, and on the other hand there are the rights of a foetus within the mother's body, whose life has not been definitively determined as long as the process leading to the birth is not yet complete, and whose participation in social interaction has not even started.

Justice Ginsburg herself could not have said it any better.

The dissent believed that the Court had zero obligation to answer the "scientific, religious or philosophical question of the beginning of life," because the vast majority of European states already had legalized abortion to protect a woman's well-being and health, and certainly her life.

Two concurring judges—from Spain and Andorra—expressed concern that the majority had not considered "the degree of intensity and gravity" of A or B's situation as a factor in its analysis. While these two judges were not persuaded that either woman had faced severe enough circumstances to find a violation of their Convention rights, they left open the door to future challenges by women who faced "grave dangers" to their health or well-being. When I spoke with B by phone later that day, she was gratified by this acknowledgment, and that so many people in Ireland had recognized the unfairness of her experience.

In contrast to the split on A and B, the Court was unanimous in finding that Applicant C's privacy rights had been violated. Although C faced no immediate threat to her life, the State would not permit her to have an abortion until such an emergency was obvious. Even if her life was at risk, there were no government guidelines for her physicians to make such a determination. Like Michelle Lee in Louisiana and my client left untreated in a coma in New York, if C had not traveled to England, she likely would have been left to deteriorate, while her doctors feared providing her an abortion without legal protection. Throughout the case the government, in fact, was unable to produce any evidence that any woman had ever received a legal lifesaving abortion in Ireland, although the IFPA knew that individual physicians had in rare cases quietly provided "pregnancy terminations" to their individual patients.

The Court held that the fact that C could not obtain sufficient information about the impact of the pregnancy on her health or life was sufficient to constitute a violation of her privacy rights. It rejected the state's demand that C further substantiate the alleged medical risk. The government was ordered to pay C compensation of €15,000 and to enact legislation to provide a pathway to lifesaving abortion for women in Ireland.

At the end of the day, I had failed to persuade the Court that twenty years after the initial referendum the Irish people no longer held extreme anti-abortion values, as the government claimed. That just felt wrong. I was frustrated and angry that the Court had let a powerful religious minority stigmatize and silence what I knew was strong Irish support for access to legal abortion. Over one hundred thousand women had traveled abroad from Ireland for abortion services since 1983. The Irish people had rejected further abortion restrictions in the 1992 referendum and supported the right to information and travel for abortion services. They had come on board to support a Dutch abortion ship and quietly expressed to me their support for the applicants in *ABC* even while not wanting to shout it from the rooftops.

In the immediate aftermath of *ABC*, the abortion rights movement was buoyed by an acknowledgment that abortion rights are human rights and that the state had a positive obligation to provide an effective and accessible way to use that right.

While not an immediate win for A and B, by courageously stepping forward these women had put abortion before a human rights tribunal, and the IFPA's advocacy work had created a renewed focus on human rights and greater support for legal abortion. But it would be nearly ten more years before the Irish people would be given a chance to vote on whether women could obtain abortions within Ireland.

The fact that the Court had not required the women to go through the futile and risky process of exhausting their claims in the Irish courts also sent a strong message. *ABC* was the first time the Court had done this to such a dramatic extent and, moreover, brought the claims straight to the Grand Chamber. The judges had left the door open for claims by women who might have circumstances sufficiently severe to persuade three additional judges. After giving Ireland a slap on the wrist for its harsh and harmful abortion laws, the Court ordered the country to do better.

More immediately, the government was now obligated to enact legislation creating access to lifesaving abortion. It had six months to present a plan to the Court, or it would be in violation of its obligations under the European Convention, an embarrassing position for a state that prided itself on being a leader of human rights in Europe. The government's response was political and churlish. I went back to living in the US, while my IFPA colleagues pushed against a government that dragged its heels to such an extent that it created a tragic result.

After a year of failing to respond to the Court's ruling, in November of 2011, the government finally declared it would set up a fourteen-member advisory group of medical and legal experts to create recommendations for legislation to enable access to lifesaving abortion. The group delivered its report a year after that, and still there was no legislation. In the meantime, a young pregnant woman in Galway died after being denied a lifesaving abortion.

Savita Halappanavar's heartbreaking death in November 2012 would become a rallying cry for an abortion rights movement that was far more focused on human rights and far more frustrated with the government's delay and obfuscation than it had been before the campaign around *ABC*. With her vibrant brown eyes and a tiny diamond decorating one tooth, Halappanavar became "the girl with the diamond smile," a worldwide symbol of the devastating consequences of Ireland's harsh abortion law. Halappanavar had been seventeen weeks into a wanted pregnancy when she presented at a hospital in western Ireland experiencing complications that made a miscarriage inevitable. Because her doctors detected a fetal heartbeat, they refused to provide an abortion. She and her husband repeatedly asked for an abortion, and instead her doctors waited. Her condition significantly deteriorated over days of medical indecision and cowardice. A few days later she died of sepsis, a condition that is treatable when addressed quickly. When Halappanavar's husband went public with the circumstances of his young wife's death, protestors gathered throughout Ireland and in front of Irish embassies in London, Delhi, and elsewhere, creating vivid memorials and demanding reform.

The appalling circumstances of Halappanavar's death made clear what happens when abortion is criminalized. Whether the doctors failed to provide her a lifesaving abortion because "Ireland is a Catholic country," as some claimed, or simply because the lack of legal guidelines combined with criminal abortion laws made her doctors freeze, the result was the same. Her doctors had fallen for a bogus anti-abortion distinction between an abortion needed to save a woman's life versus one to preserve her health.

Halappanavar's situation differed from that of thousands of other women who had suffered or died worldwide as a direct result of illegal abortions in that she had wanted to carry the pregnancy to term but was unable. Because Halappanavar and her family as well as the Indian government were vocal about the injustice she suffered, their protestations brought global attention to Ireland's extreme law. The Irish government was forced into action at last and passed the Protection of Life During Pregnancy Act (PLDPA) the next year, which purported to permit abortion where there was a "real and substantial" risk to the woman's life.

Unfortunately, the law was practically useless because it contained so many hurdles to abortion, lacked clarity about exactly how ill a woman had to be to qualify, and contained a fourteen-year criminal penalty.

People had reached their limits with the Irish solution. The *ABC* case and its related campaigns, a drumbeat of demands for political reform, and the shock at Halappanavar's horrific death had tipped public opinion on abortion.

Moreover, a new demographic in Ireland that included younger women and immigrants refused to accept the ban and the Irish Journey. In 2017, a parliamentary committee convened to consider the anti-abortion constitutional clause and heard extensive testimony from experts, which included the IFPA, the Center, the Guttmacher Institute, and a range of international organizations. The committee recommended repealing the constitutional provision, thus allowing unrestricted access to abortion during early pregnancy, and as a result the government called a referendum for May 2018.

Led by veteran abortion rights activists, grassroots campaigners, and the IFPA, a full-blown campaign that centered on women's human rights pushed for legalized abortion and a repeal of the constitutional provision banning abortion. Together for Yes, a coalition of seventy organizations, groups, and communities, now loudly called for the end of Ireland's ban on abortion. In the weeks leading up to the vote, the result was unpredictable, and I discussed launching more litigation with the IFPA if the popular vote failed to recognize abortion as a human right.

There was record turnout for the referendum. Young people streamed into Dublin airport, returning home from as far away as Tokyo and Buenos Aires to participate in the referendum: a reverse Irish journey. It was an overwhelming victory for the campaign to repeal a constitutional amendment that for thirty-five years had prohibited abortion in Ireland. Prime Minister Leo Varadkar, overcoming his initial reluctance, had campaigned in favor of legal abortion. He recognized what it had taken to achieve the referendum win: "What we have seen today is the culmination of a quiet revolution [that has been taking place] for the past ten or twenty years." Unable to travel to Ireland for the final vote, I texted and phoned friends as the results came in, smiling and weeping in relief across the miles.

Starting in January 2019, the IFPA was able to provide free, legal abortion services within Ireland for the first time. In the IFPA's view, it was a victory with work still to do. In the aftermath of the referendum, new abortion legislation fell short of human rights standards and best medical practices. Abortion is only available up to twelve weeks of pregnancy unless there is a risk to a woman's life or of serious harm to her health and in cases of fatal fetal anomaly. An inflexible three-day mandatory waiting period hampers access to abortion, and many locations lack services. But still the grass seems greener than in the US as Ireland heads in the right direction. Criminal provisions no longer apply to the pregnant woman. Abortion is provided free to any woman residing in Ireland.

Moreover, Ireland continues to be accountable to human rights bodies, and the Irish example has contributed to a growing acknowledgment of abortion as a human right. As the US Supreme Court erodes abortion rights, including the looming possibility of a complete abandonment of *Roe*, the human rights model is more important than ever.

A human rights framework rejects the bogus distinction between saving a woman's life and preserving her health when regulating abortion. It rebuffs inappropriate criminal sanctions for abortion and a vindictive "lock her up" approach to self-induced abortion. A human rights model rejects a system that makes health care accessible only to those who can afford to pay for it themselves. Rather, a human rights approach directs governments to support prenatal life by adopting policies that provide full access to contraception, ensure safe pregnancies and delivery, and work to implement a range of socioeconomic benefits that support women who do decide to become mothers.

As the US faces a continuing decline in our abortion rights, we would do well to look across the pond for inspiration and strategies.

CHAPTER 11

NEW TACTICS, NEW TRIUMPHS
NOW IT'S TIME FOR BIG AMBITIONS

"Would you tell me, please, which way I ought to go
from here?"
"That depends a good deal on where you want to get
to," said the Cat.

LEWIS CARROLL, *ALICE IN WONDERLAND*

SAVE *ROE*. SAVE *ROE*. SAVE *ROE* has been the rallying cry of the reproductive freedom movement for almost fifty years. *Roe* has been under relentless attack since the day it was born. It has been weakened but never toppled. But with three new Trump-branded Justices on the Supreme Court, we have entered a new, fervently anti-abortion era. The Supreme Court, the majority of the federal courts, and many state courts are no longer *Roe*'s friends. It is time for a new strategy.

Anyone who has embarked on strategic planning for companies or organizations—think endless meetings with Post-its and flip charts taped to walls—has been asked to set "big hairy audacious goals." What in your wildest dreams would be the win you want? What does success look like? However clichéd this concept has become, it is time for the reproductive freedom movement to identify new, bolder ambitions that do not depend so heavily on the courts.

Here we pose questions to consider as you determine the path you and your allies will take, and we lay out some long-term moon shots to advance reproductive freedom. One of our favorites, which we detail below, is a new Gender Equity Amendment to the US Constitution. We are dreamers, but pragmatists too. Therefore, the following chapters contain more immediately achievable strategies as well, to make a wide range of reproductive needs—from abortion to contraception to maternal and infant health care and child care—more affordable and accessible.

Our movement's future direction cannot be invented out of whole cloth. It must be informed by our history and build on the decades of hard-fought victories and excruciating losses. We are indebted to those who have been in the trenches fighting for reproductive freedom with vision and persistence. The activists, medical providers, lawyers, and academics who have been working on these issues for decades are some of the most accomplished and dedicated people out there. Similarly, the organizations working for a wide range of reproductive freedoms have done incredible work to safeguard our rights and introduce positive legislation in the face of relentless opposition. Thankfully, many of these groups are already working toward bolder, more inclusive models for expanding reproductive freedom and justice. The next wave of this movement gains from being far more inclusive than in the past and by continuing to follow and learn from each other.

OUR PRE-FLIGHT CHECKLIST

Whenever we test the waters of a new initiative, we pose three questions to ourselves and our partners before leaping in. These questions frame our goals and center the conversation around our values. Our hope is that they will help inform how to judge whether the strategies we present in these next few chapters—and others' ideas outside these pages—are the right path forward.

- First, will the strategy result in real, not just theoretical change? The test is whether it will advance the rights and well-being of real people, not just the rhetoric.

- Next, will the change you seek be long-lasting and not just a quick, temporary fix? Will the next president/governor/mayor be able to flip the switch and undo your good work the day they take office? Some temporary initiatives may still be worth doing, but it is far better to use Super Glue rather than Scotch Tape.

- Finally, is the end goal something that you *really* want, not just what is winnable because you have the votes for it now? You're going to have to work hard to make real changes that align with your values, so set the goal as something to celebrate, not just settle for. In reproductive rights litigation we've had to spend a lot of time on defense; it's important to make sure some of the team is on offense too. In short, if we are all going to spend considerable time and energy working for social change, let's make sure we're doing more than filling sandbags to shore up *Roe*.

Before we settle on new goals and strategies, we must ask whether they reflect the values of our movement. Does the strategy build toward elimination of systemic racism that limits bodily autonomy and the right to raise a child in a safe and sustainable community? Will the changes we push for include transgender and non-binary people and everyone else under the LGBTQ+ umbrella? Is the commitment to being inclusive reflected in the leadership of the coalition? Are the people most affected by the problem involved in designing solutions? Will the strategies not only help advance everyone's right to control when, whether, and with whom they have children, but to realize those choices as well? Are we being asked to make compromises that will exclude or harm the most marginalized or vulnerable? If our goals reflect these core values, then achieving them will be a celebration of our commitment to human rights and dignity.

Models of other successful social justice activism inspire us and contain lessons relevant to winning reproductive freedom. The decades-long campaign for marriage equality reinforces the importance of dreaming big. Attorney Evan Wolfson set out his pioneering vision in a law school paper he wrote in the early 1980s, more than ten years after the Supreme Court had already refused to consider the issue. By the mid-1990s, the HIV/AIDS epidemic had forced some LGBTQ+ people out of the closet but also fueled the development of a vibrant community that engaged in politics and demanded more rights and engaged more allies, with creative direct action and street protests driving the movement for justice. There was resistance from some activists who saw marriage as a fool's errand—or worse, a hetero-patriarchal trap. Because goals like enacting state anti-discrimination statutes or repealing laws that criminalized sex between LGBTQ+ people seemed almost in reach, there was significant resistance to chasing legal "I dos."

When in 1993 Hawaii's Supreme Court preliminarily ruled that prohibitions on same-sex marriage might violate the state constitution, LGBTQ+ activists were elated. Unfortunately, the backlash was swift. Hawaii passed a constitutional amendment banning same-sex marriage before anyone had a chance to walk down the aisle. At the federal level, President Clinton signed the Defense of Marriage Act: if same-sex couples won the right to marry in any state, the federal government would not have to honor those marriages.

But Wolfson and his allies envisioned the bigger-picture gains that marriage could bring and so created a road map to get there. They launched a nationwide campaign that would pursue marriage equality in as many states as possible before ultimately seeking rights at the federal level. A decade of legislative and referenda battles, community organizing, Pride marches, and more were bricks in the path that finally in 2015 led to the Supreme Court's decision legalizing same-sex marriage nationwide in *Obergefell v. Hodges*. As President Obama, himself a late convert to supporting marriage equality, noted on the day that the Supreme Court legalized it, "sometimes there are days like this, when that slow, steady effort is rewarded with justice that arrives like a thunderbolt." Indeed. But don't mistake that thunderbolt for anything other than a result of hard work by countless activists who created the necessary barometric pressure.

Coalition is queen. As you look at the new goals, ask whether they can inspire a broader coalition of allies. Movement building across identities and issues is the lodestar. First, can we engage our allied activists who are working for gender equity—those toiling to end gender-based violence, gain equal pay and better work-life balance, increase the minimum wage, and elect more women to political office? And crucially, can the strategy build bridges to other social justice movements, including but not limited to those working for LGBTQ+ equality, racial and economic justice, rights and access for people with disabilities, voting rights, and immigration reform? Ask not what your coalition partners can do for you but what we can do for each other's movements.

The recent efforts of Black Lives Matter (BLM) are a prime example of how a protest movement can build coalitions across a wide range of activists. What began in 2013 in response to the acquittal of George Zimmerman for fatally shooting an unarmed Trayvon Martin grew with the protests in Ferguson and St. Louis, Missouri, in 2014 into a robust and historic movement. Seeded as an online platform and organizing tool, the BLM hashtag created by three Black female organizers—Alicia Garza, Patrisse Cullors, and Opal Tometi—by 2020 had grown into a member-led network of more than forty chapters with millions of supporters across the globe, spurred to take action in the wake of the deaths of George Floyd, Breonna Taylor, and others at the hands of the police.

Black Lives Matter has accelerated the call for tangible policy reforms including oversight and accountability in policing, the end of mass incarceration and stop-and-frisk policies, and the reallocation of resources or defunding of police. Importantly, BLM and its allies have been able to unite people of different races, genders, and ages to protest injustice nationwide. Together these groups highlight and condemn systemic racism, made even more stark by the disproportionate and violent reaction of the police in major cities and the disparate health outcomes during the COVID-19 pandemic. The movement has made consistent demands at the local, state, and federal levels and before international human rights bodies, and it has spurred activists to organize politically and run for office.

As both the Freedom to Marry and BLM campaigns teach us, advancing goals in a wide range of settings improves your chance of success and enables you to tailor initiatives to local needs and options. Look for ways to make change via legislative reform, executive action, and litigation at the federal, state, and local level. Whatever forum provides the best chance of winning is where you want to be. Don't overlook the private sector, such as corporations and the media, as a resource if not a genuine ally, or otherwise as a target of your activism. Remember that game of whack-a-mole that the Center played as it fought against the onslaught of abortion restrictions? It's time for us to be the moles popping up all over the yard.

When we were at the Center, our colleagues at the Guttmacher Institute were outraged that their health insurance company refused to include birth control in their employee health policy. We realized that the Center's policy excluded contraception as well. In response, we launched a campaign to ensure that all FDA-approved contraception would be included in public and private health insurance plans. We mapped out a combination of strategies: litigation, legislative reform, administrative action at the state and federal level, and corporate advocacy.

Launched in the mid-1990s, the strategy engaged partner organizations and activists nationwide, winning hard-fought incremental gains and changing the conversation around insurance coverage for contraception. It led women in particular to question why the medication they relied on daily was being excluded from the guest list. Finally, nearly fifteen years later, when Obamacare was being designed, reproductive health activists had a seat at the table and demanded that contraception be included—without copays—under Medicaid and in all insurance sold in federal and state insurance marketplaces.

When the ACA later came under attack by the Trump administration, activists in the states responded with legislative strategies they had spent years sowing. Protection for contraceptive and abortion care was shored up in Oregon in 2017 by the state's Reproductive Health Equity Act, which mandated access to affordable reproductive health and preventative care in any state-regulated plan and expanded coverage to the undocumented immigrants shut out of the ACA.

A multidimensional campaign provides more avenues for victory and along the way creates broader engagement. It allows activists to move forward in their own way toward a common goal and not get too distracted by the opposition's plans or resources. If you've seen that photo of Olympic medalist Michael Phelps butterflying past his archrival, Chad le Clos of South Africa, you know the importance of staying in your lane, eyes forward on the goal. The image of le Clos losing valuable time by glancing over to check Phelps's progress floats over the slogan "Winners focus on winning; losers focus on winners."

Can the reproductive freedom movement coalesce around one or more audacious goals that will meet many of these criteria? Absolutely. Our dream list includes goals that advance reproductive freedom directly but also those that create the proverbial rising tide to lift all boats. At the top of our wish list is what we have dubbed the Gender Equity Amendment, a supercharged constitutional addition that could provide heightened and enduring protection for reproductive freedom.

A NEW WAY, A NEW CONSTITUTION

It's no surprise that as lawyers we look to legal strategies and constitutional reform as a central part of our long-term plans for social change. The US Constitution is the backbone that shapes the fundamentals of our country's legal rights and political system. Overall, constitutions are more permanent than legislation or policy directives, and they provide mechanisms to hold our government accountable, enforce our human rights, and solidify our values with a government stamp of approval.

While protections against gender discrimination have increased dramatically in recent generations, there remains a long way to go. Our current Constitution is insufficient to take us there. Drafted by our so-called founding fathers, the Constitution reflects their times and their biases. As such, the US Constitution has never been a place that reproductive freedom can call home. Instead, reproductive rights have found shelter just outside, in the penumbra of rights that the Supreme Court first recognized to protect privacy or in a notion of substantive due process. We need a room of our own, a provision that makes gender equity and procreative liberty its top priority and acknowledges how interconnected race, gender, and sexuality are in our current system of discrimination and disadvantage.

The strategy to seek a Gender Equity Amendment is not going to be easy, risk-free, or short-term. Indeed, some of the people we talked with, lawyers and activists we know and trust, thought a campaign would take too much work over too long a time and its success would be too speculative. They worried that the drive could detract from energies needed to secure shorter-term victories like the passage of state or federal omnibus legislation or the repeal of funding restrictions. They fretted that a drive for a new constitutional amendment could inspire our opponents to seek their own Human Life Amendment, enshrining protection for fetal life from the moment of fertilization.

We agree that the process for enacting a new constitutional amendment is cumbersome and can be daunting, requiring the passage of the proposed language by a two-thirds vote of Congress and ratification by three-quarters of the states. Given where we are today, we are certain that this is no immediate slam dunk. Nevertheless, we believe that the time to discuss, debate, and agree on proposed language is now. The proposal can be a rallying call for gender equity and reproductive justice and serve as a model for state constitutional change. We are playing the long game. It may take a decade or more to build enough support for this change. But if that is the case, then let's get started.

But wait—haven't feminists already tried this? Yes, with the ERA. First written in 1923, the Equal Rights Amendment states that "equality of rights under the law shall not be denied or abridged on account of sex." There was a lot to like about the ERA in 1972, when it was passed by Congress with bipartisan support before being sent to the states for ratification. Ultimately, the ERA failed to garner sufficient support within the ten-year time limit Congress imposed. It fell just three states short of passage, although an effort to revive it has had increasing support in more recent years.

There are numerous reasons why the ERA was defeated. It faced major opposition from Phyllis Schlafly's Eagle Forum, which rallied opposition among the conservative, churchgoing homemakers who later became the mainstay of the Christian right. Claims that the ERA would send women into combat and unisex bathrooms, deny them alimony and child support, and enshrine abortion and same-sex marriage in the Constitution scared away support from conservatives and eventually Republican state lawmakers.

But the ERA campaign also failed to unify people in the middle and on the liberal end of the spectrum. Some thought the amendment didn't go far enough to protect the most disempowered women, rectify the losses the Supreme Court dealt to low-income women and teens seeking abortion, and protect against LGBTQ+ discrimination. Others believed that Supreme Court rulings like *Roe*, federal statutes like the Equal Pay Act, and anti-discrimination prohibitions in the Civil Rights Act already provided all the legal protections women need. The campaign failed to organize effectively at the state level and account for significant regional differences and concerns other critics claimed. Although Americans supported the ERA by wide margins, there was little urgency for its passage beyond a core group of deeply committed activists.

In the end, the ERA was a near miss but an incredibly important building block, one that continues to draw attention to the need for constitutional muscle on the side of gender equity. It successfully introduced the idea that the federal Constitution should provide greater protections for women, building a strong foundation for the Gender Equity Amendment we propose. As the ultra-conservative Supreme Court seeks to diminish or completely eradicate reproductive freedom, LGBTQ+ rights, and racial justice, many of the rights we have come to rely on will be unenforceable, with stark consequences and real harm. The need for constitutional change will be more obvious, a critical antidote to countermand the Court's hostile jurisprudence. Moreover, because the Gender Equity Amendment is broader than the ERA, its more inclusive, intersectional aims will enable activists to build a wider supporting coalition that will have the political power to win this time around.

We envision an amendment that will broadly and clearly protect personal and private decision making from governmental interference. The rights to choose or refuse contraception, pregnancy, childbirth, and parenthood and to voluntarily engage in sex and make important decisions about marriage and family life would be explicitly protected as would equal access to governmental benefits based on these protected rights. Unlike the privacy right in *Roe* that belonged to the woman "in consultation with her doctor," the rights protected by the Gender Equity Amendment would be vested in individuals who could make decisions without consulting with or obtaining permission from spouses, partners, parents, or medical professionals. Moreover, an individual's autonomy, bodily integrity, and equality would not be sacrificed to the state's interest in promoting motherhood; the government's goal could be pursued only by affirmative family-friendly policies like universal child care and family leave.

Poof, Supreme Court decisions that permit the government to deny Medicaid funding for abortion would disappear forever. Laws that impose parental involvement on teens would dissolve into the ether. Coercive governmental policies such as forced contraception and sterilization; mistreatment during pregnancy, labor, and delivery; and outright denial of reproductive health care would be unlawful. The right to engage in sex free from coercion and to make life decisions and marry the person of your choice regardless of gender, race, LGBTQ+, or immigration status would be given full armor and not subject to the shifting sands of the Supreme Court. The Court's long history of denying that pregnancy discrimination actually is discrimination against women would be discarded as the ridiculous misconception that it is.

By design, the amendment also will provide greater gender equity protection beyond the area of reproductive freedom. While there are some valuable protections against gender discrimination planted in the Constitution's Equal Protection Clause and found within federal statutes and case law, this amendment would give them a much-needed boost. It would permanently prohibit discrimination on the basis of sex, gender, and LGBTQ+ status in a host of arenas from education to employment to governmental contracting to fair credit. It would usher in equal pay and equal access to government benefits far more effectively than is possible under current law. The amendment would prohibit not just acts that are intended to discriminate but also those policies that apply to everyone yet have a disproportionate harmful effect on a protected group such as women and LGBTQ+ folks.

While the ERA mandates gender *equality*, the amendment we envision furthers gender *equity*. Equality means that you have the right to be treated the same as people in the same circumstance, to have the same opportunities and resources; everyone gets the same slice of pie.

Equity, on the other hand, provides for baseline equality but also welcomes some differential treatment based on an individual or group's various circumstances and the need to remedy historical discrimination. You get the slice of pie that's the right size for your appetite, but if some people already have lots of pie in the fridge and you're still hungry, then you should get a bit extra.

Equity is based on the recognition that our social, economic, political, and cultural systems historically have been designed and implemented to favor specific groups and individuals at the expense of others and are so deeply rooted in discriminatory practices and beliefs that the resulting inequalities appear natural or inevitable. The solution is for the government to focus on programs that overcome these historical inequities: provide access to essential health care and basic education, alleviate poverty, and provide opportunities for economic advancement of marginalized groups.

The Gender Equity Amendment also would provide the highest level of legal protection—the same as is afforded free speech and religious freedom and initially provided in *Roe*—what lawyers call strict scrutiny. If a *fundamental* right is abridged, the government must prove that its actions are justified by a *compelling* state interest. This strong protection would be a big improvement from current law, in which abortion rights are governed by *Casey*'s less protective undue burden test and gender-based discrimination is evaluated by a lower, less protective standard (*middle-level scrutiny*) that unfortunately has never been adequate.

The Gender Equity Amendment should be drafted in a precise enough fashion that an originalist, textualist Court would be compelled to respect the full range of protections it mandates. The Supreme Court has a shameful history of closing its eyes to gender bias. Thus the amendment must be carefully structured to make it difficult for judges to arrive at conclusions that undermine protections for gender equity and reproductive freedom.

But the amendment also must be broad enough to offer critical protections for generations of circumstances to come, many that we cannot yet envision. Our forefathers could not imagine in vitro fertilization or predict the morning-after pill—and we're not exactly sure they would have cared to protect access for all anyway. Likewise, we know we cannot plan for all the developments and changes that will impact gender equality and procreation in the next year, never mind the next century. Lawyers love caveats, and so we suggest including one in the amendment to leave the welcome mat out for future developments. The phrase "These rights shall include but not be limited to" could do quite nicely.

We are purposefully refraining from proposing specific language for this new amendment. Instead, we aim to spur a conversation about gender equity, debate the pros and cons of specific concepts and wording, and sketch out in greater detail how hostile courts might interpret the language. We can draw on and expand an extensive array of constitutional models and language when writing the amendment, including state and federal ERAs, state constitution equality and privacy provisions, existing or proposed state or federal statutes, language used in Supreme Court decisions, and human rights doctrine.

Worth considering is the language proposed to amend the Vermont Constitution: "An individual's right to personal reproductive autonomy is central to the liberty and dignity to determine one's own life course and shall not be denied or infringed unless justified by a compelling state interest achieved by the least restrictive means."

The "shopping list approach" used in the Progressive Constitution created for the National Constitution Center's Constitution Drafting Project includes potential language striving for gender equality:

> The right of persons in the United States shall not be denied or abridged by the United States or by any State on account of sex, sexual orientation, performance of sexual or gender identity, sexual preference, or pregnancy, childbirth, and all attendant conditions, including the decision to become pregnant or terminate a pregnancy.

By specifically including definitions of "privileges and immunities," "liberty," "due process," and "equal protection of the laws" in the Fifth and Fourteenth Amendments, we could upgrade the Constitution's gender protections and give the textualist Court stronger direction. Several nations worldwide have done just this in response to their commitment to fulfilling their obligations under the Convention on the Elimination of All Forms of Discrimination Against Women (CEDAW). UN Women has created an entire Global Gender Equality Constitutional Database for hobbyists like us who collect bright, shiny gender equity clauses from around the globe.

The inclusive language contained in South Africa's Constitution, adopted after the end of apartheid, is worth a gander. It states: "The state may not unfairly discriminate directly or indirectly against anyone on one or more grounds, including race, gender, sex, pregnancy, marital status, ethnic or social origin, colour, sexual orientation, age, disability, religion, conscience, belief, culture, language and birth."

Alternatively, we could adopt language that establishes affirmative rights contained in human rights doctrine and in such documents as CEDAW and the Beijing Declaration and Platform for Action, a blueprint for gender equity inspired by the international gathering in 1995, where Hillary Clinton famously proclaimed that "human rights are women's rights and women's rights are human rights." Representatives from 189 nations adopted the Beijing Declaration's vision of equal rights, liberty, and opportunity for all women, and it continues to serve as a model for constitutions worldwide.

As we discussed earlier, the drafters in Philadelphia created a constitution that gave (themselves) freedom *from* government interference as they broke off from King George III. By comparison, the human rights framework creates an obligation for the government not only to respect and protect human rights but to remove obstacles to the realization of them. It holds the state responsible for its own discriminatory actions but also when its inaction allows others to impede rights. If the police are alerted to domestic violence and fail to respond adequately, then the state has failed to provide the protections required under human rights law, even though the conduct occurs between family members and in the privacy of the home. The ACLU and several other human rights groups obtained a favorable ruling from the Inter-American Commission on Human Rights in just such circumstances.

One noteworthy approach proposed by law professors Catharine MacKinnon and Kimberlé Crenshaw is informed by this human rights framework. It starts with introductory "Whereas" clauses that frame the document in the context of historical inequalities based on gender and race—and calls for the Constitution to treat all people in accordance with human rights principles. A key section of its text affirmatively grants women equal rights: "Women in all their diversity shall have equal rights in the United States and every place subject to its jurisdiction," echoing the Universal Declaration of Human Rights language that first established that all people, regardless of sex, "are born free and equal in dignity and rights."

There are definitely challenges to gaining traction with a human rights approach, but advantages as well. The US constitutional model has been an exemplar of freedom from government intrusion on individual rights since its beginning, and altering its structure to afford more affirmative rights will meet resistance from many quarters. But also deeply embedded in the US Constitution is an abhorrent history including the enslavement, persecution, and discrimination against African Americans and women, neither of whom had rights under the original document. An injection of affirmative rights designed to address centuries of structural racism and gender inequity might be the best way to guarantee greater equity for the next generation.

Moreover, a human rights approach aligns with values that many already embrace—such as a right to health care, racial and LGBTQ+ equity, and greater recognition of the importance of women's dignity and full participation in society. The US Supreme Court invoked the global human rights consensus when it (finally) decriminalized homosexuality in its 2003 ruling in *Lawrence v. Texas*. Bringing the US more into the international human rights community is an appropriate step and one aligned with today's global economy and its continued role as an international arbiter. But because this human rights model remains somewhat foreign to the US Constitution, it would need to be carefully constructed so as not to sabotage broad acceptance of the Gender Equity Amendment.

WE PROPOSE ACTIVISTS come together to thrash out specific constitutional concepts and language at a convening to rival the discussions held by the original drafters in 1787 in Philadelphia. This modern, feminist version will include activists and attorneys, campaigners and crusaders, organizers and orators from a wide range of social justice spaces to plan how to open up our constitution's doors to include procreative liberty and an inclusive vision of equity. No white powdered wigs this time, and a far more diverse range of participants—but for ease of commute, Kitty is fine with it still being held in Philadelphia. Lawyers and legislators could put pen to paper; medical personnel could weigh the pros and cons of each model; community organizers could lead our discussion toward consensus. Everyone would bring their expertise and their unique perspective. Each possible word choice contains different risks and benefits that must be put to a collaborative, robust planning process. With many fresh voices, the convening can provide space for dreaming big, working collaboratively, and ultimately proposing model language that aligns with our values. It may take time to implement, but developing and adopting a Gender Equity Amendment is a golden ring worth pursuing.

That doesn't mean we put all our ova into one basket. There are also pragmatic and shorter-term strategies to win wider access to safe and legal abortion, expand reproductive freedoms, and build a powerful social movement for change.

CHAPTER 12

GIVE ME AN *A*!
ABORTION ACCESS FOR ALL

> Young women need to know that abortion rights and abortion access are not presents bestowed or retracted by powerful men (or women)—Presidents, Supreme Court justices, legislators—but freedoms won, as freedom always is, by people struggling on their own behalf.
>
> KATHA POLLITT, JOURNALIST AND AUTHOR

TODAY, TOO MANY women *already* are unable to obtain abortion and other vital reproductive health care in ever-wider swathes of the US. If the new Supreme Court allows a gradual pile-on of more abortion restrictions, access to safe abortion will not just decrease but could become entirely unavailable in many states. If the Court leaps to quickly snuff out *Roe* and *Casey* altogether, abortion will be outlawed in as many as a third of the states before long. *Roe* status quo is insufficient.

We have sketched out below some strategies that we hope will inspire you to take action. We do not claim ownership or authorship of these suggestions. Think of it as Pinterest, not a prescription—an idea board, not a recipe. Some of these ideas might encourage you to embrace that old saying, "The best defense is a good offense," while for others you will need to gear up to repeal the anti-abortion initiatives that have been so harmful. By the time you read this it is possible that some of these ideas may have even been implemented—we can only hope. Nonetheless, there is plenty of work for everyone, and it takes assessing your state, your coalition, and your resources to determine the best path.

For starters, if you care about abortion, then you have to care about who has legislative and executive power. If we don't control who is in the driver's seat, we have about as much power as kids clamoring in the backseat, asking, "Are we there yet?"

Congressman Hyde used his political power to create an amendment that outlived him, denying Medicaid recipients abortion services to this day. Senator Mitch McConnell stacked the Supreme Court. President Obama and the Democratic Congress passed the Affordable Care Act and provided health coverage for twenty million Americans. The Virginia legislature flipped blue and passed the Reproductive Health Protection Act in 2020. Elections matter. If you care about preserving abortion, you have to engage in electoral politics.

Our best policy initiatives will stay in the closet like an old prom dress unless an elected official invites them to the legislative dance. To block harmful legislation takes only one branch of government—either a governor/president's veto or a House/Senate vote can hold back a new abortion restriction. Real affirmative legislative reform, however, requires control of both legislative chambers—except in Nebraska, which has only one—and an executive branch willing to sign a measure into law. Even with control of a legislative body, if the party leaders who set the legislative agenda are not on board, no new reforms are likely to flow.

For the most part, the Reds (Republicans) oppose abortion, and the Blues (Democrats) support it. The days of pro-choice Republican activists are gone, and those few remaining Republican pro-choice politicians tend to play "follow the anti-abortion leader." Similarly, anti-abortion Democrats are hard to find. Because abortion is a polarizing issue living in a partisan time, however, we need candidates from the Democratic team who are true allies—not just those who check the pro-choice box, but those who bring a real understanding of why abortion matters.

While federal legislation protecting abortion rights nationwide is big and sexy, a closely divided Congress and a Biden administration focused on restoring democratic norms and digging us out of a pandemic and recession may put immediate federal reform on the back burner. In contrast, the state level is an often-overlooked option, and winning there is more important than ever. Organizing and winning state-level reforms are an excellent way to build momentum and secure tangible gains. Many state-level actions can have a national impact by creating abortion oases and serving as testing grounds for new policies. For the foreseeable future, the action will be mostly in the states.

After the 2020 elections, Republicans control all three branches of government in twenty-three states and will gear up to pass new laws banning or severely restricting abortion. If your state is irredeemably red, you have our sympathies—but all is not lost. You can make a big stink when they move to take away your rights, and you can work to change the faces of power over the long term. Resistance can be inspiring. Texas senator Wendy Davis's solitary eleven-hour filibuster in 2013 brought worldwide attention to Texas's severe abortion bill and her bright pink running shoes.

Democrats hold power in fifteen true-blue states. If you live in these trifecta-blue locales, you're sitting pretty. These are the best places to shore up abortion rights and broader reproductive freedoms and make sure your majorities are firm going forward.

In the purple states with divided governments—twelve of them as of 2020—action on abortion rights proposals may be highly unlikely, at least until the legislature flips. For more than a decade, Stacey Abrams, LaTosha Brown, Nsé Ufot, Helen Butler, Lauren Groh-Wargo, and countless activists in Georgia registered hundreds of thousands of new voters, successfully turning their red state blue and galvanizing others to do the same. Their work is an excellent model for other purple states. And while you are focusing electoral energies on flipping states blue, let Democratic leadership know you're working for a pathway to reproductive freedom—and you expect them to be champions when they take power.

Because Republicans have been more successful than Democrats in getting out the vote in the off years between presidential elections, they control more state legislative races and gubernatorial seats when these elections are held. Abortion rights would be well served if we put some of our supporters' muscle toward voting in off years.

Ballot initiatives are another tactic used by abortion opponents to convince voters to directly enact abortion funding restrictions, parental involvement laws, late abortion bans, and more. In West Virginia in 2018 and Louisiana in 2020 voters said yes to referenda that excluded the right to abortion and funding from their state constitutions. The tide may be turning, though. In 2020, Colorado voters rejected a referendum that would have prohibited abortions at twenty-two weeks. The Vermont legislative effort that adds state constitutional protections for abortion could appear in a ballot battle in 2022. Twenty-four states have an initiative process that enables a citizen or state legislature to put a law or constitutional amendment up for a public vote. While referenda are extremely costly and time consuming, if used cautiously they can be an effective way to garner public support and enact meaningful change.

If we are going to use state constitutions to advance gender equity, we will need judges who are on board. State court judges are selected for the bench in a variety of ways—through statewide elections or by the legislature or governor—and serve terms that vary in length. Shoring up state courts with progressive jurists who have diverse real-life experiences can help advance reproductive freedom along with a whole slew of other rights. In 2015, Pennsylvania flipped control of its State Supreme Court, leading to a redrawing of gerrymandered congressional districts. In 2020, Michigan Democrats were able to gain a 4–3 Supreme Court majority, despite other significant losses in state elections, and we expect that this win will have an important role in protecting abortion rights as well as instituting criminal justice reforms.

The moral of the story is simple: be politically active. Vote in every election—not just the presidential ones—and vote all the way down-ballot for state legislative and judicial candidates. Pick your candidates carefully and early, and support their campaigns with your energy (phonebank, postcards, canvass) and dollars. Elected officials who simply declare they are pro-choice are fine, but we really need champions for abortion rights.

PROACTIVE PROPOSALS:
HOW TO GAIN NEW GROUND IN THE STATES

One of our favorite ways to safeguard abortion rights is with omnibus bills—state-level initiatives we've been pleased to see gain ground in blue states lately. These laws provide an amalgam of statutory protections for abortion as well as the repeal of existing restrictions in one fell swoop. It's important to make sure they do not leave impoverished women or teenagers behind as a trade-off for other rights.

The Reproductive Health Equity Act passed in 2017 in Oregon really does welcome everyone on board the reproductive health care bus. This comprehensive law codifies the right to abortion and expands coverage for reproductive health services in all state health care plans. It also ensures health care access for transgender and gender-nonconforming people and for undocumented immigrants excluded from the ACA—all while prohibiting out-of-pocket costs for reproductive health services. The National Institute for Reproductive Health calls it an "amazing omnibus law, which we think is one of the best around."

The Illinois omnibus law from 2019 also shines because it not only puts the standards of *Roe* into state law but provides that "every individual has a fundamental right to make autonomous decisions about one's own reproductive health," which includes the "fundamental right to continue the pregnancy and give birth or to have an abortion." It deletes from the books a number of anti-abortion restrictions (some unenforced), ditching spousal consent requirements, waiting periods, a partial birth ban, barriers to the provision of abortion by mid-level practitioners, and many more. Illinoisans now have broad access to abortion and insurance coverage and, as a result of an earlier court ruling, Medicaid funding to pay for it.

Unfortunately, Illinois's law still requires that a parent or adult family member be notified about a teen's abortion. In contrast, Massachusetts's ROE Act, passed in 2020 over Governor Charlie Baker's Christmas Eve veto, now permits sixteen- and seventeen-year-olds to make their own decisions about abortion and allows remote hearings for those under sixteen (eliminating the need for young people to travel to a courthouse). The law also provides shelter for *Roe* in Massachusetts state law and reduces restrictions on late abortion, among other reforms.

To date, a dozen states have laws or court orders explicitly permitting previability abortion or a postviability procedure whenever it is necessary to protect the health or life of the woman. Another three—Vermont, Oregon, and DC—provide a right to abortion throughout pregnancy.

To put these newly enacted rights to good use requires an ample number of abortion providers. Some states recently have moved to repeal their doctor-only requirements, while others have proactively created pathways for mid-level providers—physician assistants, midwives, and advanced practice nurses—to provide abortions. In Maine, a law introduced in 2019 by then Speaker of the House Democrat Sara Gideon permits mid-level practitioners to provide medication or surgical abortions, expanding abortion services to the more rural parts of the state. Massachusetts enables mid-level clinicians to provide abortion care consistent with their training. As of 2020, eighteen states and DC allow mid-level practitioners to dispense medication abortions, and thirteen of those permit them to perform surgical abortions as well. Since licensing medical providers is a state responsibility, this approach, paired with training and other supports, can be an effective way to expand the number of abortion providers in your state.

Increasing the number of providers goes hand in hand with expanding access to medication abortion more broadly and more creatively. College and university health clinics already provide a range of reproductive health care, including birth control, emergency contraception, pregnancy tests, and STI and HIV/AIDS screenings. A recently passed measure in California mandates the provision of medication abortion at University of California and California State University campus-based health centers, serving 750,000 students. We hope this type of requirement will be replicated in other states. In addition, activists should demand that health centers at private colleges and universities provide medication abortion and negotiate these changes with the head of health services, a dean, or the president. While you're there, if the university has a medical school, make sure the program trains students and mid-level providers in surgical and medication abortion. Medical Students for Choice is a great resource. Activism starts in the dorm.

Health care venues such as urgent care centers or "docs in a box" shopfront clinics have proliferated nationwide, and medication abortion aligns well with the services they already provide. Over 9,200 such clinics nationwide (compared to just 800 abortion clinics) that are open daily as well as evenings and weekends already provide nearly a third of all primary care visits and serve patients in rural areas, millennials, and Medicaid and Medicare recipients who do not have regular doctors. Adding medication abortion to their offerings would vastly improve access to care. Urgent care centers may be run by university hospitals already training abortion doctors or providing medication abortions in their student health centers or owned by large health systems, pharmacy companies, or investor-owned or hospital corporations ripe for social media or lobbying campaigns. CVS has over 1,100 MinuteClinics that already offer contraceptives, pregnancy and STI testing, and primary care to patients in over thirty-three states. Imagine the possibilities.

Speaking of new locations for abortions: consider establishing reproductive health centers in locations that are not subject to either federal or state laws restricting abortion. Women on Waves, the project created by Dr. Gomperts, planned to offer a full range of reproductive health services including abortion to Irish women twelve miles out to sea, where, in international waters, legal medication abortions would be provided by an onboard medical staff. How about setting sail off the coasts of Texas, Alabama, Mississippi, or Louisiana, where abortion likely will be banned? At a minimum, such a plan could bring much-needed worldwide attention to these states' harsh abortion laws.

Reproductive health centers also might partner with Indigenous tribes to provide a full range of services, including abortion on tribal lands, which are independent nations under US law. These tribal governments have the ability to establish their own health regulations that can provide greater protections for women's health than state law. The Indian Health Service's sordid history of exploiting, harming, and neglecting Indigenous women's reproductive health and their right to parent points up the vast need for these services.

Cecilia Fire Thunder, an activist and the first female president of the Oglala Sioux, was opposing a harsh South Dakota law criminalizing almost all abortion in 2004 when she remarked that she would consider opening a women's health clinic providing abortions on the reservation, bringing national attention to the idea. Working with Indigenous leaders to establish independent health services that provide quality comprehensive reproductive health care, including abortion, may be just what the doctor ordered to serve both Indigenous women and the women living in states where abortion may soon be banned or highly restricted. Charon Asetoyer of the Native American Women's Health Education Resource Center emphasizes how "for indigenous peoples of this country, [health care] is *our right*. . . . Think about that—what we gave up, what was taken from us, and [the government's] obligation, because of these treaty agreements, and how they are reneging on those agreements."

Another way to conveniently and safely bring reproductive health care providers to patients far removed from abortion clinics is through telemedicine. During the pandemic, using telemedicine for medication abortion counseling and prescribing first came into widespread use. When states require that pre-abortion counseling be done in person— as twelve states do—women may need to make two separate trips to the facility, with no corresponding health benefit. Through legislation or administrative rulings, states can modify these restrictions to allow counseling via telemedicine to ease these burdens.

From bills and ballots to clinics and abortion locations, the proactive possibilities are many.

OUR "KICK IT TO THE CURB" LIST: RESTRICTIONS THAT HAVE OVERSTAYED THEIR WELCOME

While we generally focus on affirmative legislation to move the ball forward for reproductive freedom, some state legislation currently on the books is too cruel to ignore and should be on your do-away-with list. Legislative reform, advocacy with sympathetic state or local health departments, and state budget debates offer alternative routes—far away from the hostile new lineup at the Supreme Court.

At the top of our kick-it list is the repeal of the Hyde Amendment and Hyde-like restrictions. These prohibitions on state funding for abortion under Medicaid and other state insurance programs are being targeted by groups like All* Above All, the driving force behind Hyde repeal. A few states that already provide abortion funding under Medicaid are going even further: Maine requires private health insurance plans to cover abortion, while, as mentioned earlier, California and Washington require all insurers that cover maternity care to also cover abortion. Some municipalities are stepping up to provide monies for abortion as well as related travel, child care, or accommodation expenses, even for women from out of state. If your state is not likely to repeal its restrictions, creation of local abortion funds within blue-city coffers can be an excellent way to organize support in your hometown.

When you do succeed in eliminating a funding ban, make sure not to overlook how the abortion providers' reimbursement rate is set by the state. Some states are so stingy in reimbursing Medicaid providers that clinics lose money on each Medicaid abortion they perform—not a model for sustainability of your local providers.

Teenagers are hit hard by funding bans as well as by harmful parental involvement laws, which put up barriers delaying abortions, increasing costs, and exacerbating their health risks. Ideally states would repeal their parental involvement laws in toto. Where that is not possible, activists can try to make these laws less onerous by eliminating the requirement for teens who are sixteen or older, changing consent to notification, reducing the number of parents who need to be involved from two to one, or permitting a teen to involve a stepparent, grandparent, other relative, or trusted adult. Rather than requiring a judge to certify that a teenager is mature enough to make the abortion decision, a state could allow a physician, social worker, or mental health professional to make the determination. Allowing judicial bypass proceedings to take place by videoconference—as two counties in Pennsylvania did during the pandemic—could also ease the way for teens while still ensuring that they receive the support they need.

Similarly, activists might also kick to the curb state waiting-period laws that require a twenty-four- to forty-eight-hour delay between the provision of counseling and the abortion. By necessitating two trips to the clinic in states that prohibit remote counseling, these laws are particularly arduous for teens and women living in abusive relationships, since repetitive travel increases the likelihood that unsupportive parents or dangerous spouses will prevent their abortions or react with violence.

Informed consent for abortion is absolutely the appropriate standard of care—so long as the patient's medical provider, not their legislator, controls the conversation. Unfortunately, the vast majority of these (twenty-nine) laws specify a litany of biased and medically inaccurate information that doctors must repeat, including dangerously false assertions that a medication abortion can be stopped after the first dose of pills, that abortion causes breast cancer, or that personhood begins at conception. Such interference between patients and providers should be abolished or at least amended to require that any information provided be unbiased and medically accurate.

Lastly, troublesome TRAP laws that have shuttered clinics or increased costs, moving abortion out of reach in twenty-three states, should be eliminated. In the aftermath of the Supreme Court decision in *June Medical v. Russo*, these laws may be ripe for additional litigation or reform by friendly health regulators.

NOW BACK IN WASHINGTON, DC . . .

While abortion rights have few friends left at the Supreme Court, allies and opportunities still exist in Washington, DC—particularly with a new administration in power. A national omnibus statute and repeal of funding restrictions are two long-term legislative goals, while a friendly executive branch provides an opportunity for a few key administrative actions to expand abortion access in the short term.

Even though Democrats control all three branches of the federal government, Republicans have leveraged federal rules and legislative procedures to their advantage. Three key political roadblocks continue to impede action by Congress. First, the filibuster rule (enabling a minority party to block votes on bills it's sure to lose) and, second, voter suppression and gerrymandering by state legislatures will require concentrated effort to reform. The third barrier, a disproportionate representation of rural states in the Senate gives Republicans an outsized advantage. Possibly granting statehood to the District of Columbia and Puerto Rico, two Democratic strongholds, or Democratic wins in more rural states could ensure that the Senate would be a more reproductive freedom–friendly forum.

With Democratic control of the Senate in 2021, we hope to see a rush to confirm new judges, but alas, the imbalance at the Supreme Court will persist. We're intrigued by proposals to increase the number of Justices on the Supreme Court, as President Franklin Delano Roosevelt attempted without success in 1936 with his "court-packing scheme." Some suggest adding four new jurists. Others favor a court design with fifteen Justices, five each appointed by either Republicans and Democrats, and then those Justices pick the other five. Or the current lifetime tenure could be replaced with eighteen-year terms staggered so that every president has two appointments for each four years in office. Other countries such as Spain, Germany, and Italy have specialized constitutional courts in which judges rotate in to hear matters of constitutional interpretation. Some of these reforms can be done by Congress, while others would require a constitutional amendment. All are worth exploring if we want to secure a more balanced Supreme Court for the long haul.

When Democrats have the power to secure the votes, the EACH Woman Act to repeal the Hyde Amendment and all its copycat abortion funding restrictions is teed up and ready to go. This bill promises that every woman insured through one of the many programs that serve low-income people, military families and veterans, public employees, Indigenous people, and more will have coverage for abortion services. Moreover, the EACH Woman Act prohibits any state or federal government from placing funding restrictions on state programs or private insurance plans, including those available through the ACA marketplaces. The passage of the EACH Woman Act is the highest priority of reproductive justice organizations, reproductive health clinics, and Planned Parenthood.

A sibling bill, the Women's Health Protection Act, is designed to cover everything other than the money. The bill would prohibit states, Washington, DC, and US territories from restricting, banning, or otherwise treating abortion differently from other health care. This seems-simple-enough law also recognizes the long history of harmful abortion restrictions, specifically prohibiting eleven different types of mandates—waiting periods, limits on telemedicine, TRAP laws, and more. In practice it would legislatively restore the protections of *Roe* and reverse many anti-abortion gains.

These proposals have the support of President Biden and Vice President Harris, who was a cosponsor of both bills when she served in the Senate. Needless to say, the bills face opposition from most Republicans in both chambers and likely from a few Democrats who consistently vote against abortion rights. Passage of either bill is unlikely unless there is a change to the filibuster rule and more members who strongly support abortion rights are elected.

WE PROMISED TO focus on big, audacious goals and not get tied up with initiatives that flip and flop with every change of administration. But after four lonnnnnng years under President Trump, we would be remiss if we did not mention a few federal fixes that President Biden could do relatively easily—as a thank-you gift to the women who were so key to his election.

The aptly named "gag rule" prohibits family planning clinics nationwide that receive federal Title X funds from providing, discussing, or referring for abortion, even if that service is requested by the patient and paid for with private funds. The Supreme Court upheld this Reagan-era muzzle in 1991. Both Presidents Clinton and Obama rescinded it by executive order and rule changes immediately upon taking office. Unfortunately, like other Republican presidents, President Trump reinstituted the rule soon after he took office. Unable to temporarily block the rule in the courts, Planned Parenthood and other clinics have refused to comply, forsaking millions of dollars of support and reducing the Title X network's capacity by 46 percent. During his first weeks in office President Biden ordered the Department of Health and Human Services to review Trump's Title X policy with an eye to rescinding it.

The adoption of a new rule repealing the gag rule and requiring comprehensive family planning under Title X is critical. Not only would this restore monies for Planned Parenthood, but it would make fake clinics ineligible for that funding. We are hopeful this will be done soon, perhaps before this book is published. But importantly, Congress should make this change permanent when the votes are there to avoid the restriction being revived someday by an anti-abortion administration. Biden's American Rescue Plan also added $50 million in Title X funding, a great boon.

In addition, administrative rule changes by the Food and Drug Administration, Department of Health and Human Services, Justice Department, Department of Homeland Security, and other federal agencies present opportunities to advance reproductive health and rights. The pesky Risk Evaluation and Mitigation Strategies (REMS)— the ones that make medication abortion available only at a doctor's office or clinic have been temporarily suspended by the FDA during the pandemic and should be withdrawn immediately.

Given the recent uptick in violence at abortion facilities, policy changes at the FBI, ATF, and Justice Department should include reviving the National Task Force on Violence Against Reproductive Health Care Providers, more strategizing by folks at the J. Edgar Hoover Building to beef up federal investigations and enforcement of the Freedom of Access to Clinic Entrances Act (FACE), and unifying state and federal law enforcement efforts to keep abortion providers and their patients safe.

WE END WITH one bold, smart, and humane goal for abortion: an explicit shield against the prosecution and jailing of women who have one.

Whatever way a woman obtains an abortion, she should not be held criminally liable. This was true in most states before *Roe*. As we enter the post-*Roe* era, every state ought to enact such a policy. Criminal charges related to abortion stigmatize health care and cause devastating harm to those who need abortions and their families.

History has proven that when abortion is banned, women will go to great lengths and take untoward risks to terminate an unintended pregnancy. This time (we hope) they will not be forced to resort to back-alley abortionists of the pre-*Roe* era, the Janes clandestinely performing abortions, or even an Irish solution of traveling abroad. Today it is more likely that women will use abortion medications to manage their own care—commonly called either self-managed, self-induced, or at-home abortion. We hope they will be able to do so safely and with access to medical care as needed.

Women will obtain the drugs any way they can: from legal clinics or supportive doctors, through online gray markets or illicit suppliers. A recent national study in *JAMA Network Open* estimates that already "approximately 900,000 to 1.3 million U.S. women of reproductive age have experience with self-managed abortion" and "projects that 7% of U.S. women will attempt them in their lifetime." It confirms that "people of color, those with lower incomes, and those who face barriers to care" were more likely to attempt self-managed abortions. The researchers conclude that with "a growing demand for convenience, privacy, and the comfort of self-managed abortion and self-care more broadly, coupled with increased restrictions on abortion, it is likely that self-managed abortion will become more prevalent in the U.S., as it is today in other countries." In a post-*Roe* era, if nearly a third of states ban abortion, the use of self-managed medication abortion will grow exponentially.

Criminal laws on abortion vary by state and often are murky as to whether a woman may be charged with a crime for attempting to self-induce or self-manage an abortion. According to the SIA Legal Team (now If/When/How: Lawyering for Reproductive Justice), five states—Arizona, Oklahoma, South Carolina, Delaware, and Nevada—have laws that directly put women at risk of prosecution. Laws in an additional thirty-eight states that allow a person to be charged with "fetal homicide" or "feticide" if a person is responsible for the unlawful death of a fetus offer prosecutors legal theories under which to charge women. Any of the abortion bans we expect to be passed when *Roe* and *Casey* are overruled also may give prosecutors an opening, particularly when laws do not clearly exempt those who are pregnant. And while criminal prosecution is not common, over the last twenty years at least twenty-four people have been prosecuted for using abortion pills on their own or helping a woman to do so. As the number of women using these methods increases, the likelihood of prosecutions will as well.

The dangers of criminalization are starkly drawn by the story of Jennifer Whalen, a Pennsylvania mother who in 2013 ordered medication abortion pills online for her pregnant daughter. Whalen said she had purchased the pills not knowing it was illegal. She could not afford the in-person abortion, lost days of work, and transportation costs needed to make two separate trips to a clinic. When her daughter sought medical help and admitted to taking the pills, hospital staff reported the pair to child protective services. Whalen was criminally charged with providing an abortion without a medical license and endangering the welfare of a child. She received a nine- to eighteen-month prison sentence, leaving her children at home with her husband while she was incarcerated.

That same year in South Bend, Indiana, Purvi Patel, a thirty-three-year-old Indian American woman, was convicted of feticide and sentenced to twenty years in prison for allegedly inducing her own abortion. Although the Indiana feticide statute exempts legal abortions, prosecutors argued that it was against the law to order abortion pills online, as Patel apparently did, and thus she didn't fall into the exemption. Patel's jury verdict was reversed on appeal after she had served eighteen months in prison. Bei Bei Shuai, a woman of Chinese descent, also was prosecuted under Indiana's feticide law after a suicide attempt in 2011 resulted in the loss of her pregnancy. National Advocates for Pregnant Women were cocounsel representing Shuai as she pled to misdemeanor criminal recklessness and avoided a possible sentence of forty-five years to life.

It is clear that bringing criminal charges against those who have abortions serves zero public health benefit and is unlikely to deter anyone from turning to medication abortions or other methods. Indeed, the threat of criminal prosecution is likely to have just the opposite effect. Fearing arrest, they will not seek timely medical attention, to say nothing of the concerns raised by police and zealous prosecutors probing how and why they are terminating their pregnancies or having a miscarriage.

Moreover, we know that prosecutions will not fall equally. Those who are already at greater risk of criminalization because of their gender identity, economic status, substance abuse or race, like Patel and Shuai, or those who live in very conservative areas, like Whalen, will have a higher risk of prosecution. Seventy-five percent of pregnancy-related criminal cases in Florida were brought against Black women, even though they comprise only 15 percent of the state's population.

Medication abortion has made self-managed abortion safer than ever before. The World Health Organization has indicated support for self-induced abortion in circumstances in which the medication and instructions are reliable and backup care is available from a health care provider. Today's medications are far simpler to obtain and self-administer. A number of sources ship medications from overseas pharmacies or US locales, provide online clinician support, or make the drugs available legally through local clinics and primary care providers in some states. The cost of the pills ranges from $40 for misoprostol if bought in a bodega or shipped from other countries to $750 or more for the two-drug option and telemedicine services, tests, and bloodwork. In contrast, the cost of medication abortions obtained from a legal independent clinic or Planned Parenthood averages $500 to $600 but can vary based on where the clinic is located and whether insurance coverage is available. Travel from a state where abortion is banned to a legal state will add to the cost.

Aid Access, also founded by Dr. Gomperts, has been providing reliable medication, information, and direct access to a physician for self-managed abortion since 2005. Patients provide their medical history and length of pregnancy and pay a $95 fee (those too poor to pay can still receive the medication), after which Gomperts writes a prescription and has the medication delivered from a reliable pharmacy in India. A *BMJ* study of women who used the service in Ireland and Northern Ireland found outcomes comparable with in-clinic protocols and a strong safety record. But the ability of Aid Access to continue to operate has been in jeopardy since 2019, when the FDA issued a cease and desist letter warning regulatory action including seizure or injunction if it did not cease distributing "misbranded and unapproved new drugs."

Over the longer term, legally allowing the purchase of medication abortion over the counter (OTC) is the best solution. Misoprostol is already available OTC in many countries around the world and has significantly reduced the stigma and burdens now associated with abortion. Researchers here in the US are currently looking at whether women can accurately determine their gestational age, rule out other complications, self-administer safely, and obtain help when necessary. We will await these studies. But as a first step, we must push to ensure that women who self-manage medication abortions or obtain abortions in any other way are not criminally prosecuted while we simultaneously work to remove barriers to abortion in all states.

The proactive proposals and kick-to-the-curb actions can keep activists busy for years to come, but to save reproductive freedom we cannot focus on abortion alone. Even if it takes decades of work, we need to enact laws that give everyone full access to health care, including reproductive health care and fertility treatment, and the social services and workplace benefits that support parenthood. Abortion rights must be part of an alliance of advocacy focused on reducing maternal and infant mortality, unintended pregnancy, and sexual assault and coercion, so that all of us have both the human rights and the economic means needed to fully chart our lives and destinies.

CHAPTER 13

AND THE NOMINEES ARE...
TEN STEPS FORWARD

If your dreams do not scare you, they are not big enough.

ELLEN JOHNSON SIRLEAF,
FORMER PRESIDENT OF LIBERIA,
2011 NOBEL PEACE PRIZE LAUREATE

ONLY A GENERATION ago, abortion was illegal in most states. There were no rape crisis centers or shelters for battered women. Most LGBTQ+ people lived in the closet, and marriage equality was unimaginable. Job postings were divided by gender, and apartment listings specified "no single women, children, or pets."

Much progress has been made on what was once viewed as impossible.

Yet there remain significant financial, racial and gender biases that align to create powerful obstacles to full equality. Some barriers have been deliberately constructed by anti-abortion forces; others grow organically out of the structural racism and historical sexism at the core of US law. When we consider how many individuals and families are still denied the ability to make free reproductive choices because they are too young, their income is too low, or the color of their skin is too dark, or because they live in rural communities, are persons with disabilities, or are transgender, non-binary, or in same-sex relationships, it becomes obvious that an agenda that guarantees reproductive freedom is a very long one, and much work remains.

Some activists argue that widening the reproductive rights agenda to include issues beyond abortion will dilute the struggle to protect abortion rights. We disagree. Abortion rights are inextricably intertwined with other important decisions about one's body, health care, and life. It is why abortion matters. To freely choose abortion, you need to be able to consider all your options, including whether having and raising a child is feasible and right for you. Will you have access to prenatal, maternity, and well-baby care? Will you have food, affordable housing, quality child care, and educational access to raise a child in safety and shelter? Having a full range of options when facing an unintended pregnancy is what makes a choice genuine, not just deciding from the best of a bad lot.

Broadening the abortion rights movement to fight for a wide range of reproductive freedoms is also the right thing to do politically. If we are ever to win abortion rights, we must widen our base or risk becoming an isolated fringe movement. There is a natural alignment with activists working on women's, LGBTQ+, and disibility rights, racial justice, economic equity, voting rights, and immigration reform. Building strong, mutually dependent coalitions will aid all of our goals.

With this in mind, we offer here our top ten priorities for advancing reproductive freedom. It's not as prescriptive as the Ten Commandments or as data-driven as Billboard's top ten singles, but it serves to guide us toward reproductive freedom now.

Our key initiatives need advocates in many different locales, from the steps of state capitols to the halls of Congress to local school boards and even corporate boardrooms. Mayors, governors, the president, and a wide range of other decision makers can make a difference, but they need to be prodded by activists. This list serves as a starting point to inspire conversation and connection with the many activists and organizations that bring deep experience, invaluable research, and political knowledge to our work. Let's start the count.

1. HEALTH CARE FOR ALL

You've heard it before: "Health Care Is a Human Right." "Health Care for All." Easier said than done. Yet providing universal access to affordable, comprehensive health care is at the top of our agenda. Women are free to make a wide range of procreative decisions only if they have the ability to obtain safe, quality health care, including abortion, maternity care, and full reproductive health services throughout their lifespans without interruption.

The American system of health care delivery is predominantly privatized and uniquely inequitable. While our country has some of the most advanced and innovative health care available worldwide, it comes at a high cost. Currently the cost of health care is an enormous and unfair barrier to coverage for millions of families. The first year Julie launched her consulting practice, she spent over $20,000 to continue her family's health insurance. After she experienced a brain tumor at age thirty-seven, she feared she would be denied coverage for any preexisting medical condition if she switched insurance providers. Kitty always had great employer-sponsored coverage, and after recognition of domestic partnerships and same-sex marriage, Joann could be added to her plan. They now have Medicare. We are the lucky ones.

US households spend approximately 8 percent of their budgets on health care, on average nearly $5,000 a year. That number is increasing annually, with the result that medical bills are a significant factor in personal bankruptcy filings. To preserve personal health coverage, employees stay in jobs they hate or that are dead-end, limiting mobility in the labor market and stunting individual growth and innovation. For the millions without any health care, particularly preventive services, the negative impact on physical and mental health is dramatic and unfair.

The COVID-19 pandemic and the Black Lives Matter movement underscored the long-standing disparities in health and health coverage in stark terms. The US health care system remains among the most inequitable worldwide, reflecting structural racism and gender inequality in cruel ways. Disparities also occur across socioeconomic status, age, geography, language, disability status, citizenship, immigration, and LGBTQ+ status. Fixing these inequities will not only improve the quality of care and population health but significantly reduce costs.

The Affordable Care Act was a big step forward in providing a fuller range of health care to a wider population of people, leading to significant coverage gains among Black, Latinx, AAPI, and Indigenous people facing disparities, although it unfairly excluded undocumented immigrant families from most care. It has successfully enrolled twenty million new participants in public and private health care plans thus far, enabled families to keep their children on their plans up to age twenty-six, and stopped the common denial of coverage for pre-existing conditions that disproportionately affects women.

Despite the ACA's success, Republicans have repeatedly sought to repeal it and return health care delivery into the hands of the private market, free from regulation or government obligation. They also have sought to narrow the ACA's scope, discourage enrollment, and bring litigation to outright invalidate it; as of yet they have never offered a comprehensive alternative plan.

In contrast, Democrats have urged states to adopt expanded Medicaid eligibility and to make state and federal reforms that increase enrollment and make plans more affordable, but they remain divided over next steps. Some focus on reducing the price of prescription drugs or providing a public option that permits people to buy into Medicare. The vision offered by Senator Bernie Sanders and others proposes the creation of a new, national health care system ("Medicare for All"), which would provide lifetime enrollment and comprehensive benefits with no premiums, much like that available in most developed countries.

The challenges to reforming health care are well-known, the debate well polarized, and opponents well funded. Yet more than twenty-eight million people in the US remain uninsured—approximately 10 percent of the population, and predominantly people of color. We need more coverage for more people.

Soon after taking office, the Biden administration beefed up opportunities to enroll in ACA plans and ordered the Department of

Health and Human Services to reexamine restrictive Trump-era policies, like work rules, to make health insurance more accessible and affordable. By executive order, President Biden also established a new White House Gender Policy Council as part of the Executive Office of the President. The Council will work to advance broad access to reproductive health care, combat systemic biases, and improve economic equity.

In the American Rescue Plan, Congress increased subsidies for individuals to reduce the cost of coverage and provided additional incentives to the twelve states that have not yet adopted Medicaid expansion. When politically feasible, Congress also can open Medicare to all who want to enroll—the public option—which would further reduce the cost of health insurance and spur enrollment. At the state level, activists can press the twelve states that have not yet opted to expand Medicaid to get with the program.

As for reproductive health, Medicaid and the ACA's plans now mandate maternity care, well-baby care, contraceptive options, and preventative services. The time has come for abortion coverage to be welcomed on board. States can move to require ACA-mandated services in every insurance plan, not just those provided by the government or sold through the marketplaces. Federal and state governments can find ways to bring down the high price of prescription medications without leaving behind medications essential to reproductive health. Contraceptive drugs and devices, HIV/AIDS and STI treatments, medication abortion, and infertility drugs all must be made available without out-of-pocket costs.

Ultimately, the best models of health care out there are those that reflect human rights values by providing universal health care. Some national public systems like those found in Canada and throughout Europe have been very effective but may be a bridge too far for the US, at least at this time. But making the changes that are possible now will help build a consensus for additional measures that will widen the availability of health care, including reproductive health care, for all.

2. SAVE LIVES: REDUCE MATERNAL AND
INFANT DEATHS AND COMPLICATIONS

Kitty's maternal grandmother died in childbirth when her uncle was born and her mother was four years old. Throughout her life, Kitty watched her mother struggle with the catastrophic loss and how the tragedy affected two generations of the family thereafter.

While childbirth has gotten much safer in the ensuing years, Black women, regardless of their income or educational level, still face unacceptably high rates of maternal mortality. They are three times as likely to die in childbirth as white women; the disparity increases even more for older Black women (four times) and those with a college degree (five times their white counterparts).

Amber Isaac, a seemingly healthy twenty-six-year-old first-time mother, died from complications shortly after giving birth in a Bronx hospital in 2020. Isaac, a Black woman, had pressed doctors to pay greater attention to her pregnancy, but they failed to heed her warnings, only discovering a dangerous condition the day she delivered her son by emergency C-section—when it was too late to prevent her death. Just three months later in a Brooklyn hospital, a second twenty-six-year-old Black woman, Sha-Asia Washington, would die while giving birth to her daughter. These heartbreaking deaths, so close in time and circumstance, highlight that in New York City, Black women are eight times more likely to die due to complications related to pregnancy than white women, a figure over double the nationwide disparity. In addition, Black women have starkly higher rates of life-threatening complications, largely as a result of preterm births.

Black infants are dying at almost twice the rate of babies born to white women, regardless of income or educational attainment of their mothers. Recent data show that infants born to "Black women with doctorates and professional degrees have a higher infant mortality rate than white women who never finished high school."

These racial disparities are a reflection of how structural racism in the US undermines access to health care and social services and creates stressors that can become exacerbated during pregnancy and trigger a chain of negative health events. The result is that Black women often receive poorer quality care and less of it, endure more physical pain, and experience bias and disrespect from health care providers. In 2018, tennis legend Serena Williams and pop culture icon Beyoncé each experienced life-threatening complications during pregnancy within months of one another and spoke out to give credence to the fact that even highly influential Black women's voices are disregarded during labor and delivery, too often to disastrous effect.

Reforms in maternal health care at the city and state level are urgently needed. Twenty states have established maternal mortality review commissions that collect data and investigate deaths like Washington's and Isaac's to develop avenues for improvements. Other efforts, like anti-bias training for medical personnel and uniform hospital protocols for pregnant women, can help reduce bias and differential treatment. Intensive case management programs are also needed to help women who for a variety of reasons—domestic violence, mental health, and substance abuse issues—do not make their medical appointments or who, lacking a doctor of their own, seek care from multiple medical providers who then fail to coordinate with each other. Doulas—nonmedical birth coaches—provide care and support before, during, and after pregnancy. Recognizing that doulas can improve maternal health outcomes, several states have expanded their Medicaid programs to cover these costs.

The MOMobile home-visiting program run by the Maternity Care Coalition, a forty-year-old organization in Philadelphia, provides one example of a successful program to help reduce maternal and child deaths and improve the health of pregnant women. Trained advocates visit women in their homes and offer free prenatal care, counseling, and referrals to maternity care and other critical services and, when necessary, accompany high-risk women to appointments. Services during the "fourth trimester" that support infant care, access to lactation consultants, supplemental nutrition, education, and counseling services, like those available from the federal WIC program, are also provided.

While Medicaid pays for nearly half of all births and covers infants for a full year, pregnant women have only sixty days of postpartum coverage. The majority of pregnancy-related deaths happen after the day of delivery, and nearly one-quarter occur more than six weeks postpartum. States that have expanded Medicaid under the ACA are enrolling postpartum women, but in twelve states Medicaid-eligible women remain uninsured during a medically vulnerable time. The good news is that beginning in 2022, the American Rescue Plan gives these twelve states the option to enroll women up to a year postpartum.

In 2021 Congresswomen Lauren Underwood and Alma Adams, along with Senator Cory Booker, introduced a welcome Black Maternal Health Momnibus Act. Designed to fill legislative gaps and comprehensively address the Black maternal health crisis, this bill directs a number of key federal agencies to establish studies, grants, policy changes, and innovative models to support prenatal and postnatal reforms, including services for incarcerated women, who are particularly overlooked.

Sweeping reforms at the federal, state, and local level are urgently needed to stop the racial and gender discrimination in maternal health care that endangers the lives of Black women and infants during childbirth and the year thereafter.

3. PREGNANT BY CHOICE, PART 1: WIDEN AVAILABILITY OF CONTRACEPTION

Since 1960, patients in the US have needed a prescription to obtain birth control pills. Too often this requires a doctor's visit, which creates additional hurdles and, for teens especially, may be a complete barrier to obtaining contraception. This is not your mother or grandmother's pill, and it should not be treated as such. High on our list is to make birth control pills available to all over the counter, without a prescription.

It's time for the US to join the modern era by eliminating the prescription requirement for oral contraceptives altogether, as over one hundred countries worldwide already have. Women are now buying and using the pill safely without a prescription everywhere from Afghanistan to Zambia.

Making the pill available OTC will dramatically increase access to the drug, especially for those who cannot easily obtain prescriptions, such as teenagers, rural women, and those who receive health care through the Indian Health Services. Going OTC will also reduce the cost, primarily benefiting women without insurance—about 11 percent of adult women, disproportionately including women of color. The good news is that one company already is in the process of seeking FDA approval of the most commonly used pill, and plan to make it far more affordable. Another is readying an application to the FDA for the progestin-only mini-pill.

Some activists are concerned that if the pill is available OTC, Medicaid and insurance plans will no longer cover it, leading to increased out-of-pocket costs for the millions of women who have health insurance. The ACA requires that private insurance plans sold in the federal and state marketplaces cover all FDA-approved birth control for women without a copay, including OTC methods *if prescribed*. Unfortunately, a prescription might still be required to ensure that insurance will pay, unless Congress or the states make changes to the requirement.

Over the last decade, the number and rate of abortions have decreased significantly in the US, reflecting a decline in pregnancy overall. One of the contributing factors is the use of highly effective, long-acting reversible methods of contraception (LARC) including injectable Depo-Provera, contraceptive implants placed under the skin, and IUDs. There are several barriers to wider use of LARC, particularly among teens, including medical providers who are unfamiliar with the methods or have misperceptions about their use, both of which can be overcome with better training. Yet the complex history of health risks and coercive circumstances surrounding LARC and sterilization means practitioners must proceed with caution around any effort to steer women toward specific contraception methods, particularly those based on assumptions about race, age, and gender identity. Nevertheless, LARC should be fully available for women when they choose to put them in, and when they want to take them out, qualified affordable practitioners must be trained and readily accessible.

More than a dozen states have enacted measures to increase access to affordable contraception. Some require private insurers to provide coverage for the full range of contraceptive methods, counseling, and services at no cost to the patient, matching or exceeding the ACA standard. Others require that plans cover OTC contraception or up to a year's supply of prescribed pills at one time, and to cover both male and female sterilization. Many states have made it easier to get a prescription by allowing telemedicine appointments or, as thirteen states now do, enabling pharmacists to prescribe contraceptives. All great ideas and worthy of replication.

4. PREGNANT BY CHOICE, PART 2: REDUCE INFERTILITY

Julie's first daughter was "made for free with parts available at home," as they say. Her second daughter did not come so easily. After a major health condition, one early miscarriage was followed by a much more difficult second-trimester one. After that, she and Tom went to a fertility specialist they nicknamed Dr. Baby-gawd, who had offices in New York City and, fittingly, Las Vegas, the gambling capital of the world. Her employer-sponsored health insurance covered some of the exorbitant costs of in vitro fertilization (IVF), and Julie had enough control over her work schedule to duck out for multiple appointments and procedures. Fortunately, the IVF was successful despite the low odds associated with the process at her ripe old age of forty. In the end, IVF was something she was eternally grateful for yet wouldn't have wished on her worst enemy.

When Kitty and Joann wanted to start their family in the 1980s, a lesbian couple having children together was a novelty. They ultimately found several doctors who agreed to help them with artificial insemination. One required them to undergo counseling to prove they would be good parents (straight couples had no similar requirement), and another made them use the back door in order to stay out of sight of his disapproving medical partners. Thumbing through a catalog of sperm donor profiles is a memorable experience. Thankfully the whole shebang resulted in two wonderful children, and while fertility services are widely available to LGBTQ+ couples today, bias is still rampant.

US policies and conversations on reproductive freedom have focused very little on ways to help women become pregnant. Recent data show that about 10 percent of women in the United States ages fifteen to forty-four have difficulty getting or staying pregnant. Infertility is defined as not being able to get pregnant after one year of trying (six months if a woman is thirty-five or older) or in some cases not being able to stay pregnant.

Insurance plans and public programs often classify fertility treatments as "voluntary medical care" and deny coverage. A basic IVF cycle costs around $12,000, not including fertility drugs, specialized testing, and related expenses, and all-in costs can exceed $60,000 with no guaranteed result. Without coverage for artificial insemination, IVF treatments, egg freezing procedures, and medications, treatment is completely out of reach for all but the wealthiest women or requires deep debt. Fourteen states now have laws that require insurers to cover infertility diagnosis and treatment, and two more require insurers to offer coverage. However, three of the states that require insurance coverage—Texas, Arkansas, and Hawaii—exclude same-sex couples and single women by allowing coverage only if a woman's eggs are being fertilized with her husband's sperm. Often when insurance companies cover fertility treatments, they too have rules that exclude the use of donor sperm that disadvantage couples or individuals who are LGBTQ+, unmarried, or in which the man is infertile. Full coverage of fertility treatments for all persons under both public and private insurance is an important way to guarantee anyone can choose parenthood.

We also need to look more critically at the factors causing infertility—particularly the environmental and workplace hazards and toxins that are disproportionately experienced by low-income people and people of color. In urban neighborhoods and rural areas alike, a number of toxicants and hazardous industrial waste, unsafe drinking water, air pollutants, and other conditions can lead to infertility or miscarriages. By joining together with environmental justice allies, reproductive rights advocates can call for better research on the causes of these hazards, the development of appropriate treatments, and the implementation of workplace protections and environmental cleanups.

5. ACCURATE, ENGAGING, AND FUN SEX EDUCATION

Over the years Julie has had bits and pieces of conversation with her kids about puberty, sexual health, gender identity, consent, and more—not her parents' birds 'n' bees talk but nonetheless still A-W-K-W-A-R-D. She is always grateful to educators who competently assist in teaching sexuality education.

As with reading, writing, and 'rithmetic, teaching reproductive health and sex ed takes expertise. Most Americans believe every kid should have access to a positive, affirming, inclusive program of sexuality education that is comprehensive, is free from inaccuracy or bias, and gives them the tools for healthy relationships throughout their lifetimes. Yet in schools, this ideal is hardly ever realized. The practices and mandates around sex ed vary significantly from state to state, and much of the allocated federal funding has gone to those inaccurate, stigmatizing, abstinence-only programs we discussed earlier. Not all states even have sex ed requirements: only thirty mandate it in public schools, thirty-nine mandate HIV/AIDS education, and only twenty-two say that sex and HIV/AIDS education must be medically, factually, or technically accurate. Some states require notification or consent of parents for the student to participate; others allow parents to remove their children from the classes.

On the bright side, seventeen states recently have passed laws that improve sex education. Many of these initiatives were embraced in response to the #MeToo movement: Illinois, New Jersey, and DC now teach about consent, while four other states require information on the prevention of sexual assault, dating violence, and child exploitation.

Most often absent from curricula, however, is any discussion of pleasure and desire. Instead, sex is discussed as a problem behavior, especially for teens, even though evidence shows that it is the lack of a relationship that leads to negative experiences. The history of sexist and racist stereotypes, disregard of people with disabilities, and homophobia and transphobia found in society generally run throughout many sex ed programs and must be eliminated. Sex ed also must include accurate information about the full range of sexual choices, healthy relationships, and extensive discussions about consent, coercion, and exploitation. Adolescents deserve to have the education that will protect their well-being and set a path for a lifetime of healthy relationships.

While broad guidelines about sex ed are determined at the state level, implementation happens at a very local level and can be a great place to start advocating for reproductive rights. The Sexuality Information and Education Council of the United States offers a tool kit to start building support in your community, and Advocates for Youth has model curricula for comprehensive sex ed.

6. AFFORDABLE CHILD CARE AND PRE-K EDUCATION

When their children were young, Kitty and Joann spent more money on child care than on putting Joann through law school, and this is not uncommon. Today, infant child care averages more than a year's tuition at a public college.

The availability of quality affordable child care and education is one of the most important factors when families consider whether to have a child or add to their families. According to the Center on Budget and Policy Priorities, child care takes about 10 percent of an average family's monthly budget (higher than health care), and disproportionately disadvantages low-income families, eating up as much as 30 percent or more of their budget. In the US, less than a third of children have a full-time stay-at-home parent. Families make do with arrangements that include a patchwork of day care centers and preschools, tag-teaming parents and grandparents, babysitters, nannies, neighbors, and more, oh my.

Access to quality consistent child care fuels children's growth and is essential to women's ability to participate equally in the workforce and advance gender equity. When the COVID-19 pandemic made it impossible for many children to attend child care programs or school or have caregivers at home, it laid bare the exhausting balancing act that families, and particularly low-income women of color, perform on a daily basis. Millions of women who are primarily tasked with caring for their families have been driven out of the workforce in what some are calling a "shecession," which they can ill afford.

Our national policies are in deep denial about the fact that young children need caretakers year-round and full-day. The current scatter-shot government subsidies and tax credits for child care are insufficient to guarantee low-income families access to quality care. A national program that guarantees public benefits to help low-income Americans pay for child care could be a much-needed boon to those parents who need reliable, full-day child care in order to work, while also providing a living wage to women who comprise 95 percent of child care workers.

In 1971, Congress passed the Comprehensive Child Development Act, which would have been a first step toward a universal program, but the measure was vetoed by President Nixon, and until recently Congress has given too little attention to the issue. Fortunately, President Biden's stimulus plan includes billions of dollars to help child care providers bounce back after the pandemic and provide child care assistance for families. It includes a one-time, expanded tax credit for each child that can be paid monthly. This will greatly aid low-income families and should be made permanent. To fill the gap in public support for caregiving before formal schooling begins, we also need universal pre-K starting at age three. President Biden's proposed American Families Plan endorses several of these policies and could be a giant leap forward.

7. FAMILY-FRIENDLY BENEFITS IN THE WORKPLACE

Starting from the day a child is born, the US fails to meet the paid parental leave policies of developed countries worldwide. The Family and Medical Leave Act, which provides caregivers unpaid time off to care for a family member, would be greatly expanded by the proposed American Families Plan and is long overdue.

Meanwhile, at least nine states have stepped up with help for working parents. Colorado voters passed an initiative with bipartisan support in 2020 that created at least twelve weeks of paid family and medical leave to bond with a new child, recover from illness, or care for a seriously ill loved one, and it includes extra protections for those in vulnerable low-wage jobs. Employers and employees pay a sliding fee to a statewide pool that funds the program, while self-employed workers can opt in to the program, and local governments and businesses with fewer than ten employees can opt out. Democratic State Senator Faith Winters of Colorado describes how the initiative won because supporters played the long game, spending over six years developing a broad coalition of low-wage workers, unions, people of color, faith leaders, and small-business owners: "We ran this for several years with a divided legislature, even though we knew the likelihood of passing it at the time was small—I always called it 'losing forward.' Each time we ran it, we got more coalitions to support it and we got better at messaging."

These first-out-of-the-box state models combined with guidance from A Better Balance, which provides support for activists looking to make these much-needed changes, can help you bring the idea to your state and build a groundswell for federal reform.

The private sector also needs to do its part. At a minimum, employers should provide such family-friendly benefits as paid sick time and flexible work schedules. While sick time is common in middle- and upper-income jobs and where there are union contracts, the majority of food service and personal care workers, who are disproportionately women of color, have no paid sick time or flexibility. As employers implement these policies, they must ensure that a wide range of families, not just married heterosexual couples, are able to take advantage of these benefits.

8. FAIRNESS FOR PREGNANT WORKERS

Let's be frank: most US employers regard a pregnant worker as a fly in their soup, and the law has done far too little to protect these workers from being tossed out. The Supreme Court in two of its most sexist decisions of the 1970s decided that discrimination on the basis of pregnancy did not constitute sex discrimination; rather, pregnant women just happened to experience a medical condition not applicable to (cisgender) men. Fortunately Congress came to the rescue, passing the Pregnancy Discrimination Act (PDA) in 1978 to prohibit employers from firing or refusing to hire pregnant workers, denying them benefits or promotions, or otherwise treating them differently.

Although the PDA went a long way toward preventing the most blatant discrimination, today some pregnant workers, especially those in low-wage and physically demanding jobs, continue to face discrimination. Employers frequently refuse to make reasonable workplace accommodations—denying pregnant employees the same right afforded to workers with other disabilities under federal law. Too often pregnant women are fired or demoted for requesting an additional bathroom break or a light duty assignment to avoid heavy lifting in order to maintain a healthy pregnancy.

A Better Balance and the National Women's Law Center are leading efforts to remedy this problem by supporting the Pregnant Workers Fairness Act, a proposed federal law that would require employers to make reasonable accommodations for a worker who has a medical need as a result of pregnancy or childbirth, ending the cruel dilemma of choosing between a paycheck or a healthy pregnancy. In 2020, the measure passed the House with bipartisan support, and it is expected to be considered in Congress again soon. Meanwhile, several states—both red and blue—already model strong laws to prevent pregnancy discrimination: Kentucky's law bans pregnancy discrimination in employment as sex discrimination, while New York requires even small businesses to provide reasonable accommodation and prohibits discrimination on the basis of pregnancy, childbirth, and breastfeeding. Activists can join those working at the state level to enact similar provisions where needed, inspiring crucial federal-level changes.

9. REDUCE SEXUAL ABUSE, VIOLENCE, AND HARASSMENT

Kitty started her first job out of law school at Community Legal Services just as Pennsylvania passed the first law in the nation that empowered women to seek a court order to evict a violent partner from their home. Kitty quickly learned that survivors of abuse come in all ages, genders, incomes, educational levels, races, ethnicities, and religious groups, and that only survivors can decide what is best for themselves. Judges, social workers, lawyers, doctors, and family members can give support and expert advice, but as with reproductive decision making, the final pathway to handle abuse and coercion is personal and must remain solely with the survivors.

Fortunately, the rate of reported sexual assault and rape has fallen in recent decades. Perpetrators are being held criminally liable more frequently. Workplaces are less tolerant of abuse than in decades past. Universities and other educational institutions increasingly are being held liable when they fail to take appropriate action. Yet sexual assault, coercion, and harassment still occur all too often: every seventy-three seconds in the United States, according to one study. Domestic or intimate partner violence remains an epidemic and frequently increases during pregnancy, which can be a flashpoint.

The #MeToo movement has significantly exposed a wide range of circumstances in which people feel pressured into sex without their consent and has launched an international movement calling for an end to sexual abuse and harassment. A combination of legal and cultural change; new views of gender roles, particularly eradicating the toxic masculinity that permeates our culture; criminal and civil justice reforms; safe spaces; and fair compensation for survivors are all key to reducing violence.

Progress is being made as a result of this activism. Some states have placed limits on nondisclosure agreements when perpetrators settle cases of abuse, sped up the testing of rape kits, and extended the statute of limitations for survivors who want to file civil lawsuits against their abusers or the institutions that shielded them. Hotel workers are getting panic buttons, and Hollywood sets now have intimacy directors. In 2019, Congress passed a five-year reauthorization of the federal Violence Against Women Act and the American Rescue Plan included millions for rape crisis programs and domestic violence shelters. Advocates for reproductive freedom are natural allies of those who oppose interpersonal violence or sexual assault, and vice versa, so building close alliances must be a priority.

10. JOIN THE GLOBAL WOMEN'S HUMAN RIGHTS COMMUNITY

It's time for the US to get with the program on women's human rights. Our country's failure to ratify the Convention on the Elimination of All Forms of Discrimination Against Women (CEDAW), the major global treaty protecting women's rights, is a big embarrassing zit on the face of our democracy. President Jimmy Carter signed CEDAW long ago, but the Senate has refused to ratify it—putting us in the company of a tiny handful of anti-ratification, anti-feminist governments: Sudan, South Sudan, Somalia, Iran, and two small Pacific Island nations, Palau and Tonga.

First adopted in 1979 by the UN General Assembly, the treaty is often described as an international bill of rights for women. In a preamble and thirty articles, it defines discrimination against women and elaborately describes ways to end discrimination in all aspects of society. Signatories agree to respect, protect, promote, and fulfill the human rights of women. To do so, many countries have included language in their domestic laws and constitutions that embodies the principle of gender equality. Every four years, each signatory must report what actions they are taking to prevent and eradicate discrimination against women in their country. These reports and the self-examination they require, followed by a review conducted by a CEDAW committee of independent experts, are critical for ensuring nations live up to their duties under the Convention. The CEDAW reporting process helped Julie convince the National Women's Council of Ireland to join the Irish Family Planning Association in raising the issue of abortion as a human right well before abortion was legalized in Ireland. It has enabled nongovernmental organizations to spur investigations of missing and murdered Indigenous women in Canada and to question restrictions on contraception in the Philippines.

As part of an organized Cities for CEDAW initiative, cities nationwide have adopted sample resolutions, ordinances, and executive directives that implement or model the treaty in their local area. In Los Angeles, Mayor Eric Garcetti required city departments to collect, analyze, and make public data on sex and gender in recruitment, employment, contracting, and city services as a key step for implementing the city's sustainable development goals. Join or start a campaign for ratification in your city, or urge your senator to support the long-overdue ratification of CEDAW.

While CEDAW is not a substitute for the direct enforcement mechanism a US constitutional amendment or statute could provide, ratification would bring the US into the world community and allow it to participate in or even help lead efforts to guarantee women's human rights around the world. It is the wave of the future.

THIS BOOK PROMISED to tell you what we must do *now* to save reproductive freedom. While our list is extensive, it just touches the surface of the work that needs to be done. We cannot tell you what to do—that would be arrogant and moreover might not fit your community's needs or priorities. But we can tell you how important it is to do something now. Pick one of the options and strategies laid out here, or pick many. And don't go it alone—consult with groups already doing the work, grab a friend or make a new friend, and hit the streets with us. There's plenty of work to be done and lots of progress to be made.

CHAPTER 14

FUELING AN AUDACIOUS AND INCLUSIVE MOVEMENT
REPRODUCTIVE FREEDOM IN THE TWENTY-FIRST CENTURY

Every moment is an organizing opportunity, every person a potential activist, every minute a chance to change the world.

DOLORES HUERTA,
LABOR AND FEMINIST ORGANIZER,
COFOUNDER, UNITED FARM WORKERS

WE STARTED THIS book standing in protest in front of the Supreme Court. It was one of the many, many marches and actions in favor of abortion rights that we have participated in over the years. Neither of us is very good at chanting or making signs, and we both feel more comfortable in a courtroom than in a street dance. While we always enjoy being with friends, kids, and colleagues for a good cause on a sunny day, that's not the reason we show up.

Every lawyer fighting for social change knows that progress does not happen without popular support, direct action, and outrage in the streets. History has taught us, both in the US and across the globe, that activists loudly calling for social change is a movement's lifeblood. It can provide a much-needed boost to a stagnant cause or blocked initiative, or birth an entirely new vision of change. A bold, loud, strategically targeted movement creates a sense of urgency, gains broader allies, and propels progress.

Our post-*Roe* world will demand that many people engage in activism in many different forms. The best way is the one that works for you, something that is sustainable and hopefully fun too. In college Julie used to hide behind the lens of the camera at protests and then publish the photos in the campus newspaper. Kitty and Joann owned a microphone and portable sound system that they loaned out to activists who literally wanted to amplify their voices.

More than ever, women seeking abortions need direct help to obtain them. In many states, abortion is already too far out of reach for too many, restrictions are unduly burdensome, and providers scarce. And when the Supreme Court further undermines or outright overrules *Roe* and *Casey*, things will be even worse.

In the days before *Roe*, women with means were able to travel to New York, London, or Japan for legal abortion or to Puerto Rico or Mexico, where abortion was more accessible or affordable, even if not entirely legal. Unfortunately, those left behind—low-income women, teens, those in violent relationships—turned to back-alley providers or were forced to carry their pregnancies to term. In a post-*Roe* world, such a discriminatory and inequitable system should not stand.

Some activists can help women obtain abortion services, much like Rosa Hartford, who took a teenager facing an unintended pregnancy to a clinic in a nearby state. With all the restrictions on teens' access to reproductive health care, particularly waiting periods and parental involvement laws, many teens are in need of a trusted adult to support them, help them navigate the system, and connect with professional counselors and providers. Providing teens with information, transportation, or funding is crucial to their ability to obtain reproductive health care and services. We must set up networks of supporters who will assist teens in making their decision whether to abort or not and help them to implement that decision whether by obtaining an abortion or by finding the resources they will need to succeed as a teen parent.

Teens are not the only ones who need help now and who will require assistance in the future. Low-income and undocumented women, who are disproportionately women of color, as well as survivors of domestic violence or women with disabilities, have an increased need for access to resources and counseling in order to find services, including funds and support to travel to a nearby state if necessary. In a post-*Roe* era, that need will skyrocket. Travel across state lines, overnight stays, additional child care, and other expenses create further strain and needs. In the days before *Roe*, the Clergy Consultation Service on Abortion, founded by a group of Protestant ministers and Jewish rabbis in New York, counseled women and made referrals for safe abortions. The Service grew to include some three thousand clergy in thirty-eight states, who referred at least four hundred fifty thousand people for safe abortions. When abortion was illegal in Ireland, the Abortion Support Network based in London would provide women in Ireland with funds and information about clinics abroad, help schedule appointments, arrange travel, and connect them with volunteers who could offer a place to stay. In the US, the National Network of Abortion Funds works to remove financial and logistical barriers to abortion access through a network of funds that help abortion patients in almost every state.

As the availability of abortion decreases, there will be a growing urgency for volunteers to help provide vital services like driving abortion patients to clinics, offering housing, food, or child care, and working with local abortion funds and clinics to raise money. In the process activists can meet other activists, further building and expanding our movement together.

Remember all the women seeking abortions who have filled the pages of this book? Sherry from Illinois, who survived rape only to be harassed and harmed by an illegal abortion provider in the days before *Roe*. Rosie Jimenez from Texas, who died because she could not afford a safe abortion. Vicki Wilson and Tammy Watts, who needed late abortions that would have been outlawed by the federal ban on partial birth abortions. Michelle Lee, whose own cardiac doctors refused to provide a lifesaving abortion because she had a less than 50 percent chance of dying without one. Julie's New York City hospital client, who fell into a coma and went untreated not because she was seeking an abortion but because her doctors were afraid to act. With limited access to abortion in so many communities, if we step up to keep abortion legal and available, and to aid women when it's not, we can stop such tragic results.

Time and time again, in country after country, research has shown that as abortion gets harder to obtain, it does not go away—it goes underground. The good news is that with self-managed medication abortion now an option, women need not return to the pre-*Roe* days when back-alley abortions were performed by scary practitioners in unsanitary and unsafe conditions. As state restrictions, provider shortages, and outright bans put abortion further out of reach, more and more women are likely to use medication abortion on their own to terminate an unintended pregnancy.

Increasingly, women will obtain medication abortion pills online from foreign countries or through underground networks that buy the medication in states where prescriptions are legally available and bring it elsewhere. While medication abortion has been proven to be a safe and effective way to terminate an early pregnancy, women who do this on their own will need appropriate information, counseling, and medical backup.

Activists are already developing ways to help women who choose to self-manage or self-induce their abortions. Plan C provides information about the online availability of medication abortion from reliable sources. If/When/How: Lawyering for Reproductive Justice provides free legal assistance for women seeking to self-manage their care. In the same way as the Jane Collective found ways to make illegal abortion safe, today's activists are creating support networks to help women find accurate information about medication abortion and how to obtain the pills. With help providing services, funds, backup, and legal support, a large percentage of the women seeking early medication abortion outside medical settings will be able to do so safely and without shame.

Over the last several decades, activists have spent considerable time providing clinic defense—surrounding patients and escorting them into clinics to avoid the hateful, angry confrontations by abortion opponents. A report from the National Abortion Federation notes that incidents of anti-abortion picketing at clinics grew from just over six thousand in 2010 to more than a hundred twenty-three thousand in

2019. Trespassing at clinics also increased significantly over the course of a decade. Clinic defense in cities across the country has enabled activists to connect and mobilize. Now as the Supreme Court sanctions abortion restrictions and even fewer clinics provide abortion, we need more clinic defenders.

ON A SUNNY Saturday in November just after Election Day 2020, there was dancing in the streets of Brooklyn, Philadelphia, and worldwide. Four tense days of ballot counting had passed before the election was called for President Biden and Vice President Harris. Four long years had passed under President Trump's corrosive leadership, including eight months of a worsening pandemic. The January 6 Capitol attack and insurrection was followed by an Inauguration Day that brought to those same steep steps a ceremony founded on relief and hope, music and poetry.

The political activism and effective organizing of Black women in key battleground states, particularly Georgia, and support from suburban women voters helped catapult President Biden to victory. Without a doubt he is indebted to women, particularly Black women, and that gives leverage but no guarantee that gender equity and reproductive freedom will be at the top of the administration's agenda. The Biden administration will be focused on the pandemic, stabilizing the economy, restoring relationships with global allies, curbing police and gun violence, facing climate change, and reversing many of the most appalling Trump transgressions around immigration. If we don't make some noise, reproductive freedom could get lost in the crowd.

At the same time that Biden won the presidency, Republicans maintained state strongholds and made House gains. The Senate remains closely divided on partisan lines and not united on anything. As we've said throughout, convincing Republicans to support abortion rights is a horse that fled the stable long ago.

However, as the old political adage goes, if you can't change their minds, change their faces. There are over five hundred thousand elected offices across the United States for the taking, any of which could use the energy and enthusiasm of reproductive rights activists. We need to bring in those politicians who will be stalwarts, not softies, when it comes to advancing reproductive freedom.

Explore running for office yourself, and seek training and backing from organizations that recruit progressive candidates, like Vote Run Lead, Higher Heights, and Vote Mama. If running for office isn't your thing, there are plenty of other ways to become involved. Stacey Abrams's successful Fair Fight, LaTosha Brown's Black Voters Matter, and other activist organizations made it strikingly clear how important it can be to register new voters and turn out the vote. Their work was crucial in Georgia and caused national ripple effects. We can all learn from their success. Consider managing or volunteering for a local campaign for a candidate who inspires you. Most campaign work is neither difficult nor complicated and can be quite energizing. Knocking on doors, writing postcards, joining phonebanks, and raising money are things we both have done for a whole range of local, statewide, and federal elections each year, not just in presidential election years.

Don't forget to support reforms that will open the voting systems to more people, such as automatic or same-day voter registration, mail-in ballot programs, and ranked-choice voting. As we've seen with Colorado and Oregon's mail-in ballot systems and Maine's ranked-choice voting, such mechanisms increase the likelihood of more women and Democrats winning office. These wins also can counteract the voter suppression and gerrymandering that Republicans have used so heavily to their advantage. Winning political power is the first step to getting reproductive freedom to the starting line.

Whether you are the majority in power or a vocal minority, you also can use your political capital to push for proactive policies. Organize lobby days or protests in your state capital when reproductive justice legislation is pending or to highlight the need for any of the legislation you've read about here. Small photogenic groups of activists can be highly effective. Picture the women dressed as Handmaids or the ten thousand pro-choice potatoes on the Idaho capitol steps. In our digital age, photos and videos are a significant way to spread your message and gain a national or international audience. Creatively spotlighting the need for reproductive freedom gives power to our demands, emboldens our allied politicians, and keeps the pressure on those who can take action to advance reproductive freedom.

You can also take your activism online. Ultraviolet, a national advocacy organization that drives political change in the virtual space, has exposed companies who support anti-abortion candidates and demanded that Facebook stop spreading anti-abortion groups' misinformation about reproductive medicine. MomsRising, a massive grassroots effort with over a million members is organizing online to hold politicians and corporations accountable for fair treatment of women and mothers. Be clever, be creative, and be heard.

It's time to turn up the volume. Many of the successful campaigns for women's rights and reproductive freedom in recent decades in the US and across the globe have included vocal, outraged, and sometimes even outrageous activists who have successfully brought attention to the cause. Think of the galvanized women who protested during Brett Kavanaugh's Supreme Court confirmation hearings, the throngs of survivors posting their stories of degradation and abuse at #MeToo, and the 2017 Women's March, where millions joined together across generations and around the globe to highlight the misogyny and racism of newly elected President Trump.

Although some posit that vocal and angry activists undermine the reasonable politicians who need to make deals to win necessary policy reforms, we believe that both are necessary. A stronger, more insistent left flank that invokes the power of rage and outrage, employing popular culture and humor for more forceful, edgy messaging, can gain media attention and build both awareness and support. A more inclusive, more audacious movement, led by a new generation of leaders, can not only push for policy reform but amass the political power to demand the change we seek.

The Black Lives Matter movement demonstrates how activists can leverage power in the streets for cultural change and legal and policy reforms. In addition to significantly raising awareness of and commitment to racial equity, the protests have brought forth reforms that include an increase in the use of body cameras (once considered unthinkable), the disclosure of police misconduct records, and budget reallocations that prioritize the hiring of mental health workers or de-escalation training, with more to come. The Black Lives Matter protests turbocharged adoption of reforms that activists had been working on for years.

Similarly, #MeToo was revolutionary in providing a space for women to speak up about their experiences with sexual harassment, abuse, and assault. The movement has halted such serial perpetrators as movie mogul Harvey Weinstein, Fox's Bill O'Reilly, NBC's Matt Lauer, and almost two hundred others who leveraged their positions of power to sexually harass, abuse, or assault others. #MeToo also ushered in new workplace procedures to address allegations of abuse. Seeded by large donations from women in Hollywood's entertainment industry, the TIME'S UP Legal Defense Fund partners with the National Women's Law Center to pursue lawsuits and campaigns to free employees from workplace harassment everywhere "from farm fields to the C-suite," building on decades of activism.

The Women's March of 2017 undoubtedly sent a very powerful message the day after President Trump's inauguration. It brought millions to the streets with bright hats and a show of strength. The movement's leadership deliberately included women of color and transgender and non-binary people in key organizing positions after it had initially failed to do so. We'd love to see this become an annual outpouring each year as in other countries, where it fires up activists on International Women's Day, March 8. Kitty's son, Sam, has made International Women's Day a paid holiday at the Portland-based video events company he runs, so employees may celebrate or protest.

Internationally, we have witnessed how the fight for reproductive freedom has galvanized broader movements for women's rights and large-scale political change. In Ireland, decades of activism in the courts and legislative and human rights arenas built a pyre that was ignited by protests in response to the tragic death of Savita Halappanavar. News of her death highlighted that the Irish government had utterly failed to make lifesaving abortion available as the European Court of Human Rights had ordered in Julie's case almost two years earlier.

The outrage over Halappanavar's death gave momentum to the call for legalizing abortion—marches were emboldened and brash, demanding no less than the human right to abortion. The abortion campaign and successful referendum vote were fueled by protests in the streets and vocal activism by women across the nation. The Irish legalization efforts aligned with and inspired movement demands for legalization of abortion worldwide, most recently in Poland and Argentina.

We have marched to support a wide range of issues over the years, yet watching the abortion rights protests in Poland in the fall of 2020 was unlike anything we've ever seen. The protests were an immediate reaction to a decision by the Polish Constitutional Court striking fetal anomaly as a permissible reason for abortion, thereby making legal abortion available only in cases of rape or incest or when a woman's life is at risk. As women poured into the streets, the government delayed implementing the Court's anti-abortion decision. Yet the marches and civil disobedience continued, drawing large and diverse crowds with creative, attention-grabbing tactics that included blasting Darth Vader's theme music and setting off red flares. Protesters decorated themselves with bright red lightning bolt symbols of the movement and staged sit-ins at Catholic churches, interrupting Sunday Mass dressed in red Handmaid robes to protest the Roman Catholic Church's enormous influence in Poland.

In response, the Justice Ministry ordered prosecutors nationwide to target the organizers with gathering illegally and endangering public health during the pandemic. Right-wing nationalist opponents threatened them with violence, and the police forcefully used pepper spray against them. In the parlance of US feminists, "nevertheless, they persisted," and the marches continued and spread. In January 2021 the government implemented the fetal anomaly ban, and activists across the country again took to the streets.

Although Ireland's and Poland's social movements were narrowly focused on abortion rights, Argentina's women's rights movement started as a call to end violence against women. The first Argentinian women's march in 2015 was organized by a group of female journalists and activists who met each other through Twitter. They were determined to burst through the digital wall to make their presence felt in the streets. Their hashtag Ni Una Menos—as in, "not one more" can be lost to violence—quickly grew. A year later it was a mass movement with multinational engagement for advancing women's rights and demand-ing steps to curb gender-based violence. Marches took place in every major city in Argentina and quickly inspired demonstrations in Bolivia, Chile, El Salvador, Mexico, Paraguay, and Uruguay.

The marches drew attention to the violent murders of two young women, fourteen-year-old Chiara Páez in 2015 and sixteen-year-old Lucía Pérez in 2016, and developed into a wide cry for an end to femicide—a concept defined in law four years earlier to encompass cases of domestic violence, so-called honor killings, and other categories of hate crimes against women that were widespread across the country. Argentina already had laws criminalizing gender-based violence on its books, but they had not been adequately enforced, funded, or imple-mented. As a result of the marches, the courts established a registry of femicides, and the government's Human Rights Secretariat began to compile statistics.

The women marching in Argentina also recognized that abortion rights were at the core of gender equality. As public attention focused on reports of deaths and hospitalization resulting from unsafe abortion, and data that girls as young as ten years old were giving birth, calls for legalized abortion grew despite opposition from the politically powerful Catholic Church. The movement pushed abortion rights to the top of the national agenda and swiftly moved to implement much-needed le-gal reform. Waving green bandanas in the tradition of the Argentinian Mothers and Grandmothers of the Plaza de Mayo, who had demanded justice for children and grandchildren who were disappeared during the country's earlier dictatorship, they pushed for a legislative solution. They rejected the referendum approach used in Ireland because their law already allowed for some limited abortions and also because they feared the voters might not support a change.

In December 2020, the Argentine senate, in a landmark vote, made Argentina the largest nation in Latin America to legalize abortion. Tens of thousands of supporters demonstrating outside the capitol erupted in elation as a grassroots movement leveraged rallies into political change. In an emotional speech after the vote, Senator Silvia Sapag recounted,

When I was born, women did not vote, we did not inherit, we could not manage our assets, we could not have bank accounts, we didn't have credit cards, we couldn't go to university. When I was born, women were nobody. Now, for all the women who fought for those legal rights and more, "Let it be law."

Argentina's women's rights movement is an example of successfully uniting a diverse group of activists and supporters with focused demands. Rather than relying on a top-down strategy, the movement engaged thousands of feminist collectives nationwide, which took up local grass-roots organizing, coming together for powerful mass demonstrations.

Mass movements often start with a singular individual protest that captures attention and motivates others to join. Every US student learns how Rosa Parks's arrest for her refusal to give up her seat to a white man was instrumental in launching the Montgomery Bus Boycott. More recently, high school senior Emma González's passionate speech at a gun control rally three days after the mass shooting at Marjory Stoneman Douglas High School in Parkland, Florida, lit a movement. Emanating fury and sorrow in a speech that went viral, González decried the "thoughts and prayers" expressed by politicians who support gun access and shouted for students to "call B.S." The student activists, working closely with existing gun control organizations, went on to organize the massive DC March for Our Lives, where over a million protestors demanded commonsense gun control measures that led to passage of laws in several states.

A tragic or unjust event—the killing of George Floyd, the death of Savita Halappanavar, or a judicial ruling that smacks of injustice—can be a spark that generates widespread outrage, quickly bringing attention to issues that advocates may have been quietly and daily working on for years. When these two forces come together to spread the message, and a broad coalition makes tangible demands of policy makers, change can appear to be swift—and magical.

In the next few years, the Supreme Court will likely provide that spark by overruling *Roe*. As individual states then move to ban nearly all abortions, there will be additional opportunities to drive more outrage and build momentum for change. Many states have already spurred anger by passing extreme bills that ban abortion early in pregnancy, allow men to sue to stop their wives or partners from having an abortion, or appoint lawyers to represent fetuses when teens seek court permission for an abortion—all in direct contradiction of *Roe*. Let's capitalize on our anger and outrage with additional protests and concrete demands.

In addition to small actions and mass protests against government policies, activists can put pressure on hospitals, pharmacies, insurers, or other corporations, where a change of policy could go far to advance reproductive health. Let's see what happens if activists expose Fortune 500 companies that refuse to provide family-friendly benefits to their employees. How about a holiday-themed protest at one of the over nine hundred Hobby Lobby craft stores that deny contraceptive and abortion coverage in their employees' health insurance? Could activists find ways to pressure urgent care clinics to provide medication abortion as a standard part of care? What if there were demonstrations at colleges and universities calling for wider availability of medication abortion at student health clinics, and the training of medical students on how to perform abortion?

The possibilities are endless. Pick your issue, brainstorm with your creative allies, expand your coalition, and join the movement.

It's time *now*.

ACKNOWLEDGMENTS

OVER THE YEARS we have had the privilege and pleasure of representing courageous women, medical providers, clinics, and organizations—too numerous to list here—that have agreed to be a public voice for reproductive freedom. We are in awe of the righteous indignation they demonstrated when their rights were trampled and by their bravery in the face of personal risk. We hope that this book reflects our deep respect for them and our gratitude for their commitment to making health care and freedoms more available to others.

Our colleagues and cocounsel with whom we have collaborated over decades of this work, especially the attorneys and staff of the Center for Reproductive Rights, ACLU, Guttmacher Institute, Irish Family Planning Association, Legal Momentum, Ms. Foundation, National Abortion Federation, National Institute for Reproductive Health, Planned Parenthood Federation of America and its affiliates, Women's Law Project, Women's Link Worldwide, Women on Waves, and so many more, have informed our thinking, brightened our days, and earned our admiration for their work in the trenches that came before us and continues well after us.

Many thanks to all those at Hachette Books who made these pages possible and lively even while working on an expedited "crash" schedule during the stress of a global pandemic. Our marvelous editor Mollie Weisenfeld brought her infectious enthusiasm, expert editing eye dedicated to "advancing the narrative" and avoiding rabbit warrens of legalese, and passion for the rights at the heart of this book's mission—all invaluable and always swaddled in kindness. We were delighted with the extensive toiling on our behalf by the skilled team at Hachette, including publisher Mary Ann Naples, associate publisher Michelle Aielli, marketing director Michael Barrs, publicist Lauren Rosenthal, marketing manager Julianne Lewes, managing editor Monica Oluwek, senior production editor Cisca Schreefel, copyeditor Beth Wright, attorney Elisa Rivlin, creative director Amanda Kain, and designer Trish Wilkinson. We hope we do you right by this book.

We are thankful to our wonderful agent, Joy Tutela at the David Black Literary Agency, for believing in the need for a book of this kind *now*, pushing us full speed ahead, always being supportive (or blunt as needed), and ensuring that the book found the right home. We are also grateful for the tireless work of Megan Noes at the David Black Literary Agency for helping us to find and secure permissions for the book's photographs that bring our stories to life.

Many of our friends and colleagues read portions of this book at a rapid pace and gave us invaluable insight and advice, as well as much-needed support. They include Elana Sigall and Kim Chirls, who diligently read multiple drafts, as well as Bette Begleiter, Susan Bolotin, Janet Crepps, Catherine Heaney, Andrea Miller, Michelle Exline Minovi, Nathalie Molina Niño, Melissa Silverstein, Phoebe Taubman, Gillian Thomas, and Linda Wharton. Our mistakes are our own, but there are far fewer because of their generous input.

I, Kitty, am particularly thankful for the love and support of my wife, Joann, who has been by my side for over forty years. Her willingness to do more than her share on the home front has made it possible for me to have an extraordinary career. Her insight and sense of humor have made our life together a joy. Our immediate family—Sam, Sarah, Ari, and Sylvia; Kate, Chris, and Zoe—make me happy every day and give me confidence that the world (and our freedoms) are in good hands.

I, Julie, feel lucky to have a community of friends and family near and far who encouraged me in writing this book as they have throughout life, especially Jacqueline Cessou, Adam Weinstein, Lisa Cohen, Stephen Kay, and Lis Tarlow, and my mother, who would have loved to have lived to edit this book. So many others are not named here but much depended on for coffees and walks together that give meaning to my life. My two fabulous daughters mock me when I tell them how much I love them but must know how much joy and pride they each bring me. Tom and I have journeyed through life together since law school, and I would not be where I am today without his love, reassurance, and humor, nor would it have been nearly as much fun.

AUTHORS' NOTE

WE ARE HOPEFUL that this book inspires you to take action to preserve reproductive freedom. If you have interest in working with, volunteering, or supporting existing efforts to preserve reproductive freedom, local organizations in your area provide a great starting point. You can find additional information about organizations working for reproductive freedom at controllingwomenthebook.com, or email us at controllingwomen@gmail.com.

NOTES

A NOTE ON SOURCES

This book is based on our own professional experience and analyses, colored by our personal opinions, and influenced by the insights and experiences our colleagues have generously shared over the years and in the writing of this book. Throughout this book we rely on a range of sources, including our own recollections and contemporaneous accounts and analysis by others. We have referenced additional sources where more information may be of interest to the reader.

INTRODUCTION

1   *June Medical Services v. Russo*: 591 U.S. __ (2020).
2   *Roe v. Wade*: 410 U.S. 113 (1973).
2   *Thornburgh v. American College of Obstetrics and Gynecologists*: 476 U.S. 747 (1986).
2   *Planned Parenthood v. Casey*: 505 U.S. 833 (1992).
4   **are the foundation of anti-abortion sentiment:** The Guttmacher Institute's estimate that between 462 and 530 transgender and non-binary individuals had abortions in 2017 supports the need to implement and expand gender-inclusive and gender-affirming care at abortion facilities nationwide. Rachel K. Jones, Elizabeth Witwer, and Jenna Jerman, "Transgender Abortion Patients and the Provision of Transgender-Specific Care at Non-Hospital Facilities That Provide Abortions," *Contraception: X* 2 (2020): 100019. See also Options for Sexual Health, "Trans-Inclusive Abortion Services: A Manual for Providers on Operationalizing Trans-Inclusive Policies

and Practices in an Abortion Setting," July 2019, www.optionsfor
sexualhealth.org/wp-content/uploads/2019/07/FQPN18-Manual
-EN-BC-web.pdf.

CHAPTER 1

7 **such as colonoscopies and dental surgery:** Ushma D. Upadhyay
et al., "Incidence of Emergency Department Visits and Complications After Abortion," *Obstetrics & Gynecology* 125, no. 1 (2015):
175–183; E. G. Raymond and D. A. Grimes, "The Comparative
Safety of Legal Induced Abortion and Childbirth in the United
States," *Obstetrics & Gynecology* 119, no. 2 pt. 1 (2012): 215–219;
Mandy Oaklander, "Abortion Complication Rates Are 'Lower Than
That for Wisdom Tooth Extraction,' Study Says," *Time*, Dec. 9,
2014.

8 **and define yourself as pro-life.":** Nicholas Kristof, "She's Evangelical, 'Pro-Life' and Voting for Biden," *New York Times*, Oct. 21,
2020.

8 **should be legal in all or most cases:** Jesse Bering, "God's Little
Rabbits: Religious People Out-Reproduce Secular Ones by a Landslide," *Bering in Mind* (blog), *Scientific American*, Dec. 22, 2010,
blogs.scientificamerican.com/bering-in-mind/gods-little
-rabbits-religious-people-out-reproduce-secular-ones-by-a-land
slide.

8 **with those of their religious hierarchies:** Dalia Fahmy, *8 Key
Findings About Catholics and Abortion*, Pew Research Center,
Oct. 20, 2020, www.pewresearch.org/fact-tank/2020/10/20/8-key
-findings-about-catholics-and-abortion.

9 *Frontiero v. Richardson:* 411 U.S. 677 (1973).

10 **that perpetuate traditional gender roles:** Kristin Luker, *Abortion
and the Politics of Motherhood* (Berkeley: University of California
Press, 1985); "'Pro-Choice' or 'Pro-Life,' 2018–2020 Demographic
Tables," Gallup, news.gallup.com/poll/244709/pro-choice-pro-life
-2018-demographic-tables.aspx.

10 **abortion as an important part of those values:** Ruth Graham and
Sharon LaFraniere, "Inside the People of Praise, the Tight-Knit
Faith Community of Amy Coney Barrett," *New York Times*, Oct. 8,
2020.

10 **should she stray from the proper path.":** Emma Brown, Jon
Swaine, and Michelle Boorstein, "Amy Coney Barrett Served as a

'Handmaid' in Christian Group People of Praise," *Washington Post*, Oct. 6, 2020.

11   **drug use and other behaviors during pregnancy:** Dorothy E. Roberts, "Punishing Drug Addicts Who Have Babies: Women of Color, Equality, and the Right of Privacy," *Harvard Law Review* 104, no. 1419 (1991); Lynn M. Paltrow, *Criminal Prosecutions Against Pregnant Women: National Update and Overview*, National Advocates for Pregnant Women, Jan. 31, 1992, www.national advocatesforpregnantwomen.org/criminal_prosecutions_against _pregnant_women.

11   **include broader social justice concerns.":** Dorothy E. Roberts, "Representing Race, Unshackling Black Motherhood," in *Feminist Legal Theory: An Anti-Essentialist Reader*, 2nd ed., Nancy Levit and Robert R. M. Verchick (New York: New York University Press, 2016).

12   **as an independent, self-sustaining, equal citizen:** Ruth Bader Ginsburg, "Some Thoughts on Autonomy and Equality in Relation to *Roe v. Wade*," *North Carolina Law Review* 63, no. 2 (Jan. 1, 1985): 375.

13   **whether or not they have another child:** Jenna Jerman, Rachel K. Jones, and Tsuyoshi Onda, *Characteristics of U.S. Abortion Patients in 2014 and Changes Since 2008*, Guttmacher Institute, May 2016, www.guttmacher.org/report/characteristics-us-abortion-patients -2014.

13   **can also affect their choice:** Lawrence B. Finer et al., "Reasons U.S. Women Have Abortions: Quantitative and Qualitative Perspectives," *Perspectives on Sexual and Reproductive Health* 37, no. 3 (2005): 110–118.

14   **define homosexuality as "unnatural.":** "Who We Are," Concerned Women for America, concernedwomen.org/about/who-we-are, accessed Jan. 21, 2021.

15   **whether bodily or mental and spiritual.":** John Stuart Mill, *On Liberty* (London: John W. Parker and Son, 1859), 6, 8.

15   **for childbirth exceed that for abortion:** Raymond and Grimes, "The Comparative Safety of Legal Induced Abortion."

16   **the health of the patient and the welfare of society.":** Buck v. Bell, 274 U.S. 200 (1927).

16   **Detention Center in Georgia in 2020:** Caitlin Dickerson, Seth Freed Wessler, and Miriam Jordan, "Immigrants Say They Were Pressured into Unneeded Surgeries," *New York Times*, Sept. 29, 2020.

16   **to carry a pregnancy to term:** Marin Roger Scordato, "Under-
      standing the Absence of a Duty to Reasonably Rescue in American
      Tort Law," *Tulane Law Review* 82 (2008): 1447.

18   **who has children with whom, and how many:** Emma Brockes,
      "Gloria Steinem: 'If Men Could Get Pregnant, Abortion Would Be
      a Sacrament,'" *Guardian*, Oct. 17, 2015.

19   **leaves true equality off the table:** A term coined by law professor
      Kimberlé Crenshaw, intersectionality takes into account the pres-
      sures and structural inequities an individual faces as a result of the
      cumulative effect of race, gender, religion, sexual orientation, nation-
      ality, and other biases. Kimberlé Crenshaw, "Mapping the Margins:
      Intersectionality, Identity Politics, and Violence Against Women of
      Color," *Stanford Law Review* 43, no. 6 (1991): 1241–1299.

CHAPTER 2

21   **in the lawsuit that legalized abortion:** Louis DeLuca, "Career in a
      Year Photos 1995: Jane Roe (Roe v. Wade) Baptized by Former
      Adversary," *Dallas Morning News*, Aug. 9, 2015.

21   **now a common practice:** A companion case to *Roe* was filed on
      behalf of John and Mary Doe, pseudonyms for a childless woman
      and her husband who sought access to abortion in the event Mary
      became pregnant. She suffered from a "neural-chemical" disorder
      for which her doctor advised her to stop using birth control but also
      to avoid becoming pregnant. Their case was later dismissed for lack
      of standing. *Roe v. Wade*, 410 U.S. at 127–129 (1973).

21   **a letter from Sherry:** *The Voices of Women: Abortion in Their Own
      Words* (National Abortion Rights Action League, undated), 5.

22   **1.2 million women sought back-alley procedures:** Rachel Benson
      Gold, "Lessons from Before Roe: Will Past Be Prologue?," *Gutt-
      macher Policy Review* 6, no. 1 (March 2003): 8–11.

23   **attributed to pregnancy and childbirth that year.":** Ibid.

23   **deaths among nonwhite and Puerto Rican women.":** Ibid.

24   **abortion providers who worked with them:** Clyde Haberman,
      "Code Name Jane: The Women Behind a Covert Abortion Net-
      work," *New York Times*, Oct. 14, 2018.

24   **helped women locate safe abortion services:** "History," Religious
      Coalition for Reproductive Choice, rcrc.org/history, accessed
      Jan. 21, 2021.

24   **when the fetus had a severe anomaly:** Gold, "Lessons from Before
      Roe."

24   **effects of illegal abortion while living in Peru:** Erica Meltzer, "50 Years Ago, Colorado Became the First State to Liberalize Its Abortion Laws," *Denverite*, Feb. 10, 2017.

25   **of efficiency with incompetence, of humanity with cruelty":** Susan Edmiston, "A Report on the Abortion Capital of the Country," *New York Times*, April 11, 1971.

25   **from the airport, lodging, and meals:** Gold, "Lessons from Before Roe."

25   *United States v. Vuitch:* 402 U.S. 62 (1971).

26   **would protect a woman's health and well-being:** People v. Belous, 71 Cal. 2d 954 (California Sup. Ct.) (1969); Doe v. Scott, 321 F. Supp. 1385 (N. D. Ill. 1971); Babbitz v. McCann, 310 F. Supp. 293 (E.D. Wis. 1970); State v. Munson (South Dak. Circuit Court, Pennington Cty, April 6, 1970).

26   *Griswold v. Connecticut:* 381 U.S. 479 (1965).

26   *Eisenstadt v. Baird:* 405 U.S. 438 (1972).

26   *Doe v. Bolton:* 410 U.S. 179 (1973).

27   **failed to obtain confirmation of two previous picks:** Judges Clement F. Haynsworth Jr. and G. Harrold Carswell.

27   **500,000 deaths in the past year.":** Tinsley Yarborough, *Harry A. Blackmun: The Outsider Justice* (New York: Oxford University Press, 2008).

27   **he deserves to go to hell.'":** Michael Specter, "Shot Fired Through Blackmun's Window," *Washington Post*, March 5, 1985; Wanda Martinson to Robert Borruso, March 5, 1985, Blackmun Archives, Box 1455, Library of Congress.

31   **moved further back toward conception:** Akron v. Akron Center for Reproductive Health, 462 U.S. 416 (1983).

32   **just like Norma McCorvey:** David Treadwell, "Abortion Plaintiffs Now on Opposite Sides: Similar Pasts, Different Viewpoints for Roe, Doe." *Los Angeles Times*, June 25, 1989.

32   **the pregnancy resulted from rape.":** O.C.G.A. § 26–1202(a) (1968).

32   **beliefs she had been taught as a child:** "Margie Pitts Hames and the Other Landmark Abortion Rights Case: Recalling a 'Swashbuckling' Woman Lawyer," *Legal History Blog*, Feb. 27, 2011, legalhistoryblog.blogspot.com/2011/02/margie-pitts-hames-and-other-landmark.html.

33   **pregnancy for almost any reason":** "What Did Doe v. Bolton Decide?," Pro-Life Action, prolifeaction.org/fact/boltondecide, accessed Jan. 21, 2021.

34 **Justice William Rehnquist:** Justice Rehnquist was elevated to Chief Justice in 1986 by President Reagan, upon the retirement of Chief Justice Burger.

35 **example in recent decades is *Roe v. Wade*.":** Ruth Bader Ginsburg, "Speaking in a Judicial Voice," *New York University Law Review* 67 (Dec. 1992): 1186.

35 **lower the temperature of the abortion debate.":** Linda Greenhouse and Reva B. Siegel, "Before (and After) *Roe v. Wade*: New Questions About Backlash," *Yale Law Journal* 120 (2011). Kali Borkoski, "Ask the Author: Linda Greenhouse on 'Before (and After) *Roe v. Wade*: New Questions About Backlash,' " *SCOTUSblog*, March 6, 2013, www.scotusblog.com/2013/03/ask-the-author -linda-greenhouse-on-before-and-after-roe-v-wade-new-questions -about-backlash.

37 ***Webster v. Reproductive Health Services*:** 492 U.S. 490 (1989).

CHAPTER 3

38 **posed a real threat to these freedoms:** We rely on our own recollections and contemporaneous accounts by others for the discussion of Justice Thomas's confirmation hearings. For an in-depth analysis, see Jane Mayer and Jill Abramson, *Strange Justice: The Selling of Clarence Thomas* (Menlo Park, CA: Graymalkin Media, 1994).

40 **offered Hill only a tepid apology:** Sheryl Gay Stolberg and Carl Hulse, "Joe Biden Expresses Regret to Anita Hill, but She Says 'I'm Sorry' Is Not Enough," *New York Times*, April 25, 2019.

40 **shed light on his position on abortion:** Neil A. Lewis, "The Thomas Hearings; Thomas Declines Requests by Panel for Abortion View," *New York Times*, Sept. 11, 1991.

40 **the Court has decided since *Roe v. Wade*.":** John Paul Stevens, *The Making of a Justice: Reflections on My First 94 Years* (New York: Little, Brown, 2019).

42 **take away a settled constitutional right:** Ronald J. Ostrow, "U.S. to Seek Reversal of Abortion Decision: Decides to Ask High Court to Overturn Ruling Making Act a Constitutionally Protected Right," *Los Angeles Times*, July 13, 1985.

42 **had vetoed an earlier version:** Planned Parenthood v. Casey, 744 F. Supp. 1323 (E.D. Pa. 1990).

43 **restrictions at issue in *Casey*—for now:** Ibid.

43 **still perpetuated by anti-abortion crusaders:** Molly Ball, "I've Never Heard a Woman Say, I'm So Glad I Had an Abortion," *Atlantic*, Nov. 4, 2011.

46 **confirmed to the Supreme Court:** Planned Parenthood v. Casey, 947 F. 2d 682 (3d Cir. 1991).

46 **Justice O'Connor had written in 1983:** Akron v. Akron Center for Reproductive Health, 462 U.S. 416 (1983).

47 **now five votes to overrule *Roe*:** Chief Justice Rehnquist, Justices Byron White, Antonin Scalia, and Anthony Kennedy had already voted to forsake the heightened protections of *Roe* just two years earlier in their dissent in *Webster v. Reproductive Health Services*.

50 **where the Court voted to accept review:** Jeffrey Toobin, *The Nine: Inside the Secret World of the Supreme Court* (New York: Doubleday, 2007), 40–42. See also Edward Lazarus, *Closed Chambers: The Rise, Fall, and Future of the Modern Supreme Court* (New York: Times Books, 1998), 459–486. But see David J. Garrow, "Dissenting Opinion," *New York Times Book Review*, April 19, 1998.

51 **Bill Clinton and Edmund G. Brown Jr.:** Karen de Witt, "Huge Crowd Backs Right to Abortion in Capital March," *New York Times*, April 6, 1992.

54 **Solicitor General Kenneth Starr:** Yes, the infamous Ken Starr who became a household name for his 222-page report detailing President Clinton's affair with White House intern Monica Lewinsky, was fired as Baylor University's president for ignoring sexual assault and gang rape allegations against members of the football team, and defended accused child sex trafficker Jeffrey Epstein and President Trump at his first impeachment trial. Naomi Andu, "Texan Ken Starr Joins Donald Trump's Impeachment Defense Team," *Texas Tribune*, Jan. 17, 2020.

60 **Justice John Paul Stevens's memoir:** Stevens, *The Making of a Justice.*

62 **marriage of two people of the same sex:** Romer v. Evans, 517 U.S. 620 (1996); Lawrence v. Texas, 539 U.S. 558 (2003); United States v. Windsor, 570 U.S. 744 (2013); and Obergefell v. Hodges 576 U.S. 644 (2015).

CHAPTER 4

63 ***Reversing* Roe v. Wade *through the Courts*:** Dennis J. Horan, *Abortion and the Constitution: Reversing* Roe v. Wade *Through the*

Courts (Washington, DC: Georgetown University Press, 1987). See also Robert Barry, "[Book Review of] *Abortion and the Constitution: Reversing 'Roe v. Wade' Through the Courts*, edited by Dennis J. Horan, Edward R. Grant, and Paige C. Cunningham," *Linacre Quarterly* 56, no. 12 (1989).

64   **Justice O'Connor had suggested in a 1983 case:** Akron v. Akron Center for Reproductive Health, 462 U.S. 416 (1983).

67   **other single five-year period since *Roe*:** "Last Five Years Account for More Than One-Quarter of All Abortion Restrictions Enacted Since Roe," *News in Context*, Guttmacher Institute, Jan. 2016, www.guttmacher.org/article/2016/01/last-five-years-account-more -one-quarter-all-abortion-restrictions-enacted-roe#.

CHAPTER 5

70   **Enacted in 1976, the Hyde Amendment:** The amendment was a rider to the 1977 appropriations bill for what was then the Department of Health, Education and Welfare. "Access Denied: Origins of the Hyde Amendment and Other Restrictions on Public Funding for Abortion," ACLU, www.aclu.org/other/access-denied -origins-hyde-amendment-and-other-restrictions-public-funding -abortion, accessed Jan. 21, 2021.

71   **Medicaid-eligible family of three:** *Medicaid Funding of Abortion: Evidence You Can Use* (New York: Guttmacher Institute, 2020), www.guttmacher.org/evidence-you-can-use/medicaid-funding -abortion.

71   **$3,000 or more if past that:** Ibid.

72   **Jimenez's death received national attention:** Alexa Garcia-Ditta, "Reckoning with Rosie," *Texas Observer*, Nov. 3, 2015. See also F. Kissling and E. Frankfort, "Investigation of a Wrongful Death," *Conscience* 17, no. 3 (1996): 23–24.

72   **instead give birth when this funding is unavailable:** Stanley K. Henshaw et al., *Restrictions on Medicaid Funding for Abortions: A Literature Review* (New York: Guttmacher Institute, 2009), www .guttmacher.org/report/restrictions-medicaid-funding-abortions -literature-review.

72   **just 15 percent of white women:** Megan K. Donovan, "In Real Life: Federal Restrictions on Abortion Coverage and the Women They Impact," *Guttmacher Institute Policy Review* 20 (Jan. 5, 2017).

73   **neighborhood legal services lawyers:** Rhonda Copelon and Sylvia Ann Law, "Nearly Allied to Her Right 'to Be'—Medicaid Funding

for Abortion: The Story of *Harris v. McRae*," in *Women and the Law Stories*, ed. Elizabeth M. Schneider and Stephanie M. Wildman (New York: Foundation Press, 2011).

73   **constitutional claims in *Beal* and *Maher*:** Beal v. Doe, 432 U.S. 438 (1977); Maher v. Roe, 432 U.S. 464 (1977).

74   ***Harris v. McRae*:** 448 U.S. 297 (1980).

74   **for a family on welfare at the time:** "Harris v. McRae at a Glance," Center for Constitutional Rights, Oct. 2007, ccrjustice.org/home /what-we-do/our-cases/harris-v-mcrae. See also McRae v. Califano, 491 F. Supp. 630, 660 (E.D.N.Y. 1980).

75   **potential life and therefore was upheld:** The Court rejected any notion that the ban was religiously based. Although the funding restrictions in the Hyde Amendment might coincide with the religious tenets of the Roman Catholic Church, that was insufficient to find an Establishment Clause violation. And the claims of the Women's Division of the United Methodist Church that the ban impeded the religious dictates of its members (under their faith, choosing abortion was the best moral decision) in violation of the Free Exercise Clause were dismissed for lack of standing.

75   ***Fischer v. Department of Public Welfare*:** 509 Pa. 293 (1985).

76   **state constitutions or other state laws:** Committee to Defend Reproductive Rights v. Myers, 625 P.2d 779 (Cal. 1981); Doe v. Maher, 515 A.2d 134 (Conn. Super. Ct. 1986); Moe v. Sec'y of Admin. & Fin., 417 N.E.2d 387 (Mass. 1981); Right to Choose v. Byrne, 450 A.2d 925 (N.J. 1982); Planned Parenthood Ass'n v. Dep't of Human Resources, 663 P.2d 1247 (Or. Ct. App. 1983), aff'd on statutory grounds, 687 P.2d 785 (Or. 1984); Doe v. Celani, No. S81-84CnC (Vt. Super. Ct. May 26, 1986). See also Kathryn Kolbert and David H. Gans, "Responding to *Planned Parenthood v. Casey*: Establishing Neutrality Principles in State Constitutional Law," *Temple Law Review* 66, no. 4 (1993): 1151–1170.

76   **litigation successfully expanded Medicaid funding:** Alaska v. Planned Parenthood, 28 P.3d 904 (Alaska 2001); Simat Corp. v. Ariz. Health Care Cost Containment Sys., 56 P.3d 28 (Ariz. Oct. 22, 2002); Women of Minn. v. Gomez, 542 N.W.2d 17 (Minn. 1995); Jeannette R. v. Ellery, No. BDV-94-811 (Mont. Dist. Ct. May 19, 1995); New Mexico Right to Choose/NARAL v. Johnson, 975 P.2d 841 (N.M. 1998); see also Women's Health Ctr. v. Panepinto, 446 S.E.2d 658 (W. Va. 1993).

77   **still conform to the severe federal Hyde standards:** "State Funding of Abortion Under Medicaid," Guttmacher Institute, Jan. 1, 2021,

www.guttmacher.org/state-policy/explore/state-funding
-abortion-under-medicaid#. For information on an individual
state's coverage of abortion, the ACLU provides a helpful online
interactive map here: www.aclu.org/issues/reproductive-freedom
/abortion/public-funding-abortion.

78   **had tipped off to the case:** Tamar Lewin, "Medicaid Fraud Is New
Weapon in the Abortion Battleground," *New York Times*, Aug. 3,
1997.

79   **was overturned on appeal:** Britell v. United States, 150 F. Supp. 2d
211 (U.S. Dist. Ct. Mass., 2004), rev'd 372 F.3d 1370 (Fed. Cir. 2004).

80   **may be impossible to secure an abortion:** Ellen Haring et al.,
*Access to Reproductive Health Care: The Experiences of Military
Women*, Service Women, 2018, www.servicewomen.org/wp
-content/uploads/2018/12/2018ReproReport_SWAN-2.pdf.

80   **other appropriate reproductive health services:** Allison Herrera,
"Indigenous Women Face Extra Barriers When It Comes to Reproductive Rights," *High Country News*, Feb. 14, 2020.

80   **dependent on authorities for health services:** Donovan, "In Real
Life."

80   **the policy was put on hold:** "Victory: After Three Years of Battling
in Court, the Trump Administration Abandons Its Policy of Banning Abortion for Unaccompanied Immigrant Minors," ACLU,
Sept. 30, 2020, www.aclu.org/news/immigrants-rights/victory-after
-three-years-of-battling-in-court-the-trump-administration-aba
ndons-its-policy-of-banning-abortion-for-unaccompanied-imm
igrant-minors.

82   **coverage in these private employer-sponsored plans:** Donovan,
"In Real Life."

82   **insurance marketplaces and in private health plans:** Anusha
Ravi, *How the U.S. Health Insurance System Excludes Abortion*, Center for American Progress, July 20, 2018, www.americanprogress
.org/issues/women/reports/2018/07/20/453572/u-s-health
-insurance-system-excludes-abortion.

83   **ACA gives states the option to expand Medicaid coverage:**
Madeline Guth, Rachel Garfield, and Robin Rudowitz, *The Effects
of Medicaid Expansion Under the ACA: Updated Findings from a
Literature Review*, Kaiser Family Foundation, March 17, 2020,
www.kff.org/report-section/the-effects-of-medicaid-expansion
-under-the-aca-updated-findings-from-a-literature-review-report.
See also Center on Budget and Policy Priorities, "Chart Book: Ac-
complishments of Affordable Care Act," March 19, 2019, www

.cbpp.org/research/health/chart-book-accomplishments-of
-affordable-care-act.

83 **the first ten years of the program:** Jennifer Tolbert et al., "Key
Facts About the Uninsured Population," Kaiser Family Foundation, Dec. 13, 2019, www.kff.org/uninsured/issue-brief/key-facts
-about-the-uninsured-population; Katie Keith, "Final Marketplace
Enrollment Data for 2020," *Health Affairs Blog*, April 2, 2020,
www.cbpp.org/research/health/chart-book-accomplishments
-of-affordable-care-act.

84 **no longer a pre-existing condition.":** Nancy Pelosi (@Speaker
Pelosi), "#ACA means being a woman is no longer a pre-existing
condition. We won't go back! #ProtectOurCare," Twitter, Feb. 18,
2017, 10:45 a.m., twitter.com/speakerpelosi/status/83302467813
4444032.

84 **states have leaped at the opportunity:** Caroline Rosenzweig, Laurie Sobel, and Alina Salganicoff, *Abortion Riders: Women Living in
States with Insurance Restrictions Lack Abortion Coverage Options*,
Women's Health Policy, Kaiser Family Foundation (Feb. 13, 2018),
www.kff.org/womens-health-policy/issue-brief/abortion-riders
-women-living-in-states-with-insurance-restrictions-lack-abortion
-coverage-options.

CHAPTER 6

86 **seven years in prison if convicted:** Hartford was charged with interference with custody of a minor, Pennsylvania Criminal Code,
Interference with Custody of Children, 18 Pa. Cons. Stat. § 2904(a)
(1984).

87 **her pregnancy or abortion decision:** Testimony of Robert A.
Graci, Assistant Deputy Attorney General of Pennsylvania, Hearing
on the Child Custody Protection Act (H.R. 3682), Subcommittee
on the Constitution, Committee on the Judiciary, House of Representatives, May 21, 1998.

87 **able to obtain the abortion at her appointment:** Lane testified at
trial that she was neither coerced into traveling to Binghamton nor
coerced into having the abortion. The details of the Hartford trial
recounted here are based on Kitty's recollection as well as the testimony of Graci at the Hearing on the Child Custody Protection Act
(cited above) and coverage from the time of the trial, including
Sandy Banisky, "Trial Ties Parental Custody, Abortion: Woman
Who Helped Girl Get Abortion Is on Trial in Pa.," *Baltimore Sun*,

Oct. 29, 1996; Sandy Banisky, "Woman Who Helped Teen Get Abortion Is Convicted; Pa. Jury Finds She Interfered with Custody of a Child," *Baltimore Sun*, Oct. 30, 1996; David Stout, "Woman Who Took Girl for Abortion Is Guilty in Custody Case," *New York Times*, Oct. 31, 1996.

87   **motivated by anti-abortion animus:** Kitty argued that a parent has no right of "custody" to control their daughter's decision to choose abortion and that the prosecution violated Lane's constitutionally protected right to abortion, as well as her right to travel to a state whose laws permit her to obtain an abortion without parental consent.

90   **higher than in the Netherlands:** "Adolescent Pregnancy and Its Outcomes Across Countries," Guttmacher Institute, 2015, www .guttmacher.org/fact-sheet/adolescent-pregnancy-and-its-out comes-across-countries; "U.S. Teen Birth Rate Hits New Low, Still Higher Than Europe's," Population Reference Bureau, April 26, 2012, www.prb.org/us-teen-birth-rate.

90   **among Asian and Pacific Islander teens:** Gretchen Livingston and Deja Thomas, "Why Is the Teen Birth Rate Falling?," Pew Research Center, Aug. 2, 2019, www.pewresearch.org/fact-tank/2019/08/02 /why-is-the-teen-birth-rate-falling.

90   **among young women ages fifteen to nineteen:** Kathryn Kost, Isaac Maddow-Zimet, and Alex Arpaia, *Pregnancies, Births and Abortion Among Adolescents and Young Women in the United States, 2013: National and State Trends by Age, Race and Ethnicity* (New York: Guttmacher Institute, 2017), www.guttmacher.org/report /us-adolescent-pregnancy-trends-2013.

91   **changing the world . . . not changing diapers":** Margot Peppers, "Change the World . . . NOT Diapers: Carly Rae Jepsen Stars in Teen Pregnancy Prevention Campaign for Candie's," *Daily Mail*, May 1, 2013.

92   **even if the sex is consensual:** Carolyn Cocca, *Jailbait: The Politics of Statutory Rape Laws in the United States* (New York: State University of New York Press, 2004).

93   **their decision to have an abortion:** For this discussion about teenagers' access to abortion we have relied on "Laws Restricting Teenagers' Access to Abortion," ACLU, www.aclu.org/other/laws -restricting-teenagers-access-abortion, accessed Jan. 19, 2021. See also Lauren Ralph et al., "The Role of Parents and Partners in Minors' Decisions to Have an Abortion and Anticipated Coping After Abortion," *Journal of Adolescent Health* 54 (2014): 428–434.

93   **unable or unwilling to discuss their pregnancy:** Stanley K. Henshaw and Kathryn Kost, "Parental Involvement in Minors' Abortion Decisions," *Family Planning Perspectives* 24 (1992): 196. See also Lawrence B. Finer and Jesse M. Philbin, "Sexual Initiation, Contraceptive Use, and Pregnancy Among Young Adolescents," *Pediatrics* 131, no. 5 (2013): 886–891.

93   ***Planned Parenthood of Central Missouri v. Danforth:*** 428 U.S. 52 (1976).

94   **Through a series of cases:** Bellotti v. Baird, 443 U.S. 622 (1979) (Bellotti II); Akron v. Akron Ctr. for Repro. Health, 462 U.S. 416 (1983); Webster v. Reproductive Health Services, 492 U.S. 490 (1989); Hodgson v. Minnesota, 497 U.S. 417 (1990); Ohio v. Akron Center, 497 U.S. 502 (1990); Planned Parenthood v. Casey, 505 U.S. 833 (1992).

95   **she will be unable to have an abortion:** Caitlin Myers and Daniel Ladd, "Did Parental Involvement Laws Grow Teeth? The Effects of State Restrictions on Minors' Access to Abortion," IZA DP No. 10952, IZA Institute of Labor Economics, 2017, www.iza.org /publications/dp/10952/did-parental-involvement-laws-grow -teeth-the-effects-of-state-restrictions-on-minors-access-to-abortion.

96   **expose their decisions to have abortions:** "Laws Restricting Teenagers' Access to Abortion."

96   **half a million teen births:** Ibid.

97   **programs that exclusively promote abstinence:** *A History of Abstinence-Only Until Marriage (AOUM) Funding,* SIECUS (May 2019), www.advocatesforyouth.org/storage/advfy/documents/fshi storyabonly.pdf.

97   **groups that promote and sell these programs:** Society for Adolescent Health and Medicine and the North American Society for Pediatric and Adolescent Gynecology, "Crisis Pregnancy Centers in the U.S.: Lack of Adherence to Medical and Ethical Practice Standards," *Journal of Adolescent Health* 65, no. 6 (Dec. 2019); Julie F. Kay with Ashley Jackson, "Sex, Lies & Stereotypes: How Abstinence-Only Programs Harm Women and Girls," *Legal Momentum* (2008), www.americanprogress.org/issues/education-k-12 /news/2008/03/27/4082/whats-not-being-said-about-sex-and -who-its-hurting.

98   **had terminated grants illegally:** Ariana Eunjung Cha, "Nine Organizations Sue Trump Administration for Ending Grants to Teen Pregnancy Programs," *Washington Post,* Feb. 15, 2018; See also "Trump's Teen Pregnancy Prevention Programs Shift: A Timeline,"

SIECUS, 2019, siecus.org/resources/trump-shifts-teen-pregnancy
-prevention-program.

CHAPTER 7

101   **letters threatening anthrax poisoning:** The FBI notes that terrorism is defined in the Code of Federal Regulations as "the unlawful use
of force and violence against persons or property to intimidate or coerce a government, the civilian population, or any segment thereof, in
furtherance of political or social objectives." U.S. Dept. of Justice,
FBI, "Terrorism 2002–2005."

101   **six of these have only one:** R. K. Jones, E. Witwer, and J. Jerman,
Abortion Incidence and Service Availability in the United States (New
York: Guttmacher Institute, 2019), www.guttmacher.org/report
/abortion-incidence-service-availability-us-2017.

101   **even two hundred miles to reach services:** J. Barr-Walker, R. T.
Jayaweera, A. M. Ramirez, and C. Gerdts, "Experiences of Women
Who Travel for Abortion: A Mixed Methods Systematic Review,"
PLOS One 14, no. 4 (2019): e0209991.

102   **clinics that are being targeted for violence:** Michelle Batchelor,
"Clinic Violence Is a Reproductive Justice Issue," In Our Own Voice:
National Black Women's Reproductive Justice Agenda, Jan. 21,
2016, blackrj.org/clinic-violence-is-a-reproductive-justice-issue.

102   **"cutting edge of the abortion issue.":** "Who We Are," Operation
Rescue, www.operationrescue.org/about-us/who-we-are, accessed
Jan. 21, 2021.

102   **mounted horses tried to dispel the large crowds:** Isabel Wilker-
son, "Drive Against Abortion Finds a New Symbol: Wichita," *New
York Times*, Aug. 4, 1991.

102   **names and photographs around town:** Jennifer Warren, "Seven
Target Cities Brace for Operation Rescue Protests: Clinics and
Doctors from San Jose to Philadelphia Will Be Focus of Abortion
Foes' Onslaught. Both Sides Say They Will Apply Lessons from the
Past," *Los Angeles Times*, July 9, 1993.

103   **number of babies' lives will be saved.":** History.com editors,
"Dr. David Gunn Is Murdered by Anti-Abortion Activist," History
Channel, Nov. 13, 2009, www.history.com/this-day-in-history
/dr-david-gunn-is-murdered-by-anti-abortion-activist.

103   **liberal states were immune from the violence:** Yvonne Abraham,
"Remembering the Horror of the Brookline Clinic Shootings, 25
Years Later," *Boston Globe*, Dec. 28, 2019.

104 **injured Emily Lyons, a nurse at the clinic:** "2019 Violence and Disruption Statistics," National Abortion Federation, July 30, 2020, 5aa1b2xfmfh2e2mk03kk8rsx-wpengine.netdna-ssl.com/wp-content/uploads/NAF-2019-Violence-and-Disruption-Stats-Final.pdf; Liam Stack, "A Brief History of Deadly Attacks on Abortion Providers," *New York Times*, Nov. 29, 2015; Tom Brady, "Suspected Abortions Killer Worked at Govt Agency Here," *Independent* (Ireland), March 31, 2001.

104 **against Planned Parenthood in July 2015:** "2019 Violence and Disruption Statistics"; Sabrina Tavernise, "Planned Parenthood Awarded $2 Million in Lawsuit over Secret Videos," *New York Times*, Nov. 15, 2019.

104 **thank him for saving unborn babies.":** Trevor Hughes, "Planned Parenthood Shooter 'Happy' with His Attack," *USA Today*, April 11, 2016.

104 **twenty-four attempts since 2000 alone:** "2019 Violence and Disruption Statistics."

105 **the population of providers continued to age:** Sarp Aksel et al., "Unintended Consequences: Abortion Training in the Years After *Roe v Wade*," *American Journal of Public Health* 103, no. 3 (2013): 404–407; *Bottom Feeder: The Abortionists' Jokebook* (Lewisville, TX: Life Dynamics Inc., 1993), 1–16.

105 **NOW's claims were dismissed:** National Organization for Women v. Scheidler, 510 U.S. 249 (1994); Scheidler v. National Organization for Women, Inc., 537 U.S. 393 (2003) (NOW II); Scheidler v. National Organization for Women, 547 U.S. 9 (2006).

105 *Bray v. Alexandria Women's Health Clinic:* 506 U.S. 263 (1993).

106 **but the law stood strong:** Norton v. Ashcroft, 298 F.3d 547 (6th Cir. 2002); U.S. v. Hart, 212 F.3d 1067 (8th Cir. 2000); United States v. Gregg, 226 F.3d 253 (3d Cir. 2000); United States v. Weslin, 156 F.3d 292 (2d Cir. 1998); U.S. v. Wilson, 154 F.3d 658 (7th Cir.1998); United States v. Bird, 124 F.3d 667 (5th Cir. 1997); Hoffman v. Hunt, 126 F.3d 575 (4th Cir. 1997); Terry v. Reno, 101 F.3d 1412 (D.C. Cir. 1996); U.S. v. Soderna, 82 F.3d 1370 (7th Cir. 1996); United States v. Dinwiddie, 76 F.3d 913 (8th Cir. 1996); Cheffer v. Reno, 55 F.3d 1517 (11th Cir. 1995); American Life League, Inc. v. Reno, 47 F.3d 642 (4th Cir. 1995).

106 **President George W. Bush's administration:** "Little-Enforced Law Opens Window for Suits Against Extremist Groups," *Washington Independent*, June 3, 2009; "2019 Violence and Disruption Statistics."

107   **following Dr. Tiller's murder in 2009:** Rebecca A. Hart and Dana Sussman, *About FACE: Using Legal Tools to Protect Abortion Providers, Clinics, and Their Patients* (New York: Center for Reproductive Rights, 2009), reproductiverights.org/press-room/about-face-using -legal-tools-to-protect-abortion-providers-clinics-and-their-patients.

107   **more than one hundred twenty-three thousand incidents in 2019:** Jessica Grose, "The New Abortion Rights Advocates Are on TikTok," *New York Times*, Dec. 10, 2020.

107   **in the midst of . . . the 2020 election.":** Federal Bureau of Investigation, *Strategic Perspective: Executive Analytical Report, Abortion-Related Violent Extremist Threats and Freedom of Access to Clinic Entrances Act Violations Increase, Likely in Reaction to Recent Legislative Activities* (Washington, DC: FBI, 2020), 5aa1b2xfmfh2e2mk 03kk8rsx-wpengine.netdna-ssl.com/wp-content/uploads /200122-Abortion-Related-Violent-Extremist-Threats-FBI.pdf.

107   **transphobic ideologies of the extreme right:** Alex DiBranco, "The Long History of the Anti-Abortion Movement's Links to White Supremacists," *Nation*, Feb. 3, 2020.

107   **an insurrectionist shot by police:** "Anti-Choice Violence and the U.S. Capital Insurrection," NARAL Pro-Choice America, Jan. 8, 2021, www.prochoiceamerica.org/report/anti-choice-violence-us -capitol-insurrection/; Tayler Hansen (@TaylerUSA), "A young woman was just shot in the neck right besides me in the Capitol Building," Twitter, Jan. 6, 2021, 3:16 p.m., twitter.com/Tayler USA/status/1346913549898149888.

107   **their racist support for eugenics:** Aaron Winter, "Anti-Abortion Extremism and Violence in the United States," in *Extremism in America*, ed. George Michael (Gainesville: University Press of Florida, 2013), 218–248.

107   **rob white male Americans of their rightful power:** "White Supremacists' Anti-Semitic and Anti-Immigrant Sentiments Often Intersect," Anti-Defamation League, 2018, www.adl.org/blog /white-supremacists-anti-semitic-and-anti-immigrant-sentiments -often-intersect; "White Supremacists' Mixed Reactions to Alabama Abortion Law Reflect Divide on Issue," Anti-Defamation League, 2019.

108   **by the Nazis during World War II:** Ruth Graham, "The Long, Weird History of Comparing Abortion to the Holocaust," *Slate*, March 15, 2017.

108   **fixed thirty-five-foot buffer around clinics:** McCullen v. Coakley, 573 U.S. 464 (2014).

109 **that number had risen to 95 percent of abortions:** J. D. Forrest, C. Tietze, and E. Sullivan, "Abortion in the United States, 1976–1977," *Family Planning Perspectives* 10, no. 5 (1978): 271–279; R. K. Jones et al., "Abortion in the United States: Incidence and Access to Services," *Perspectives on Sexual and Reproductive Health* 40, no. 1 (2008): 6–16.

109 **go to a physician's office for an abortion.":** Erin Schumaker, "Clinics Where Majority of US Patients Get Abortions Are Rapidly Closing," *ABC News*, Dec. 11, 2019.

110 **surgical and medication abortions to their patients:** Aksel et al., "Unintended Consequences."

110 **routinely dedicate time to abortion training:** Jody E. Steinauer et al., "Abortion Training in US Obstetrics and Gynecology Residency Programs," *American Journal of Obstetrics and Gynecology* 219 (2018): 86.e1-6.

110 **comprehensive reproductive health care:** Reproductive Health Care and Advocacy Fellowship, Reproductive Health Access Project, www.reproductiveaccess.org/programs/fellowship, accessed Jan. 21, 2021.

110 **have led to its continued dominance:** Elaine L. Hill et al., "Reproductive Health Care in Catholic-Owned Hospitals," *Journal of Health Economics* (Sept. 2019).

110 **tubal ligations and vasectomies:** Hayley Penan and Amy Chen, *The Ethical & Religious Directives: What the 2018 Update Means for Catholic Hospital Mergers* (Washington, DC: The National Health Law Program, 2019), healthlaw.org/resource/the-ethical-religious -directives-what-the-2018-update-means-for-catholic-hospital -mergers.

110 **necessary treatment to their own patients:** Sarah Watts, "Your Ob/Gyn Might Not Perform Your Abortion—Here's Why," *Glamour*, June 5, 2019.

111 **in order to avoid being targeted themselves:** Aksel et al., "Unintended Consequences." Thankfully, ACOG and the AMA continue to advocate for safe abortion practices in lawsuits challenging restrictive policies.

111 **where they are sorely lacking:** David Garrow, "From the Front Line of the Abortion Wars: Susan Wicklund Explores Abortion and Her Role as a Provider in a Memoir That Often Surprises," *Christian Science Monitor*, Feb. 26, 2008; Susan Wicklund with Alan Kesselheim, *This Common Secret: My Journey as an Abortion Doctor* (New York: PublicAffairs, 2007); Vegas Tenold and Glenna

Gordon, "On the Frontline: 12 Hours in a Besieged Abortion Clinic," *Guardian*, July 24, 2019.

111 **medication abortions in thirty-two states:** "The Availability and Use of Medication Abortion," Women's Health Policy Fact Sheet, Kaiser Family Foundation, 2020, www.kff.org/womens-health -policy/fact-sheet/the-availability-and-use-of-medication-abortion. Since the date of this article, Massachusetts amended its law to permit mid-level practitioners to perform abortions.

112 **World Health Organization and practices worldwide:** United Nations Development Programme et al., *Mid-level Health-Care Providers Are a Safe Alternative to Doctors for First-Trimester Abortions in Developing Countries* (Geneva: World Health Organization 2008), www.who.int/reproductivehealth/publications/unsafe_abortion /rhr_hrp_08_15/en/; Marge Berer, "Provision of Abortion by Mid-Level Providers: International Policy, Practice and Perspectives," *Bulletin of the World Health Organization* 87, no. 1 (2009): 58–63.

112 **are as safe as when performed by physicians:** Tracy A. Weitz et al., "Safety of Aspiration Abortion Performed by Nurse Practitioners, Certified Nurse Midwives, and Physician Assistants Under a California Legal Waiver," *American Journal of Public Health* 103, no. 3 (2013): 454–461.

112 **New York to Montana:** Robin Marty, "Why This Longtime Abortion Provider May Never Reopen Her Practice," *Cosmopolitan*, April 10, 2015.

112 **without oral argument or full briefing:** Mazurek v. Armstrong, 520 U.S. 968 (1997).

113 **I'm not that brave of a person.'":** Corin Cates-Carney, "How Vandalism and Fear Ended Abortion in Northwest Montana," National Public Radio, July 21, 2015.

113 **Cahill as its "pioneering foremother.":** "About Us," All Families Healthcare, www.allfamilieshealth.org/about-us, accessed Jan. 21, 2021.

113 **could provide abortions:** In April 2019, the Montana Supreme Court affirmed the granting on a preliminary injunction by the lower court, and as of Jan. 2021, the matter was awaiting further proceedings. Center for Reproductive Rights, Weems v. State of Montana, Aug. 25, 2020, reproductiverights.org/case/helen-weems-v-state-of-montana.

113 **expanding the availability of early abortion:** "An Overview of Abortion Laws," State Laws and Policies, Guttmacher Institute, Jan. 1, 2021, www.guttmacher.org/state-policy/explore/overview -abortion-laws.

114   **abortions at eight weeks' or less gestation:** "The Availability and Use of Medication Abortion," Women's Health Policy, Kaiser Family Foundation, 2020, www.kff.org/womens-health-policy/fact-sheet/the-availability-and-use-of-medication-abortion.

114   **feel more natural than surgery:** "Medical vs. Surgical Abortion," UCSF Health, www.ucsfhealth.org/education/medical-versus-surgical-abortion, accessed Jan. 21, 2021.

114   **or as an abortion kit with mifepristone:** "Our View: Self-Managed Abortion with FDA-Approved Medication Is Safe and Effective," National Women's Health Network, 2018, nwhn.org/taking-abortion-pills-nwhns-position-self-induced-abortion-using-fda-approved-medication.

114   **dissuade them from offering the drug:** Elizabeth G. Raymond et al., "Sixteen Years of Overregulation: Time to Unburden Mifeprex," *New England Journal of Medicine* 376 (2017): 790–794.

115   **FDA expertise on whether to lift them:** Food and Drug Administration v. American College of Obstetricians and Gynecologists, US Supreme Court, Docket No. 20A34, Application for stay granted (Jan. 12, 2021), www.aclu.org/legal-document/supreme-court-order-granting-stay. See also Chelius v. Azar, www.aclu.org/cases/chelius-v-azar.

115   **through the duration of the COVID-19 public health emergency:** Justine Coleman, "FDA Ends Restrictions on Mailing Abortion Pills During Pandemic," *The Hill*, Apr. 13, 2021.

CHAPTER 8

117   **to return to her day job back east:** Guam Society of Obstetricians & Gynecologists v. Ada, 776 F. Supp. 1422 (D. Guam 1990) aff'd 962 F.2d 1366 (9th Cir. 1992).

118   **ten thousand pounds of spuds on the capitol steps:** Marty Trillhaase, "Abortion Ban Puts Idaho on the Media Map," *Lewiston Tribune* (Idaho), March 30, 1990.

118   **stricter bill banning nearly all abortions:** The measure banned all abortions except to save the life of the pregnant woman or the "unborn baby" or in cases of rape or incest if the crimes were reported to police and the woman was within her first trimester of pregnancy. The law subjected doctors to a sentence of ten years in prison and fines up to $100,000. 1991 La. Acts 26.

118   **We do not have that right.":** Frances Frank Marcus, "In Louisiana, Veto on Abortion Bill," *New York Times*, July 7, 1990.

119   **despite his own views on abortion:** Sojourner v. Roemer, 772 F. Supp. 930 (E.D. La. 1991) aff'd Sojourner T v. Edwin W. Edwards, 974 F.2d 27 (5th Cir).

119   **far more than any other state:** Elizabeth Nash, "Louisiana Has Passed 89 Abortion Restrictions Since *Roe*: It's About Control, Not Health," Guttmacher Institute, 2020, docs.google.com/document /d/1Gm2YYHN6VnQI8ND4On_FDp8beOP4-5nj6V8ivoe5ryA /edit#heading=h.k4cfn6omjgpo.

120   **a child "just two inches from birth.":** Helen Alvare, former head of the National Conference of Catholic Bishops Pro-Life Office, interview with Ed Bradley, "Partial-Birth Abortion," *60 Minutes*, June 2, 1996.

120   **certainly would apply later in pregnancy:** Julie Rovner, "'Partial-Birth Abortion': Separating Fact from Spin," National Public Radio, Feb. 21, 2006.

121   **successfully blocked Ohio's partial birth ban:** Women's Medical Professional Corp. v Voinovich, 911 F. Supp. 1051 (S.D. Ohio 1995), affirmed, 130 F.3d 187 (6th Cir. 1997).

121   **magic wand and it's not there.":** "Bill Clinton on Vetoing the Partial Birth Abortion Ban," *PBS News Hour*, April 10, 1996, www.pbs.org /newshour/politics/white_house-jan-june96-abortion_veto_04-10.

121   **and thus harming future fertility:** Rovner, "'Partial-Birth Abortion.'"

121   **thankfully he vetoed the measure:** "Bill Clinton on Vetoing the Partial Birth Abortion Ban," *PBS News Hour*. An identical bill that was passed the following year was again vetoed by President Clinton.

122   **an exception to preserve the woman's health:** Stenberg v. Carhart, 530 U.S. 914 (2000).

122   **a 5–4 ruling that upheld the federal ban:** Gonzales v. Carhart, 550 U.S. 124 (2007).

123   **any second-trimester abortion providers:** "Bans on Specific Abortion Methods Used After the First Trimester," State Laws and Policies, Guttmacher Institute, Jan. 1, 2021, www.guttmacher.org /state-policy/explore/bans-specific-abortion-methods-used -after-first-trimester. See also Megan K. Donovan, "D&E Abortion Bans: The Implications of Banning the Most Common Second-Trimester Procedure," Guttmacher Institute, Feb. 21, 2017. Although two bans are operative in Mississippi and West Virginia, they have little effect because there are no providers in either state

who perform second-trimester abortions. A North Dakota law will only go into effect when *Roe* is reversed.

126 **used race as a determining factor:** Additionally, several states passed bans on abortion where a fetus has a genetic anomaly—for example, when Down syndrome is detected later in pregnancy. "Abortion Bans in Cases of Sex or Race Selection or Genetic Anomaly," State Laws and Policies, Guttmacher Institute, Jan. 1, 2021, www.guttmacher.org/state-policy/explore/bans-specific-abortion-methods-used-after-first-trimester. Other states have prohibited doctors or genetic counselors from providing abortion information to families after a diagnosis of a fetal anomaly or genetic condition.

126 **stereotypes that South Asian cultures "don't value women.":** Miriam Yeung, "How Asian American Women Became the Target of Anti-Abortion Activism," *Washington Post*, Nov. 4, 2015.

126 **address a problem that likely does not exist:** "Sex Selective Abortion Bans," Factsheet, National Asian Pacific American Women's Forum, Jan. 11, 2021, www.napawf.org/reproductive-health-and-rights/sex-selective-abortion-bans; *Replacing Myths with Facts: Sex Selective Abortion Laws in the United States* (Washington, DC: National Asian Pacific American Women's Forum, 2014), www.napawf.org/our-work/content/replacing-myths-with-facts.

127 **the race of the men that impregnated them:** "Race and Sex Selection Abortion Bans Are Harmful to Women," Fact Sheet, National Women's Law Center, www.nwlc.org/wp content/uploads/2015/08/prendafactsheet.pdf; see also Sneha Barot, "A Problem-and-Solution Mismatch: Son Preference and Sex-Selective Abortion Bans," *Guttmacher Policy Review* 15, no. 2 (2012).

127 **abortion providers, particularly Planned Parenthood:** Box v. Planned Parenthood of Indiana and Kentucky, Inc., 587 U.S. ___ (2019) (Thomas, J. concurring).

127 **which abortion opponents claim "aborts 360 Blacks every day.":** "Black Preborn Lives Matter Billboards Launched Across the Country, with Calls for Defunding Planned Parenthood," Students for Life of America, Sept. 1, 2020, studentsforlife.org/2020/09/01/black-preborn-lives-matter-billboards-launched-across-the-country-with-calls-for-defunding-planned-parenthood.

127 **abortion rights organizations adamantly disavow:** Nikita Stewart, "Planned Parenthood in N.Y. Disavows Margaret Sanger over Eugenics," *New York Times*, July 21, 2020; "The Layered, Complex

History of Margaret Sanger—Planned Parenthood Founder and Reproductive Rights Trailblazer," Planned Parenthood Action Fund, Oct. 13, 2016, plannedparenthoodaction.org/blog/margaret -sanger-planned-parenthoods-founder.

127   **the moment a fetal heartbeat can be detected:** "State Bans on Abortion Throughout Pregnancy," State Laws and Policies, Guttmacher Institute, Jan. 1, 2021. The South Carolina ban was passed on Feb. 17, 2021. Jeffrey Collins, "SC Governor Signs Abortion Ban; Planned Parenthood Sues," Associated Press, Feb. 17, 2021.

128   **doors until the end of the emergency:** Laurie Sobel et al., "State Action to Limit Abortion Access During the COVID-19 Pandemic," Kaiser Family Foundation, Aug. 10, 2020, www.kff.org /coronavirus-covid-19/issue-brief/state-action-to-limit-abortion -access-during-the-covid-19-pandemic.

128   **time-sensitive medical procedure:** American College of Obstetricians and Gynecologists et al., "Joint Statement on Abortion Access During the COVID-19 Outbreak," Press Release, March 18, 2020, www.acog.org/news/news-releases/2020/03/joint-statement -on-abortion-access-during-the-covid-19-outbreak.

128   **surgical procedures, including abortion, to proceed:** Jonathan Bearak, et al., "COVID-19 Abortion Bans Would Greatly Increase Driving Distances for Those Seeking Care," Guttmacher Institute, April 2020, www.guttmacher.org/article/2020/04/covid-19-abor tion-bans-would-greatly-increase-driving-distances-those-seeking -care; J. Barr-Walker, et al., "Experiences of Women Who Travel for Abortion: A Mixed Methods Systematic Review," *PLOS One* 14, no. 4 (2019): e0209991.

CHAPTER 9

131   *Whole Woman's Health v. Hellerstedt:* 579 U.S.__(2016).

131   **much less invasive, low-risk procedure:** "Evidence You Can Use: Targeted Regulation of Abortion Providers (TRAP) Laws," Guttmacher Institute (2020), www.guttmacher.org/evidence-you -can-use/targeted-regulation-abortion-providers-trap-laws. Procedures performed in ambulatory surgical centers include colonoscopies, cataract and gallbladder removal, tonsillectomies, and hernia repairs.

132   **opposed by ACOG and the AMA:** Sarah McCammon, "Major Medical, Legal Groups Oppose Louisiana Abortion Law Before U.S. Supreme Court," National Public Radio, Dec. 2, 2019.

133 **Obama nominated Merrick Garland:** Judge Garland was confirmed as the attorney general shortly after President Biden took office.

133 **with the nation for generations to come":** Lisa Mascarol, "McConnell Tries to Salvage Senate Majority with Court Vote," *AP News*, Oct. 10, 2020.

135 **did not reveal their views of *Roe* or *Casey*:** Gorsuch had ruled on two abortion cases while a Court of Appeals judge, but neither involved a direct challenge to *Roe* or *Casey*. In one he would have permitted the governor of Utah to terminate funding for Planned Parenthood. Planned Parenthood Ass'n of Utah v. Herbert, No. 15-4189 (10th Cir. 2016). In another, brought by the Center, he permitted the lower court to consider further a challenge to an Oklahoma law that gave proceeds from specialty license plates to anti-abortion but not abortion rights groups. See Hill v. Kemp, 478 F.3d 1236 (10th Cir. 2007).

136 **of the four liberal Justices:** The more liberal Justices who support abortion rights have interpreted the standard of *Casey* to require courts to determine not just whether a law creates an "undue burden" but that any burden the law imposes must be weighed against the benefits it confers. If there is no benefit from the law, then it cannot pointlessly place a burden on abortion access.

138 **first woman and first Jewish person to lie in state:** Rosa Parks was honored with a public viewing in the Capitol, but because she was not a government official, she did not formally lie in state.

138 **single vote from the minority party:** Sarah Binder, "Barrett Is the First Supreme Court Justice Confirmed Without Opposition Support Since 1869," *Washington Post*, Oct. 27, 2020.

139 **"Who does laundry in your house?":** Julie Kantor, "The 'Mominee': Supreme Expectations and Gender Bias in Amy Coney Barrett's Confirmation," *National Law Journal*, Oct. 26, 2020.

139 **precluded from enforcing the death penalty.":** Amy Coney Barrett and John H. Garvey, "Catholic Judges in Capital Cases," *Marquette Law Review* 81 (1997–1998): 303.

139 **the tenets of her religion:** Several weeks later, she joined the liberal Justices and refused to lift a hold on an execution in order to allow a prisoner an opportunity to have his pastor present during his execution. Dunn v. Smith, 592 U.S. ____ (2021).

139 **at the time it was ratified:** Amy C. Barrett, "Originalism and Stare Decisis," *Notre Dame Law Review* 92 (2017): 1921.

140   **and their selfish views.":** Madison Debates, Sept. 17, 1787, available at Yale Law School Goldman Law Library, avalon.law.yale.edu/18th_century/debates_917.asp.

140   **into the super-precedent category:** Brian Naylor, "Barrett Says She Does Not Consider *Roe v. Wade* 'Super-Precedent,'" National Public Radio, Oct. 13, 2020.

141   **overturning its "barbaric legacy.":** Stephanie Kirchgaessner, "Revealed: Amy Coney Barrett Supported a Group That Said Life Begins at Fertilization," *Guardian*, Oct. 1, 2020. See also Rebecca R. Ruiz, "Amy Coney Barrett Signed an Ad in 2006 Urging Overturning the 'Barbaric Legacy' of *Roe v. Wade*," *New York Times*, Oct. 1, 2020.

142   **case law is wrongly decided:** Amy C. Barrett, "Stare Decisis and Due Process," *University of Colorado Law Review* 73 (2003): 1011.

143   ***Burwell v. Hobby Lobby Stores*:** 573 U.S. 682 (2014).

143   **to no-cost contraceptive services:** Little Sisters of the Poor Saints Peter and Paul Home v. Pennsylvania: 591 U.S. ___ (2020).

143   ***Roman Catholic Diocese of Brooklyn v. Cuomo*:** 592 U.S. ___ (2020).

143   ***Masterpiece Cakeshop, Ltd. v. Colorado Civil Rights Commission*:** 584 U.S. ___ (2018).

143   **which legalized same-sex marriage:** Obergefell v. Hodges, 576 U.S. 644 (2015) (Scalia, dissenting); see also Ruth Marcus, "Amy Coney Barrett's Alignment with Scalia Has Implications Far Beyond *Roe v. Wade*," *Washington Post*, Oct. 2, 2020.

143   ***Lawrence v. Texas*:** 539 U.S. 558 (2003).

144   ***Bostock v. Clayton County*:** 590 U.S. ___ (2020). By an executive order issued within a few days of President Biden taking office, this ruling has now been applied to revise and clarify that federal policies and regulations that prohibit sex discrimination in such areas as education, housing, and immigration also prohibit discrimination based on sexual orientation and gender identity. President Joseph R. Biden Jr., "Executive Order on Preventing and Combating Discrimination on the Basis of Gender Identity or Sexual Orientation," Jan. 20, 2021, www.whitehouse.gov/briefing-room/presidential-actions/2021/01/20/executive-order-preventing-and-combating-discrimination-on-basis-of-gender-identity-or-sexual-orientation.

144   **to remain an all-male bastion:** United States v. Virginia, 518 U.S. 515 (1996).

145   **in contemporary US history:** Michael A. Bailey, "If Trump Appoints a Third Justice, the Supreme Court Would Be the Most

Conservative It's Been Since 1950," *Washington Post*, Sept. 22, 2020.

CHAPTER 10

147   **defend and vindicate that right.":** Irish Constitution Article 40.3.3° (1937).

147   **from the moment of fertilization:** Between 1973 and 2003 members of Congress introduced hundreds of proposals for a Human Life Amendment to the US Constitution that would overturn *Roe*. Rather than return the question of abortion to Congress and the states, these proposals would prohibit abortions and some forms of birth control nationwide. The Senate Judiciary Committee held numerous hearings on the proposals and in 1983 the Hatch-Eagleton Amendment was put to a floor vote. The measure was defeated 51–49, falling eighteen votes short of the sixty-seven required for passage. Since *Casey*, the strategy has largely been abandoned, although likely to return in a post-*Roe* era. Human Life Action, "Human Life Amendment: National Committee for a Human Life Amendment," www.humanlifeaction.org/issues/human-life-amendment, accessed March 1, 2021.

150   **their duties in the home.":** Irish Constitution 41.2.2. While there was some discussion of a referendum to remove this phrase from the Irish Constitution, by 2020 efforts to do so lost momentum. Sorcha Pollak, "Momentum to Remove 'Women in the Home' from Constitution 'Lost,'" *Irish Times*, Feb. 15, 2019.

151   ***Attorney General v. X:*** [1992] 1 I.R. 1 at 54–55.

155   **multiple intersecting forms of discrimination:** Joanna N. Erdman and Rebecca J. Cook, "Decriminalization of Abortion: A Human Rights Imperative," *Best Practices in Research Clinical Obstetrics and Gynaecology* 62 (2020): 11–14.

155   ***Abortion and the Law: An Irish Perspective:*** James Kingston, Anthony Whelan, and Ivana Bacik, *Abortion and the Law: An Irish Perspective* (Dublin: Round Hall Sweet & Maxwell, 1997).

157   ***A, B, and C v. Ireland:*** No. 25579/05 Eur. Ct. H.R. (2010).

158   **"success without victory,":** Jules Lobel, *Success Without Victory: Lost Legal Battles and the Long Road to Justice in America* (New York: New York University Press, 2004).

159   **grounds of a fatal fetal anomaly:** D v. Ireland, Appl. No. 26499/02, European Court of Human Rights, June 28, 2006, www.refworld.org/cases,ECHR,470376a62.html.

165   **"the girl with the diamond smile,":** Kitty Holland, "The Girl with the Diamond Smile," *Irish Times*, June 14, 2013.

166   **a reverse Irish journey:** Kate Hickey, "Irish Around the World Travel #Hometovote in Ireland's Abortion Referendum," *Irish Central*, May 25, 2018; Ciara Nugent, "Why Thousands of Irish Expats Are Flying Home to Vote in the Historic Abortion Referendum," *Time*, May 24, 2018.

166   **culmination of a quiet revolution:** Henry McDonald, Emma Graham-Harrison, and Sinead Baker, "Ireland Votes by Landslide to Legalise Abortion," *Guardian*, May 26, 2018.

167   **preserving her health when regulating abortion:** "The majority of international and regional human rights bodies have established that any prenatal protection must be consistent with the woman's right to life, physical integrity, health and privacy as well as the principles of equality and of non-discrimination." Inter-Parliamentary Union and United Nations Office of the High Commissioner for Human Rights, *Human Rights Handbook for Parliamentarians N° 26* (2016), www.ohchr.org/documents/publications/handbookparliamentarians.pdf.

CHAPTER 11

168   **"big hairy audacious goals.":** Jim Collins and Jerry I. Porras, *Built to Last: Successful Habits of Visionary Companies* (New York: Harper Business Essentials, 1994).

170   **refused to consider the issue:** Baker v. Nelson, 191 N.W.2d 185 (Minn. 1971) dismissed for want of substantial federal question, 409 U.S. 810 (1972).

171   **LGBTQ+ activists were elated:** Baehr v. Lewin, 852 P.2d 44 (1993). See also Jeffrey Schmalz, "In Hawaii, Step Toward Legalized Gay Marriage," *New York Times* (May 7, 1993).

171   **justice that arrives like a thunderbolt.":** "Transcript: Obama's Remarks on Supreme Court Ruling on Same-Sex Marriage," *Washington Post*, June 26, 2015.

171   **created the necessary barometric pressure:** Wolfson's own account of the Freedom to Marry initiative gives an in-depth account of the village it took to achieve this victory. See "Winning the Freedom to Marry: The Inside Story of a Transformative Campaign," Freedom to Marry, freedomtomarry.org/pages/how-it-happened, accessed Jan. 19, 2021. See also John F. Kowal, "The Improbable Victory of Marriage Equality," Brennan Center for Justice,

Sept. 29, 2015, brennancenter.org/our-work/analysis-opinion /improbable-victory-marriage-equality.

172 **network of more than forty chapters:** Patrisse Cullors, "6 Years Strong," Black Lives Matter, July 13, 2019, blacklivesmatter.com /six-years-strong.

172 **resources or defunding of police:** "Protests Build Momentum for Police Accountability, Reforms to Address U.S. Structural Racism: Interview with Darius Charney, Senior Staff Attorney with the Center for Constitutional Rights, Conducted by Scott Harris," *Between the Lines*, June 10, 2020, btlonline.org/protests-build -momentum-for-police-accountability-reforms-to-address-u-s -structural-racism; Martin Austermuhle, "Here's What Black Lives Matter D.C. Is Calling For, and Where the City Stands," National Public Radio, June 9, 2020; "#8Can'tWait," Campaign Zero, 8cantwait.org, accessed Jan. 19, 2021.

173 **undocumented immigrants shut out of the ACA:** Reproductive Health Equity Act, Oregon Laws 2017, Chapter 721, oregonlegisla ture.gov/bills_laws/lawsstatutes/2017orlaw0721.pdf. See also Reproductive Health Equity Act, Oregon Health Authority, oregon .gov/oha/PH/HEALTHYPEOPLEFAMILIES/REPRODUCTI VESEXUALHEALTH/Pages/reproductive-health-equity-act.aspx, accessed Jan. 19, 2021.

174 **losers focus on winners.":** Photo by Pascal Le Segretain for Getty Images, available at Scott Morrison, "A Winners [*sic*] Focus vs. a Losers [*sic*] Focus," scottdmorrison.com/winners-focus-vs-losers -focus, accessed Jan. 19, 2021.

175 **ratification by three-quarters of the states:** The Constitution also may be amended by two-thirds of the state legislatures calling for a constitutional convention and three-fourths of the states ratifying any proposals that are adopted at the convention (US Constitution, Article V). Prominent conservative groups and Republican members of Congress have been advocating for a convention to require a balanced budget, congressional term limits, and repeal of the federal income tax among other initiatives. The strategy has been gaining ground but in our view is extremely problematic, for there is no way to limit the changes that emerge from the convention and may result in even further rollbacks to the liberties we hold dear.

175 **within the ten-year time limit Congress imposed:** The original time limit for passage was seven years, although extended to ten by a congressional resolution that some thought was invalid. "Two

Modes to Ratification," Alice Paul Institute, 2018, www.equal
rightsamendment.org/pathstoratification.

175 **increasing support in more recent years:** On Jan. 15, 2020, decades after the deadline and after much work by activists, Virginia
ratified the original amendment, bringing the total number of states
supporting it to thirty-eight. Some hoped that this would enable
the amendment to take effect. But given the ten-year time limit, the
fact that some states had withdrawn their support, and the current
composition of the Supreme Court, this route may have only a limited chance of success. Even Justice Ginsburg counseled against pin-
ning hopes on such an approach. Russell Berman, "Ruth Bader
Ginsburg Versus the Equal Rights Amendment," *Atlantic*, Feb. 15,
2020. Some activists are working with Congress to try to remove
the deadline or again extend the time limit for ratification by the
states. In 2020, the House voted to remove the deadline, and there
is hope for Senate support, although an uphill battle.

175 **and eventually Republican state lawmakers:** "History of the
Equal Rights Amendment," Alice Paul Institute, 2018, www.equal
rightsamendment.org/the-equal-rights-amendment.

176 **Americans supported the ERA by wide margins:** David Dismore,
"Today in Feminist History: Public Support for ERA Is 'Overwhelming' (April 9, 1975)," *Ms. Magazine*, April 9, 2020.

177 **governmental contracting to fair credit:** In Bostock v. Clayton
County, 590 U.S. ___ (2020), Justice Gorsuch used a textualist's approach to find that the language of Title VII, the law that prohibits
employment discrimination on the "basis of sex," includes discrimination against LGBTQ+ people as well as women, a surprising and
welcome ruling. Supporters of the ERA suggest that this same rationale would ensure that the ERA protects against LGBTQ+ discrimination as well but it remains vulnerable with four ultra-conservative
Supreme Court Justices who take a contrary view.

178 **economic advancement of marginalized groups:** Savitri Goonese-
kere, *A Rights-Based Approach to Realizing Gender Equality*, UN Division for the Advancement of Women, 1998, www.un.org
/womenwatch/daw/news/rights.htm. The Division had commissioned the study as a background paper for a workshop of gender
experts from the United Nations system and from the OECD/
DAC Working Party on Gender Equality.

178 **unfortunately has never been adequate:** Craig v. Boren, 429 U.S.
190 (1976).

178   **closing its eyes to gender bias:** Gillian Thomas, *Because of Sex: One
       Law, Ten Cases, and Fifty Years That Changed American Women's
       Lives at Work* (New York: St. Martin's, 2016).

179   **achieved by the least restrictive means.":** Right to Personal Re-
       productive Autonomy Amendment, P.R. 5, Vermont (2022); Mike
       Faher, "Senate OKs Abortion-Rights Constitutional Amendment,"
       VTDigger, April 4, 2019.

179   **become pregnant or terminate a pregnancy:** Caroline Fredrick-
       son, Jamal Greene, and Melissa Murray, *The Progressive Constitu-
       tion,* National Constitution Center, constitutioncenter.org/debate
       /special-projects/constitution-drafting-project/the-progressive-con
       stitution, accessed Jan. 1, 2021.

180   **gender equity clauses from around the globe:** "Global Gender
       Equality Constitutional Database," UN Women, 2016, constitutions
       .unwomen.org/en.

180   **conscience, belief, culture, language and birth.":** Constitution of
       the Republic of South Africa 1996, as amended 2012, Global Gen-
       der Equality Constitutional Database, UN Women, constitutions
       .unwomen.org/en.

180   **women's rights are human rights.":** *Hillary Clinton Declares
       "Women's Rights Are Human Rights,"* video, 5:36, PBS, Sept. 8,
       1995.

180   **a model for constitutions worldwide:** Isabel Latz et al., "Equal
       Rights for Women and Girls in the World's Constitutions," UCLA
       Fielding School of Public Health, World Policy Analysis Center,
       2014,   www.worldpolicycenter.org/sites/default/files/WORLD
       _Policy_Brief_Equal_Rights_For_Women_and_Girls_in
       _Constitutions_2015.pdf. "On the 25th Anniversary of the Land-
       mark Beijing Declaration on Women's Rights," UN Women,
       Sept. 4, 2020, www.unwomen.org/en/news/stories/2020/9/press
       -release-25th-anniversary-of-the-beijing-declaration-on
       -womens-rights.

180   **Human Rights in just such circumstances:** S. Ramya, "Domestic
       Violence: Police Have a Duty to Protect Victims," ACLU Wom-
       en's Rights Project, Oct. 23, 2013. The police in Castle Rock, Col-
       orado, had repeatedly ignored pleas by Jessica Lenahan after her
       estranged husband, who was subject to a restraining order, had kid-
       napped their children. He later murdered them before taking his
       own life in front of the police station. While the US Supreme Court
       had found the government owed Lenahan no duty to enforce the

restraining order in Castle Rock v. Gonzales, 545 U.S. 748 (2005), the Inter-American Commission on Human Rights recommended that the government conduct an investigation, adopt reforms, and provide compensation to her.

181   **in accordance with human rights principles:** Catharine A. Mac-Kinnon and Kimberlé W. Crenshaw, "Reconstituting the Future: An Equality Amendment," *Yale Law Journal* 129 (2019–2020).

181   **"are born free and equal in dignity and rights.":** The Universal Declaration of Human Rights, United Nations, www.un.org/en /universal-declaration-human-rights, accessed Jan. 19, 2021.

CHAPTER 12

184   **"follow the anti-abortion leader.":** Anna Louie Sussman, "The Loneliness of the Pro-Choice Republican Woman," *New Yorker*, Oct. 30, 2020.

185   **galvanizing others to do the same:** As Stacey Abrams recognized after the Biden win in Georgia: "So many deserve credit for 10yrs to new Georgia: @gwlauren @fairfightaction @nseufot @New GAProject @AAAJ_Atlanta @GALEOorg @BlackVotersMtr Helen Butler @GeorgiaDemocrat @RebeccaDeHart DuBose Porter @DPGChair. Always John Lewis. Charge any omissions to my head. My heart is full," @staceyabrams Twitter, Nov. 6, 2020, 7:17 a.m., twitter.com/staceyabrams/status/1324687447259779072. Stacey Abrams and Lauren Groh-Wargo, "How to Turn Your Red State Blue: It May Take 10 Years; Do It Anyway," *New York Times*, Feb. 11, 2021.

186   **appear in a ballot battle in 2022:** Right to Personal Reproductive Autonomy Amendment, P.R. 5, Vermont (2022); Mike Faher, "Senate OKs Abortion-Rights Constitutional Amendment," *VT-Digger*, April 4, 2019. To be enacted the matter must pass the Vermont Senate by a two-thirds vote and be supported by a majority in the house in two consecutive sessions and then be placed on the ballot for approval by the voters. See VT. Const. Ch. II, § 72 [Amending Constitution].

186   **amendment up for a public vote:** "States with Initiatives or Referendum," Ballotpedia, ballotpedia.org/States_with_initiative _or_referendum, accessed Jan. 19, 2021.

186   **instituting criminal justice reforms:** Candice Williams and Karen Bouffard, "McCormack, Welch Flip Control of Michigan Supreme

Court," *Detroit News*, Nov. 3, 2020; Caroline Fredrickson and Eric Lesh, "How Progressives Can Compete for Power," Brennan Center for Justice Podcast, April 8, 2020 www.brennancenter.org /our-work/analysis-opinion/podcasts/how-progressives-can -compete-power.

187   **give birth or to have an abortion.":** Illinois Reproductive Health Act, www.ilga.gov/legislation/ilcs/ilcs5.asp?ActID=3987&Chapter ID=64.

188   **right to abortion throughout pregnancy:** "Abortion Policy in the Absence of *Roe*," Guttmacher Institute, Nov. 1, 2020, www .guttmacher.org/state-policy/explore/abortion-policy-absence-roe. Massachusetts enacted an omnibus measure, the *Roe* Act, in December 2020.

188   **more rural parts of the state:** Title 22: Health and Welfare, Subtitle 2: Part 3: Chapter 263-B: Abortions. §1598. Abortions, legislature.maine.gov/statutes/22/title22sec1598.html.

188   **perform surgical abortions as well:** Guttmacher Institute, "An Overview of Abortion Laws, State Laws and Policies," Feb. 1, 2021, www.guttmacher.org/state-policy/explore/overview-abortion-laws.

188   **health centers, serving 750,000 students:** Hannah Wiley, "Abortion Pills to Be Available at California Colleges Under Law Signed by Gavin Newsom," *Sacramento Bee*, Oct. 11, 2019.

189   **who do not have regular doctors:** Shelagh Dolan, "How the Growth of the Urgent Care Industry Business Model Is Changing the Healthcare Market," *Business Insider*, March 18, 2019; Cheryl Alkon, "What's Behind the Growth of Urgent Care Clinics?," *Medical Economics* 95, no. 17 (2018).

189   **for social media or lobbying campaigns:** Bruce Japsen, "Urgent Care Centers Eclipse 9200 Driven by Optum and Hospital Systems," *Forbes*, Dec. 12, 2019.

190   **bringing national attention to the idea:** "Help Sioux Challenge SD's Abortion Ban," *Daily Kos,* March 23, 2006, www.dailykos .com/stories/2006/3/23/196373/-. Fire Thunder's proposal and her subsequent impeachment are memorialized in the documentary film *Young Lakota*; see itvs.org/films/young-lakota.

190   **are reneging on those agreements.":** Charon Asetoyer, "Voices of Feminism Oral History Project," interviewed by Joyce Follet, Sept. 1–2, 2005, Lake Andes, South Dakota.

190   **with no corresponding health benefit:** Guttmacher Institute, "An Overview of Abortion Laws."

191   **maternity care to also cover abortion:** Anusha Ravi, *How the U.S. Health Insurance System Excludes Abortion*, Center for American Progress, July 20, 2018, www.americanprogress.org/issues/women /reports/2018/07/20/453572/u-s-health-insurance-system -excludes-abortion. Adam Sonfeld and Elizabeth Nash, "States Lead the Way in Promoting Coverage of Abortion in Medicaid and Private Insurance," Guttmacher Institute, June 2019, www .guttmacher.org/article/2019/06/states-lead-way-promoting -coverage-abortion-medicaid-and-private-insurance#.

191   **for women from out of state:** Nikita Stewart, "New York City Allocates $250,000 for Abortions, Challenging Conservative States: The Money Will Go to a Nonprofit Fund That Pays Clinics for Abortions Performed on Women Who Cannot Pay, a Third of Whom Live Outside New York," *New York Times*, June 14, 2019; Stacy Fernández, "Texas Told Cities They Couldn't Fund Abortion Providers. So Austin Is Funding Abortion Access Instead," *Texas Tribune*, Sept. 11, 2019.

191   **receive the support they need:** "How to Get an Abortion in Pennsylvania if You're a Teen During Coronavirus," Women's Law Project, 2020, womenslawproject.org/wp-content/uploads/2020 /04/WLP-JB-Updated-Corona.pdf.

192   **twenty-three states, should be eliminated:** "Targeted Regulation of Abortion Providers, State Laws and Policies," Guttmacher Institute, Dec. 1, 2020, www.guttmacher.org/state-policy/explore /targeted-regulation-abortion-providers.

193   **more reproductive freedom–friendly forum:** Thomas Schaller, "The Republican Structural Advantage: Republicans Start Every Election Cycle with Structural Advantages Regardless of the Issues and All the Other Factors That Usually Determine Who Wins Elections," *American Prospect*, Oct. 28, 2015. See also Jeff Greenfield, "Yes, the Senate Is Rigged for Small States, but Not for Republicans," *Washington Post*, Nov. 19, 2020.

193   **for each four years in office:** Russell Wheeler, "Should We Restructure the Supreme Court?," The Brookings Institution, March 2, 2020, www.brookings.edu/policy2020/votervital/should -we-restructure-the-supreme-court.

193   **have coverage for abortion services:** Each Woman Act Factsheet, All* Above All, allaboveall.org/resource/each-woman-act-fact-sheet, accessed Jan. 19, 2021.

194   **this Reagan-era muzzle in 1991:** Rust v. Sullivan, 500 U.S. 173 (1991).

195 **with an eye to rescinding it:** At the same time, President Biden repealed by executive order the "global gag rule" also known as the Mexico City policy, which banned international groups that receive US aid from performing, facilitating, or discussing abortion. Bhadra Sharma, Ruth Maclean, Oscar Lopez, and Rick Gladstone, "Health Providers Worldwide Welcome Biden Reversal of Anti-Abortion Rule," *New York Times*, Jan. 29, 2021.

195 **in Title X funding, a great boon:** E. M. August, et al., "Projecting the Unmet Need and Costs for Contraception Services After the Affordable Care Act," *American Journal of Public Health* 106, no. 2 (2016): 334–341.

195 **could be erased by an FDA ruling:** The ACLU has sought to reverse the REMS through several lawsuits. Although the Supreme Court allowed the REMS to remain in place in Food and Drug Administration v. ACOG, 592 U.S. ____ (2021), the FDA has since suspended the rules during the pandemic.

196 **likely to attempt self-managed abortions:** Lauren Ralph et al., "Prevalence of Self-Managed Abortion Among Women of Reproductive Age in the United States," *JAMA Open Network*, Dec. 18, 2020. See also "A Roadmap for Research on Self-Managed Abortion in the United States," Advancing New Standards in Reproductive Health (ANSIRH), Gynuity Health Projects, and Ibis Reproductive Health, 2018, ibisreproductivehealth.org/sites/default/files/files/publications/US%20research%20roadmap%20self%20managed%20abortion.pdf.

196 **put women at risk of prosecution:** "Self-Managed Abortion, the Law, and COVID-19 Fact Sheet," If/When/How: Lawyering for Reproductive Justice, 2020, www.ifwhenhow.org/wp-content/uploads/2020/04/20_04_Final_SMA_TheLaw_COVID-19_FactSheet_PDF.pdf.

197 **exempt those who are pregnant:** Andrea Rowan, "Prosecuting Women for Self-Inducing Abortion: Counterproductive and Lacking Compassion," *Guttmacher Policy Review* 18, no. 3 (2015).

197 **helping a woman to do so:** "The Plan C Guide to Getting Abortion Pills," Plan C, www.plancpills.org/guide-how-to-get-abortion-pills#faq, accessed Jan. 19, 2021.

197 **admitted to taking the pills:** Rowan, "Prosecuting Women for Self-Inducing Abortion"; Emily Bazelon, "A Mother in Jail for Helping Her Daughter Have an Abortion," *New York Times*, Sept. 22, 2014.

197   **served eighteen months in prison:** Emily Bazelon, "Purvi Patel Could Be Just the Beginning," *New York Times*, April 1, 2015; Miriam Yeung, "How Asian American Women Became the Target of Anti-Abortion Activism," *Washington Post*, Nov. 4, 2015.

197   **sentence of forty-five years to life:** Ed Pilkington, "Indiana Prosecuting Chinese Woman for Suicide Attempt That Killed Her Foetus," *Guardian*, May 30, 2012.

198   **15 percent of the state's population:** Jill E. Adams and Melissa Mikesell, "Primer on Self Induced Abortion," SIA Legal Team, www.google.com/url?q=www.law.berkeley.edu/wp-content /uploads/2016/01/Primer-on-Self-Induced-Abortions.pdf&sa =D&ust=1611199626796000&usg=AOvVaw13urnMQdQjG fzwoww14rGB, accessed Jan. 19, 2021.

198   **available from a health care provider:** Megan K. Donovan, "Self-Managed Medication Abortion: Expanding the Available Options for U.S. Abortion Care," *Guttmacher Policy Review* 21 (Oct. 2018); *Safe Abortion: Technical and Policy Guidance for Health Systems*, World Health Organization, Department of Reproductive Health and Research (2012), www.who.int/reproductivehealth /publications/unsafe_abortion/9789241548434/en.

198   **primary care providers in some states:** "The Plan C Guide to Getting Abortion Pills." Chloe Murtagh et al., "Exploring the Feasibility of Obtaining Mifepristone and Misoprostol from the Internet," *Contraception* 97 (2018): 287–291.

198   **whether insurance coverage is available:** "The Plan C Guide to Getting Abortion Pills." See also "Where Can I Get the Abortion Pill & How Much Will It Cost?," Planned Parenthood, www.plannedparenthood.org/learn/abortion/the-abortion-pill /how-do-i-get-the-abortion-pill, accessed Jan. 20, 2021.

198   **delivered from a reliable pharmacy in India:** Jessica Lussenhop, "The Women Looking Outside the Law for Abortions," *BBC News*, Oct. 27, 2018.

199   **and a strong safety record:** Abigail R. A. Aiken et al., "Self Reported Outcomes and Adverse Events After Medical Abortion Through Online Telemedicine: Population Based Study in the Republic of Ireland and Northern Ireland," *BMJ* 357 (April 27, 2012).

199   **"misbranded and unapproved new drugs.":** FDA Warning Letter to Aid Access, March 8, 2019.

199   **and obtain help when necessary:** "Over-the-Counter Medication Abortion," Advancing New Standards in Reproductive Health,

www.ansirh.org/research/over-counter-medication-abortion, accessed
Jan. 19, 2021.

CHAPTER 13

201   **guide us toward reproductive freedom now:** In the mid-1980s
      Kitty wrote *A Reproductive Rights Agenda for the 1990's,* much of
      which remains unfinished business. We have updated and expanded
      those ideas as they align with our priorities on today's Top Ten list
      and added many more. Kathryn Kolbert, "Developing a Reproduc-
      tive Rights Agenda for the 1990's," in *Reproductive Laws for the
      1990's, a Briefing Handbook,* ed. Nadine Taub and Sherrill Cohen
      (Clifton, NJ: Humana, 1988). See also Kathryn Kolbert, "Develop-
      ing a Reproductive Rights Agenda for the 1990's," in *From Abor-
      tion to Reproductive Freedom: Transforming a Movement,* ed. Marlene
      Gerber Fried (Boston: South End, 1990).

202   **on average nearly $5,000 a year:** Bureau of Labor Statistics, Con-
      sumer Expenditures—2019, www.bls.gov/news.release/cesan.nr0
      .htm.

202   **significant factor in personal bankruptcy filings:** Lorie Konish,
      "This Is the Real Reason Most Americans File for Bankruptcy,"
      CNBC, Feb. 11, 2019.

202   **physical and mental health is dramatic and unfair:** Jennifer Tol-
      bert, Kendal Orgera, and Anthony Damico, "Key Facts About the
      Uninsured Population," Kaiser Family Foundation Issue Brief,
      Nov. 6, 2020, www.kff.org/uninsured/issue-brief/key-facts-about
      -the-uninsured-population.

202   **remains among the most inequitable worldwide:** National Re-
      search Council, Institute of Medicine, S. H. Woolf, and L. Aron,
      eds., *U.S. Health in International Perspective: Shorter Lives, Poorer
      Health* (Washington, DC: National Academies Press, 2013).

203   **but significantly reduce costs:** Samantha Artiga, Kendal Orgera,
      and Olivia Pham, "Disparities in Health and Health Care: Five
      Key Questions and Answers," Kaiser Family Foundation,
      March 4, 2020, www.kff.org/racial-equity-and-health-policy/issue
      -brief/disparities-in-health-and-health-care-five-key-questions
      -and-answers.

203   **offered a comprehensive alternative plan:** In 2012 in National
      Federation of Independent Business v. Sebelius, 567 U.S. 519
      (2012), the Supreme Court upheld the ACA. Justice Roberts

provided the saving vote when he found that Congress's taxing authority gave it the power to enact the law. In November 2020, after Justice Barrett joined the Court, the Court heard arguments in California v. Texas (Docket No. 19-840) which raised questions about the constitutionality of the individual mandate and the fate of the entire ACA should the mandate fall. Although many feared that the new majority would invalidate the entire law, skepticism expressed by both Chief Justice Roberts and Justice Kavanaugh may make that less likely when the Court releases its decision in 2021. Nina Totenberg, "Supreme Court Appears Likely to Uphold Obamacare," National Public Radio, Nov. 10, 2020.

203   **like that available in most developed countries:** There are many different proposals for universal health care, but most would be financed with tax dollars and would replace the current Medicare system and private health insurance. Sarah Kliff, "Bernie Sanders's Medicare-for-All Plan, Explained," *Vox*, April 10, 2019.

204   **improve economic equity:** President Joseph R. Biden, "Executive Order on Establishment of the White House Gender Policy Council," March 08, 2021, https://www.whitehouse.gov/briefing-room /presidential-actions/2021/03/08/executive-order-on-establish ment-of-the-white-house-gender-policy-council/.

204   **have not yet adopted Medicaid expansion:** MaryBeth Musumeci, "Medicaid Provisions in the American Rescue Plan Act," *Kaiser Health News*, March 18, 2021, https://www.kff.org/ medicaid /issue-brief/medicaid-provisions-in-the-american-rescue-plan-act/.

204   **available without out-of-pocket costs:** There is bipartisan support for proposals that would allow the federal government to negotiate the price of drugs provided by Medicare, which would drive down costs in other plans, but to date the measure has stalled. Juliette Cubanski, et al., "What's the Latest on Medicare Drug Price Negotiations?," Kaiser Family Foundation Issue Brief, Oct. 17, 2019, www.kff.org/medicare/issue-brief/whats-the-latest-on-medicare -drug-price-negotiations.

205   **unacceptably high rates of maternal mortality:** Centers for Disease Control and Prevention, "Infographic: Racial/Ethnic Disparities in Pregnancy-Related Deaths—United States, 2007–2016," Feb. 4, 2020, www.cdc.gov/reproductivehealth/maternal-mortality /disparities-pregnancy-related-deaths/infographic.html; Cristina Novoa and Jamila Taylor, "Exploring African Americans' High Maternal and Infant Death Rates," Center for American Progress, Feb. 1, 2018, www.americanprogress.org/issues/early-childhood

/reports/2018/02/01/445576/exploring-african-americans-high
-maternal-infant-death-rates.

205 **would die while giving birth to her daughter:** Tanya A. Christian,
"Amber Isaac Died at NY Hospital After Complaining About Care,"
Essence, April 29, 2020; Tanya A. Christian, "Sha-Asia Washington
Death During Childbirth Triggers Calls," *Essence*, July 10, 2020.

205 **a figure over double the nationwide disparity:** Office of the
Mayor, "De Blasio Administration Launches Comprehensive Plan
to Reduce Maternal Deaths," City of New York, July 20, 2018,
www1.nyc.gov/office-of-the-mayor/news/365-18/de-blasio
-administration-launches-comprehensive-plan-reduce-maternal
-deaths-life-threatening; see also Centers for Disease Control and
Prevention, "Infographic"; Andreea A. Creanga et al., "Pregnancy-
Related Mortality in the United States, 2011–2013," *Obstetrics and
Gynecology* 130, no. 2 (Aug. 2017): 366–373.

205 **educational attainment of their mothers:** Jamila Taylor, et al.,
"Eliminating Racial Disparities in Maternal and Infant Mortality: A
Comprehensive Policy Blueprint," Center for American Progress, May
2, 2019, www.americanprogress.org/issues/women/reports/2019/05
/02/469186/eliminating-racial-disparities-maternal-infant-mortality.

205 **white women who never finished high school.":** Danielle M. Ely
and Anne K. Driscoll, *Infant Mortality in the United States, 2018:
National Vital Statistics Reports*, vol. 69, no. 7, Centers for Disease
Control and Prevention, July 16, 2020, www.cdc.gov/nchs/data
/nvsr/nvsr69/NVSR-69-7-508.pdf; Imari Z. Smith, et al., "Fight-
ing at Birth: Eradicating the Black-White Infant Mortality Gap,"
Duke University's Samuel DuBois Cook Center on Social Equity
and Insight Center for Community Economic Development,
March 2018, socialequity.duke.edu/wp-content/uploads/2019/12
/Eradicating-Black-Infant-Mortality-March-2018.pdf.

206 **trigger a chain of negative health events:** "These stressors and the
long-term psychological toll of racism puts African American
women at higher risk for a range of medical conditions that threaten
their lives and their infants' lives, including preeclampsia (pregnancy-
related high blood pressure), eclampsia (a complication of preeclampsia characterized by seizures), embolisms (blood vessel
obstructions), and mental health conditions." Jamila Taylor et al.,
"Eliminating Racial Disparities in Maternal and Infant Mortality."

206 **bias and disrespect from health care providers:** Dána-Ain Davis,
Reproductive Injustice: Racism, Pregnancy and Premature Birth (New
York: New York University Press, 2019).

206 **too often to disastrous effect:** Allyson Chiu, "Beyoncé, Serena Williams Open Up About Potentially Fatal Childbirths, a Problem Especially for Black Mothers," *Washington Post*, Aug. 7, 2018; Rob Haskell, "Serena Williams on Motherhood, Marriage, and Making Her Comeback," *Vogue*, Jan. 10, 2018.

206 **to develop avenues for improvements:** Maternal Mortality Review Committees, State Laws and Policies, Guttmacher Institute, Jan. 1, 2021, www.guttmacher.org/state-policy/explore/maternal-mortality-review-committees.

206 **reduce bias and differential treatment:** Jamila Taylor et al., "Eliminating Racial Disparities in Maternal and Infant Mortality."

206 **Medicaid programs to cover these costs:** Taylor Platt and Neva Kaye, "Four State Strategies to Employ Doulas to Improve Maternal Health and Birth Outcomes in Medicaid," National Academy for State Health Policy, July 13, 2020, www.nashp.org/four-state-strategies-to-employ-doulas-to-improve-maternal-health-and-birth-outcomes-in-medicaid/#toggle-id-1.

206 **improve the health of pregnant women:** Maternity Care Coalition, maternitycarecoalition.org.

207 **one-quarter occur more than six weeks postpartum:** N. L. Davis, A. N. Smoots, and D. A. Goodman, "Pregnancy-Related Deaths: Data from 14 U.S. Maternal Mortality Review Committees, 2008–2017," Centers for Disease Control and Prevention, 2019, www.cdc.gov/reproductivehealth/maternal-mortality/erase-mm/MMR-Data-Brief_2019-h.pdf.

207 **remain uninsured during a medically vulnerable time**: Jamila Taylor, "Promoting Better Maternal Health Outcomes by Closing the Medicaid Postpartum Coverage Gap," The Century Foundation, Nov. 16, 2020, tcf.org/content/report/promoting-better-maternal-health-outcomes-closing-medicaid-postpartum-coverage-gap/?agreed=1. See also Usha Ranji, Ivette Gomez, and Alina Salganicoff, "Expanding Postpartum Medicaid Coverage," Kaiser Family Foundation, Dec. 21, 2020.

207 **enroll women up to a year postpartum:** Usha Ranji, Alina Salganicoff, and Ivette Gomez, "Postpartum Coverage Extension in the American Rescue Plan Act of 2021," Kaiser Health News, March 18, 2021, https://www.kff.org/policy-watch/postpartum-coverage-extension-in-the-american-rescue-plan-act-of-2021/.

207 **Black Maternal Health Momnibus Act:** Black Maternal Health Caucus, Black Maternal Health Momnibus Act of 2021, accessed

March 1, 2021, https://underwood.house.gov/sites/underwood
.house.gov/files/Black%20Maternal%20Health%20Momnibus
%20Act%201-Pager%20%281%29.pdf.

208 **everywhere from Afghanistan to Zambia:** The Oral Contraceptives (OCs) Over-the-Counter (OTC) Working Group, Global
Oral Contraception Availability, ocsotc.org/world-map.

208 **health care through the Indian Health Services:** *Free the Pill: Native American Women and the Need for "Over the Counter" Access to
Birth Control Pills!,* Native American Community Board, June
2019, www.nativeshop.org/images/pdf/free-the-pill.pdf.

208 **in the process of seeking FDA approval:** See cadenceotc.com and
freethepill.org.

208 **reflecting a decline in pregnancy overall:** Elizabeth Nash and
Joerg Dreweke, "The U.S. Abortion Rate Continues to Drop: Once
Again, State Abortion Restrictions Are Not the Main Driver," *Gutt-
macher Policy Review* 22 (2019).

208 **implants placed under the skin, and IUDs:** "Contraceptive Pearl:
LARC for Teens," Reproductive Health Access Project, June 4,
2016, www.reproductiveaccess.org/resource/larc-for-teens.

208 **assumptions about race, age, and gender identity:** Marsha Kaitz et
al., "Long-Acting Reversible Contraception: A Route to Reproductive
Justice or Injustice," *Infant Mental Health Journal* 40, no. 5 (2019):
673–689; "Long-Acting Reversible Contraception Statement of Principles," Sister Song and National Women's Health Project, www.nwhn
.org/wp-content/uploads/2017/02/LARCStatementofPrinciples.pdf.

209 **to cover both male and female sterilization:** Insurance Coverage
of Contraceptives, State Laws and Policies, Guttmacher Institute,
Dec. 1, 2020, www.guttmacher.org/state-policy/explore/insurance
-coverage-contraceptives.

209 **enabling pharmacists to prescribe contraceptives:** For a list of
companies in the US and globally that issue prescriptions for the pill
online without requiring an in-person doctor visit, see "Who Prescribes the Pill Online?," Free the Pill, freethepill.org/online-pill
-prescribing-resources. See also "Pharmacist-Prescribed Contraceptives," State Laws and Policies, Guttmacher Institute, Dec. 7, 2020,
www.guttmacher.org/state-policy/explore/pharmacist-prescribed
-contraceptives.

210 **to help women become pregnant:** Government policies also have
failed to assist people to form families via foster care, adoption, or
surrogacy, but we do not address these complex topics here.

210 **difficulty getting or staying pregnant:** Centers for Disease Control and Prevention, "FastStats—Infertility," www.cdc.gov/nchs/fastats/infertility.htm, accessed March 1, 2021.

210 **not being able to stay pregnant:** "Infertility," *A to Z Health Topics*, Office of Women's Health, US Department of Health and Human Services, www.womenshealth.gov/a-z-topics/infertility.

210 **or requires deep debt:** Nina Bahadur, "The Cost of Infertility: How Real People Pay for IVF," *Self*, Jan. 8, 2018.

210 **two more require insurers to offer coverage:** National Council of State Legislatures, "State Laws Related to Insurance Coverage for Infertility Treatment," June 12, 2019, www.ncsl.org/research/health/insurance-coverage-for-infertility-laws.aspx.

210 **in which the man is infertile:** Erin Bried, "Could You Be Denied IVF?," *Self*, May 1, 2015.

210 **lead to infertility or miscarriages:** Elizabeth Hoover, "Environmental Reproductive Justice: Intersections in an American Indian Community Impacted by Environmental Contamination," *Environmental Sociology* 4, no. 2 (2017).

211 **relationships throughout their lifetimes:** Leslie Kantor and Nicole Levitz, "Parents' Views on Sex Education in Schools: How Much Do Democrats and Republicans Agree?," *PLOS One* 12, no. 7 (2017).

211 **must be medically, factually, or technically accurate:** National Conference of State Legislatures, "State Policies on Sex Education in the Schools," Oct. 2020, www.ncsl.org/Default.aspx?TabId=17077&language=en-US.

211 **dating violence, and child exploitation:** Sophia Naide, "State Lawmakers Say Yes to Consent Education," Policy Analysis, Guttmacher Institute, Jan. 2020, www.guttmacher.org/article/2020/01/state-lawmakers-say-yes-consent-education.

211 **that leads to negative experiences:** Eva S. Goldfarb and Lisa D. Lieberman, "Three Decades of Research: The Case for Comprehensive Sex Education," *Journal of Adolescent Health* 68, no. 1 (2021): 13–27.

212 **model curricula for comprehensive sex ed:** *Community Action Toolkit: A Guide to Advancing Sex Education in Your Community*, SIECUS, Sept. 2018, siecus.org/wp-content/uploads/2018/09/CAT-Sept-2018-Final.pdf; *Rights, Respect, Responsibility: A K–12 Sex Education Curriculum*, Advocates for Youth, Dec. 18, 2018, www.advocatesforyouth.org/resources/health-information/rights-respect-responsibility-a-k-12-sex-education-curriculum.

212 **a year's tuition at a public college:** Claire Zillman, "Childcare Costs More Than College Tuition in 28 U.S. States," *Fortune*, Oct. 22, 2018.

212   **30 percent or more of their budget:** Douglas Rice et al., *Child Care and Housing: Big Expenses with Too Little Help Available*, Center on Budget and Policy Priorities and CLASP, 2019, www.cbpp .org/research/housing/child-care-and-housing-big-expenses-with -too-little-help-available.

213   **a "shecession," which they can ill afford:** Isaac Chotiner, "Why the Pandemic Is Forcing Women out of the Workforce," *New Yorker*, Oct. 23, 2020; Alisha Haridasani Gupta, "Why Some Women Call This Recession a 'Shecession,'" *New York Times*, May 9, 2020.

213   **Childcare assistance for families:** Anna North, "Biden's Covid-19 Stimulus Plan Includes $40 Billion for Child Care," *VOX* (Jan. 20, 2021).

213   **should be made permanent:** Chuck Marr et al. "American Rescue Plan Act Includes Critical Expansions of Child Tax Credit and EITC," Center for Budget and Policy Priorities, March 12, 2021, https://www.cbpp.org/research/federal-tax/american-rescue-plan -act-includes-critical-expansions-of-child-tax-credit-and.

213   **economic disparities and family poverty:** Pre-Kindergarten Task Force, *The Current State of Scientific Knowledge on Pre-Kindergarten Effects*, The Brookings Institution, 2017, www.brookings.edu/wp -content/uploads/2017/04/duke_prekstudy_final_4-4-17_hires.pdf.

214   **and we got better at messaging.":** Jennifer Oldham, "How Colorado Got Even Libertarians to Support Paid Family Leave: Inside a Years Long Persuasion Campaign," *Slate*, Dec. 2, 2020.

215   **a medical condition not applicable to (cisgender) men:** In Geduldig v. Aiello, 417 U.S. 484 (1974), the Supreme Court ruled that the exclusion of medical benefits for pregnant women under California's disability insurance program was not sex discrimination and did not violate the Equal Protection Clause. Eighteen months later, in General Electric v. Gilbert, 429 US 125 (1976), the Court ruled that the exclusion of pregnancy-related disabilities from GE's disability plan did not violate Title VII of the Civil Rights Act. See also Gillian Thomas, *Because of Sex: One Law, Ten Cases, and Fifty Years That Changed American Women's Lives at Work* (New York: St. Martin's Press, 2016).

215   **in order to maintain a healthy pregnancy:** Dina Bakst, "Pregnant, and Pushed out of a Job," *New York Times*, Jan. 30, 2012; Joanna L. Grossman and Gillian Thomas, "Making Sure Pregnancy Works: Accommodation Claims After *Young v. United Parcel Service, Inc.*," *Harvard Law & Policy Review* 14 (2020): 319.

215 **the Pregnant Workers Fairness Act:** H.R. 1065—Pregnant Workers Fairness Act, 117th Congress (2021–2022).

215 **inspiring crucial federal level changes:** See maps of state-level by the ACLU and A Better Balance: www.aclu.org/issues/deliver ing-fairness-ending-discrimination-against-pregnant-women-and -moms-work; www.abetterbalance.org/resources/pregnant-worker-fair ness-legislative-successes.

216 **United States, according to one study:** RAINN (Rape, Abuse & Incest National Network), rainn.org/statistics accessed Jan. 21, 2021. Native Americans are more likely to experience a rape or sexual assault compared to all races. Sarah Deer, *The Beginning and End of Rape: Confronting Sexual Violence in Native America* (Minneapolis: University of Minnesota Press, 2015). Similarly Black women are at higher risk of sexual violence. As many as six in ten Black women report being subjected to coercive sexual contact by age eighteen. *Black Women and Sexual Assault,* The National Center on Violence Against Women in the Black Community, Oct. 2018, ujimacommunity.org/wp-content/uploads/2018/12/Ujima-Womens -Violence-Stats-v7.4-1.pdf.

216 **which can be a flashpoint:** Planned Parenthood v. Casey, 505 U.S. at 888-94 (1992).

217 **two small Pacific Island nations, Palau and Tonga:** Christina Morales Hansen, "It's Time for the United States to Ratify CEDAW," National Women's Law Center, Oct. 16, 2013, nwlc .org/blog/it%E2%80%99s-time-united-states-ratify-cedaw.

217 **embodies the principle of gender equality:** UN General Assembly, *Convention on the Elimination of All Forms of Discrimination Against Women*, Dec. 18, 1979, United Nations, Treaty Series, vol. 1249, p. 13, www.refworld.org/docid/3ae6b3970.html.

217 **live up to their duties under the Convention:** Committee on the Elimination of Discrimination Against Women, United Nations Office of the High Commissioner, www.ohchr.org/EN/HRBodies /CEDAW/pages/cedawindex.aspx.

217 **on contraception in the Philippines:** Report of the Inquiry Concerning Canada Women, Committee on the Elimination of Discrimination Against Women, CEDAW/C/OP.8/CAN/1, March 30, 2015, tbinternet.ohchr.org/Treaties/CEDAW/Shared%20 Documents/CAN/CEDAW_C_OP-8_CAN_1_7643_E.pdf; *Concluding Observations on the Combined Seventh and Eighth Periodic Reports of the Philippines*, UN Committee on the Elimination of Discrimination Against Women (64th sess.: 2016: Geneva).

217   **organized Cities for CEDAW initiative:** Cities for CEDAW, Women's International Network, citiesforcedaw.org.

218   **recruitment, employment, contracting, and city services:** Los Angeles Mayor Eric Garcetti, Executive Directive No. 11, Aug. 26, 2015, www.lamayor.org/sites/g/files/wph446/f/page/file/ED_11 .pdf?1440645063. See Goal 5—Gender equality, sdgdata.lamayor .org/5.

CHAPTER 14

220   **even if not entirely legal:** Yamila Azize-Vargas and Luis A. Avilés, "Abortion in Puerto Rico: The Limits of Colonial Legality," *Reproductive Health Matters* 5, no. 9 (1997): 56–65; Leslie J. Reagan, "Crossing the Border for Abortions: California Activists, Mexican Clinics, and the Creation of a Feminist Health Agency in the 1960s," *Feminist Studies* 26, no. 2 (2000): 323–348.

221   **four hundred fifty thousand people for safe abortions:** Doris A. Dirks and Patricia Relf, *To Offer Compassion: A History of the Clergy Consultation Service on Abortion* (Madison: University of Wisconsin Press, 2017); Edward B. Fiske, "Clergymen Offer Abortion Advice: 21 Ministers and Rabbis Form New Group Will Propose Alternatives," *New York Times*, May 22, 1967.

223   **increased significantly over the course of a decade:** "2019 Violence and Disruption Statistics," National Abortion Federation, July 30, 2020, 5aa1b2xfmfh2e2mk03kk8rsx-wpengine.netdna-ssl .com/wp-content/uploads/NAF-2019-Violence-and-Disruption -Stats-Final.pdf; Jessica Grose, "The New Abortion Rights Advocates Are on TikTok," *New York Times*, Dec. 10, 2020.

223   **helped catapult President Biden to victory:** Taylor Crumpton, "Perspective: Black Women Saved the Democrats. Don't Make Us Do It Again," *Washington Post*, Nov. 7, 2020.

224   **recruit progressive candidates, like Vote Run Lead:** Kitty serves on the board of directors of Vote Run Lead.

226   **de-escalation training, with more to come:** Ian Prasad Philbrick and Sanam Yar, "What Has Changed Since George Floyd," *New York Times,* Aug. 3, 2020.

226   **sexually harass, abuse, or assault others:** Audrey Carlsen et al., "#MeToo Brought Down 201 Powerful Men. Nearly Half of Their Replacements Are Women," *New York Times*, Oct. 29, 2018.

226   **building on decades of activism.:** "From Farm Fields to the C-Suite: Building Our Power," TIME'S UP Foundation, timesupfoundation

.org/work/power/from-farm-fields-to-the-c-suite-building-our
-power, accessed Jan. 1, 2021; TIME'S UP Legal Defense Fund,
National Women's Law Center, nwlc.org/times-up-legal-defense-
fund, accessed Jan. 1, 2021.

226 **in Julie's case almost two years earlier:** Marge Berere and Lesley
Hoggart, "Progress Toward Decriminalization of Abortion and
Universal Access to Safe Abortions: National Trends and Strate-
gies," *Health and Human Rights* 21, no. 2 (2019): 79–83.

227 **no less than the human right to abortion:** Megan Specia, "How
Savita Halappanavar's Death Spurred Ireland's Abortion Rights
Campaign," *New York Times*, May 27, 2018.

227 **most recently in Poland and Argentina:** José Miguel Vivanco,
"What Ireland's Abortion Referendum Means for Latin America,"
Human Rights Watch, May 31, 2018, www.hrw.org/news/2018
/05/31/what-irelands-abortion-referendum-means-latin-america.

227 **Catholic Church's enormous influence in Poland:** "Poland
Abortion Ruling: Protesters Disrupt Church Services," *BBC News*,
Oct. 24, 2020.

227 **again took to the streets:** Isabella Kwai, Monika Pronczuk, and
Anatol Magdziarz, "Near-Total Abortion Ban Takes Effect in Poland, and Thousands Protest," *New York Times*, Jan. 27, 2021.

228 **to curb gender-based violence:** Natalie Alcoba and Charis Mc-
Gowan, "#Niunamenos Five Years On: Latin America as Deadly as
Ever for Women, Say Activists," *Guardian*, June 4, 2020.

228 **categories of hate crimes against women:** Uki Goñi, "Argentina's
Women Joined Across South America in Marches Against Violence," *Guardian*, Oct. 20, 2016.

228 **that were widespread across the country:** Roberto Valent, "Tack-
ling Femicide in Argentina: A UN Resident Coordinator Blog,"
UN News, Jan. 17, 2020, news.un.org/en/story/2020/01/1055452.

228 **Human Rights Secretariat began to compile statistics:** Hinde
Pomeraniec, "How Argentina Rose Up Against the Murder of
Women," *Guardian*, June 8, 2015.

228 **opposition from the politically powerful Catholic Church:** *A
Case for Legal Abortion: The Human Cost of Barriers to Sexual and
Reproductive Rights in Argentina*, Human Rights Watch, 2020,
www.hrw.org/report/2020/08/31/case-legal-abortion/human
-cost-barriers-sexual-and-reproductive-rights-argentina.

228 **disappeared during the country's earlier dictatorship:** Lucía
Cholakian Herrera, "Decades After Argentina's Dictatorship, the

Abuelas Continue Reuniting Families," *Latino USA*, March 24, 2020, www.latinousa.org/2020/03/24/abuelascontinuereuniting.

228 **the voters might not support a change:** Valeria Perasso, "The Women Protesting in the Argentina Abortion Debate," *BBC News*, Aug. 8, 2018.

229 **for those legal rights and more, "Let it be law.":** Daniel Politi and Ernesto Londoño, "Argentina Legalizes Abortion, a Milestone in a Conservative Region," *New York Times*, Dec. 30, 2020.

229 **coming together for powerful mass demonstrations:** Amy Booth, "Women's Strike in Argentina: 'If Our Lives Are Worthless, Produce Without Us,'" *Toward Freedom*, March 10, 2020, towardfreedom.org/author/amy-booth.

229 **for students to "call B.S.":** "Florida Student Emma González to Lawmakers and Gun Advocates: 'We Call BS,'" CNN, Feb. 17, 2018.

229 **passage of laws in several states:** Lois Beckett, "From the March for Our Lives to a Background Check Bill, Activists Have Seen Success in Preventative Measures Since the Shooting," *Guardian*, Feb. 14, 2019.

INDEX

A, B, and C v. Ireland (ABC), 157–163
*Abortion and the Constitution:
   Reversing Roe v. Wade Through
   the Courts*, 63
*Abortion and the Law: An Irish
   Perspective* (Bacik), 155–156
Abortion Control Act (1982), 41–42
abortion ship, 149
Abortion Support Network, 221
"Abortionists' Jokebook, The," 105
abortions
   bans on, 116–117
   challenges to laws regarding, 1–2
   costs for, 71
   erroneous claims of risks of, 65
   factors impacting decisions
      regarding, 13–14
   forced, 16
   illegal, 21–24, 72
   liberalization of laws regarding, 24–25
   medication, 18, 113–115, 188–189,
      196, 197, 198–199, 222
   narrowing justifications for,
      126–127
   rates of, 6
   rights to, 2, 4, 6–19
   self-managed, 196, 197, 198–199, 222
   training for, 109–110
   See also individual cases regarding
Abrams, Stacey, 185, 224

abstinence-only or abstinence-based
   sex education programs, 97–98
abusive relationships, 15–16, 44
ACLU
   *Planned Parenthood v. Casey
      (Casey)* and, 50
   Reproductive Freedom Project of,
      1–2, 42, 55–56, 116
Adams, Alma, 207
Advocates for Youth, 212
Affordable Care Act (ACA)
   attacks on, 68
   attempts to repeal, 203
   contraception and, 83, 209
   EACH Woman Act and, 81
   expansion of, 7
   impact of, 64, 68, 184
   maternal and infant care and, 204,
      207
   Roberts on, 145
   Trump administration and, 173
Aid Access, 198–199
Alaskan natives, 80
Alito, Samuel, 46, 66, 122, 136–137, 144
All Families Healthcare, 112–113
All* Above All, 81, 191
American Academy of Pediatrics, 96
American College of Obstetrics and
   Gynecologists (ACOG), 65, 96,
      122, 128, 132

American Law Institute (ALI), 24
American Medical Association (AMA), 96, 132
American Psychological Association, 65
American Public Health Association, 96
American Rescue Plan, 195, 204, 207, 216
Americans United for Life, 63, 64, 117
Anderson, Bebe, 76–77
Andrus, Cecil D., 118
anthrax poisoning, threats of, 104
anti-abortion groups
  beliefs espoused by, 14
  ideology of, 107–108
  increase in picketing from, 222–223
  strategy of, 63–67
  See also clinics: domestic terrorism against
anti-bias training, 206
anti-discrimination laws, 143
anti-noise restrictions, 108
anti-Semitism, 107–108, 118–119
Argentina, women's rights movement in, 227–229
Argentinian Mothers and Grandmothers of the Plaza de Mayo, 228
Armstrong v. Mazurek, 112
Army of God, 27, 104
Arriola, Anita, 116, 117
artificial insemination, 209–210
Asetoyer, Charon, 190
Asian American and Pacific Islanders (AAPI), 13, 90, 126
assassinations of providers and clinic staff, 103–104
Attorney General v. X, 151–152
Avery, Samantha, 113

"Baby Lives Matter," 107
Bacik, Ivana, 155–156
Baker, Charlie, 187
ballot initiatives, 186

bankruptcy filings, medical bills and, 202
Barrett, Amy Coney, 10, 61, 66, 129, 130, 131, 137–139, 140–143, 144–145
Barrett, James H., 103
Batchelor, Michelle, 101–102
Beal v. Doe, 73
Behan, Niall, 156
Beijing Declaration and Platform for Action, 180
benefits, family-friendly, 213–214
Benshoof, Janet, 42, 55–56, 112, 116–117, 124
Better Balance, A, 214, 215
Beyoncé, 206
biased counseling, 45
Biden, Joe, and administration of, 40, 81, 84, 194–195, 203, 213, 223
birth control pill, 17, 207–208
Bixby Global Center for Reproductive Health (UCSF), 110
Black Lives Matter (BLM), 172, 202, 225–226
Black Maternal Health Momnibus Act, 207
Black Voters Matter, 224
Black women
  clinic violence and, 101–102
  maternal mortality and, 205–206
  Medicaid and, 72
  outsized impact of restrictions on, 13
  penalizing of, 11
  prosecution of, 198
  teen pregnancy rate and, 90
Blackmun, Harry, 12–13, 15, 27–29, 36, 37, 50–51, 59–61, 104
bodily integrity, protection of, 15–16
Bold Futures, 91–92
Booker, Cory, 207
Bostock v. Clayton County, 144
Boxer, Barbara, 39
Bray v. Alexandria Women's Health Clinic, 105

Brennan, William J., Jr., 9–10, 28
Breyer, Stephen G., 131, 132–133,
    136, 144
Britell, Maureen, 78–79, 124
Britton, John Bayard, 103, 107
Brown, Edmund G., Jr., 52
Brown, LaTosha, 185, 224
Brown, Liz, 126
"buffer zone" laws, 108
Buffet, Warren and Susan, 56
Burger, Warren E., 27, 28
Burwell v. Hobby Lobby Stores, 143
Bush, George H. W., 38, 46
Bush, George W., 46, 106–107, 122
Butler, Helen, 185

Cahill, Susan, 112–113
Candie's Foundation, 91
Cano, Mary, 32
Carhart, LeRoy, 77, 122
Carroll, Lewis, 168
Carter, Jimmy, 217
Casey. See Planned Parenthood v.
    Casey (Casey)
Casey, Robert P., Sr., 42, 55
Catholic Church, 43, 110, 147–148,
    227, 228
Cavallo, Mercedes, 159
census (2010), 66
Center for Bio-Ethical Reform, 65
Center for Constitutional Rights, 73
Center for Medical Progress, 65, 104
Center for Reproductive Rights, 1–2,
    27, 56
Center on Budget and Policy Priorities,
    212
child care, affordable, 212–213
Child Custody Protection Act, 89–90
childbearing, forced, 72–73
childbirth mortality and morbidity
    rates, 15
Children's Health Insurance Program
    (CHIP), 71
Cities for CEDAW initiative, 217–218

"Cities of Refuge," 102
Civil Rights Act, 176
Clergy Consultation Service on
    Abortion, 24, 221
clinics
    domestic terrorism against,
        100–101, 103–104
    extreme right and, 107
    increase in picketing at, 222–223
    Operation Rescue and, 102–103
    protections for, 105–107
    TRAP laws and, 131–132
Clinton, Bill, 52, 100, 106, 121, 171,
    194
Clinton, Hillary, 133, 180
Coffee, Linda, 20
Collins, Susan, 138
Community Legal Services, 215–216
compelling state interest, 29, 64, 178
Comprehensive Child Development
    Act, 213
Concerned Women of America, 14
Constitution, US
    drafting of, 153
    Gender Equity Amendment to, 169,
        174–182
    human rights model and, 180–181
    as living document, 139–140
    See also individual amendments
Constitutional Convention, 140
Contemplation of Justice, 1
contraception
    ACA and, 83, 209
    advances in, 18
    availability of, 207–209
    Barrett on, 140–141, 143
    emergency, 17
    health insurance and, 173
    legalization of in Ireland, 147
    limiting access to, 143
    right to, 36
    right to privacy and, 26
    teen pregnancy rate and, 90
contraceptive implants, 90, 208–209

contraceptive injections, 17, 90, 208–209

Convention on the Elimination of All Forms of Discrimination Against Women (CEDAW), 150, 180, 217–218

Copelon, Rhonda, 73–74, 145

Coyle, Marcia, 52

Crenshaw, Kimberlé, 181

Crepps, Janet, 88

criminal charges, need for restrictions against, 195–198

crisis pregnancy centers, 97

Cruz, Ted, 139

Cullors, Patrisse, 172

D v. Ireland, 159

D&E abortion, 123, 142

Davis, Wendy, 185

DC March for Our Lives, 229

DC statehood, 193

deaths
　caused by illegal abortions, 22–23
　infant mortality, 7, 91, 205–207
　maternal mortality, 164–166, 205, 206, 226–227, 229

Defense of Marriage Act, 171

Democratic Party, 66, 81, 84

Department of Health and Human Services, 195, 204

Department of Homeland Security, 195

Depo-Provera, 17, 90, 208–209

dilation and extraction (D&X), 120

disabled women, forced sterilization of, 16

doctor-only provisions, 111–112, 113, 188

Doe v. Bolton (*Doe*), 26–27, 31–34

domestic terrorism, clinics and, 100–101, 103–104

domestic violence, 15–16, 44, 215–216, 228

Douglas, William O., 28

doulas, 206

Duckworth, Tammy, 81

Due Process Clause, 26, 54

Duford, Jerushah, 7–8

Duke, David, 118, 119

Duplantier, Adrian G., 118–119

Eagle Forum, 175

education
　pre-K, 212–213
　sexuality, 96–98, 211–212

Edwards, Edwin, 118

Eisenstadt v. Baird, 26

electoral politics, 184–186, 192–194, 223–224

Elizabeth Blackwell Health Center (Philadelphia), 108

England, access to abortion in, 25

Equal Access to Abortion Coverage in Health Insurance Act (EACH Woman Act), 81, 193, 194

Equal Employment Opportunity Commission, 39

Equal Pay Act, 176

Equal Protection Clause, 12–13, 36, 75, 177

Equal Rights Amendment (ERA), 175–176

equity versus equality, 177–178

eugenics, 107, 127

European Convention on Human Rights, 153, 154, 164

European Court of Human Rights (ECHR), 2, 153, 155–157, 158–163, 226

Evans, Roger, 55

Facebook, 225

Fair Fight, 224

Family and Medical Leave Act, 213

family/domestic violence, 15–16, 44, 215–216, 228

family-friendly benefits in workplace, 213–214

Farley, Joyce, 87, 89
FBI, clinic security and, 100–101, 106, 107, 195
FDA, 17, 113–115, 195, 199, 208
Federal Employees Health Benefit Plan, 79
Federalist Society, 135
femicide, 228
Feminist Majority, 50
fetal anomalies, 78–79, 121–122, 159, 227
"fetal homicide"/"feticide," 196, 197
fetal life, state's interest in, 30–31, 64
Fifth Amendment, 179
filibuster rule, 192
Fire Thunder, Cecilia, 190
First Amendment, 9
Fischer v. Department of Public Welfare, 75–76
Floyd, George, 172, 229
Food and Drug Administration (FDA), 17, 113–115, 195, 199, 208
Ford, Christine Blasey, 134
Forde, Catherine, 156, 159
Fortas, Abe, 27
Fourteenth Amendment, 12–13, 26, 35, 36, 54, 62, 141, 179
"fourth trimester" services, 206
Franklin, Benjamin, 140
Free Exercise Clause, 9, 143
Freedom of Access to Clinic Entrances Act (FACE), 100, 106, 107, 195
Freedom to Marry campaign, 172
freedoms, essential, 154
Frontiero v. Richardson, 9–10
fundamental rights, 29–30, 178
funding bans, 191

"gag rule," 194–195
Gans, David, 50, 52, 88
Garcetti, Eric, 218
Garland, Merrick, 133–134, 138
Gartner, Eve, 122
Garza, Alicia, 172

gender equity advocates, 171–172
Gender Equity Amendment, 169, 174–182
gender roles
    abortion rights as threat to, 18–19
    Irish Constitution and, 150
    legal system and, 9–10
    religious belief and, 10
George III, 153, 180
Gerhardstein, Al, 121
gerrymandering, 193, 224
Gideon, Sara, 188
Ginsburg, Ruth Bader, 9–10, 12, 35, 122–123, 130–133, 136, 138, 144
Glasser, Ira, 50
Global Gender Equality Constitutional Database, 180
Gomperts, Rebecca, 149, 189, 198–199
González, Emma, 229
Good Samaritan laws, 16
Gorsuch, Neil, 66, 134–135, 136–137, 143–144
Graham, Billy, 7
Greenhouse, Linda, 35
Griswold v. Connecticut, 26, 141
Groh-Wargo, Lauren, 185
Guam, ban on abortions in, 116–117
Guardian of Law, 1
gun control, 229
Gunn, David, 103
Guste, William, 119
Guttmacher Institute, 22–23, 67, 71, 72, 90, 166, 173

Halappanavar, Savita, 164–166, 226–227, 229
Hallford, James Hubert, 21, 26, 28–29
Hames, Margie Pitts, 32
Handmaid's Tale, The, 15
Hanig, Michelle, 77–78
Hansen, Tayler, 107

Harris, Kamala, 194, 223
Harris v. McRae, 74–75, 80
Hartford, Rosa, 86–89, 99, 220
Haskell, Martin, 120–121
Haug, Vance, 77–78
health care for all, 202–204
health insurance, 82–83, 173,
    207–210. *See also* Affordable
    Care Act (ACA)
Heaney, Catherine, 158, 160
heartbeat laws, 127–128, 142
Heller, Simon, 77–78, 112, 122
Heritage Foundation, 40
heteronormativity, 96–97
Higher Heights, 224
Hill, Anita, 38–40, 61, 134
Hispanic women, 13, 72, 90
HIV/AIDS education, 211
Hollos, Sherley, 48
Holmes, Oliver Wendell, 16
homophobia, 4, 107–108, 143
homosexuality, decriminalization of, 181
honor killings, 228
Hope Medical Group for Women
    (Shreveport, Louisiana), 119, 124
Hope Pregnancy Ministries, 113
hospital admitting privileges
    requirement, 132–133
House Committee on Oversight and
    Reform, 97
Huerta, Dolores, 219
Human Life Amendment, 147
human rights/human rights approach,
    154–155, 158, 160–161, 164,
    167, 180–181, 217
husband consent/notice requirement,
    41, 43–44, 45, 46
Huyett, Daniel, III, 43, 44, 45
Hyde, Henry, 70–71, 89, 184
Hyde Amendment, 70–77, 80–81,
    82–83, 191, 193

Idaho, ban on abortions in, 117–118
If/When/How: Lawyering for

Reproductive Justice, 196, 222
immigrants
    forced sterilization of, 16
    undocumented, 173, 203, 220–221
Immigration and Customs
    Enforcement (ICE), 16, 80
In Our Own Voice, 101
in vitro fertilization (IVF), 209–210
Indian Health Service (IHS), 80, 189,
    208
Indigenous women, 13, 80, 189–190,
    217
infant mortality, 7, 91, 205–207
infertility, reducing, 209–211
informed consent, 192
insurrection at US Capitol, 107, 223
intensive care management programs,
    206
Inter-American Commission on
    Human Rights, 180
International Planned Parenthood
    Federation, 148
International Women's Day, 226
intrauterine devices (IUDs), 17, 90,
    208–209
Ireland
    abortion ban in, 146–148, 150–151
    abortion rights advocates in,
        148–149
    challenge to ban in, 152–162
    liberalization of abortion laws in,
        146
    overturning of abortion ban in,
        166–167, 226–227
Irish Constitution, 147, 149–152,
    166–167
Irish Family Planning Association
    (IFPA), 148, 155, 156–157,
    158, 159, 163, 164, 166–167,
    217
Irish Journey, 150–151
Irwin County Detention Center, 16
Isaac, Amber, 205
Ivey, Kay, 128

Jackson, Alphonse, 118
Jackson, Janet, 1
JAMA Network Open, 196
Jane Collective, 20, 23–24, 222
Jimenez, Rosie, 72, 221
Johnson, Douglas, 120
Joint Commission on Accreditation
    of Healthcare Organizations
    (JCAHO), 32, 33
judicial appointments, 65–66,
    128–129, 133–135, 138
judicial bypass procedure, 44, 94,
    95–96, 191
Judiciary Committee, 89
June Medical Services v. Russo, 1–2,
    119, 131, 135–136, 142, 192
Justice Department, 195
Juvenile Law Center, 89

Kagan, Elena, 54, 115, 131, 132–133,
    136, 144
Kaling, Mindy, 116
Kavanaugh, Brett, 61, 66, 134–135,
    136–137, 144, 225
Kennedy, Anthony M., 38, 57–58,
    60–61, 122, 131, 132–133, 134
Kennedy, John, 139
"kick it to the curb" list, 190–192
Kilmer, Michael, 86–87, 89
Klobuchar, Amy, 140
Klundt, Zachary, 112–113
Ku Klux Klan Act, 105, 106
Ku Klux Klan (KKK), 107

Lamm, Richard, 24
Lane, Crystal, 86–88, 89, 95, 99
Lauer, Matt, 226
Lawrence v. Texas, 143, 181
le Clos, Chad, 174
least restrictive means, 29–30
Lee, Barbara, 81
Lee, Michelle, 124–125, 163, 221
Legal Momentum, 97, 158
LGBTQ+ people

abortion rights supporters and,
    11
acceptance of as parents, 14–15
anti-abortion groups and, 14
extreme right and, 107–108
fertility services for, 209–210
marriage equality and, 170–171
*Masterpiece Cakeshop, Ltd.
    v. Colorado Civil Rights
    Commission* and, 143
Obergefell v. Hodges and, 62
teenage sexuality and, 96
Lilly Ledbetter Act, 67
Little, Max, 87, 89
loitering restrictions, 108
long-acting reversible methods of
    contraception (LARC), 208–209
Lorde, Audre, 6
Louisiana, ban on abortions in,
    118–119
Louisiana State University Medical
    Center (LSUMC), 124–125
Lowey, Nita, 39
low-income people
    child care and, 212–213
    EACH Woman Act and, 193
    Hyde Amendment and, 71–73
    infertility and, 209–210
    mortality rate and, 23
    outsized impact of restrictions on,
        13–14, 25
    support for, 220–221
    teen pregnancy and, 91
    two-trip requirement and, 43
    See also Medicaid
Lowney, Shannon, 103
Lyons, Emily, 104

MacKinnon, Catharine, 181
Maher v. Roe, 73
main-in ballot systems, 224
March for Women's Lives, 51–52
Markovsky, Jennifer, 104
marriage equality, 61, 143, 170–171

Marshall, Thurgood, 28, 30–31, 38
Martin, Trayvon, 172
Marzen, Thomas, 63
Masterpiece Cakeshop, Ltd.
  v. Colorado Civil Rights
  Commission, 143
maternal and infant death and
  complications, 205–207
Maternity Care Coalition, 206
McConnell, Mitch, 128, 133–134,
  138, 184
McCorvey, Norma, 20–21
McGee v. The Attorney General, 147
McMahon, James, 120
McRae, Cora, 73–74
Medicaid
  expansion of, 7, 83, 204
  maternal and infant care and,
  206–207
  restriction on funds from, 67
  teen pregnancy and, 95
  See also Hyde Amendment
Medical Students for Choice,
  109–110, 189
Medicare, 71
"Medicare for All," 203
medication abortion, 18, 113–115,
  188–189, 196, 197, 198–199,
  222
mental health, 25, 65
#MeToo movement, 19, 67, 211, 216,
  225, 226
Michelman, Kate, 50
middle-level scrutiny, 178
mid-level providers, 111–113, 188
mifepristone (RU-486), 114
military families, 78–80
Mill, John Stuart, 15
Miller, Andrea, 50
Mink, Patsy, 39
MinuteClinics, 189
misoprostol, 114, 198, 199
MOMobile home-visiting program, 206
MomsRising, 225

Montgomery Bus Boycott, 229
Moral Majority, 66
morning-after pill, 17, 90
murders of providers and clinic staff,
  103–104

NARAL Pro-Choice America, 107
National Abortion Federation (NAF),
  103, 104, 107, 124, 222
National Advocates for Pregnant
  Women, 197
National Asian Pacific Women's
  Forum, 126
National Association for the Repeal of
  Abortion Laws (NARAL), 24, 50
National Constitution Center's
  Constitution Drafting Project,
  179
National Institute for Reproductive
  Health, 50, 187
National Latina Institute for
  Reproductive Justice, 72
National Law Journal, 52
National Network of Abortion Funds
  (NNAF), 82, 221
National Organization of Women
  (NOW), 24, 51–52, 105
National Right to Life Committee
  (NRLC), 89, 120
National Task Force on Violence
  Against Reproductive Health
  Care Providers, 106, 195
National Women's Council of Ireland,
  217
National Women's Law Center,
  126–127, 215, 226
Native American women, 80,
  189–190, 217
New England Medical Center, 79
New Woman All Women clinic, 104
New York, access to abortion in, 24–25
Ni Una Menos ("not one more"),
  227–228
Nichols, Leanne, 103

Ninth Amendment, 26, 35
Nixon, Richard, 27, 213
nondisclosure agreements, limits on, 216
Norton, Eleanor Holmes, 39
NOW Legal Defense and Education
    Fund, 97, 105

Obama, Barack, and administration of,
    54, 84, 98, 107, 133–134, 171,
    184, 194
Obamacare. *See* Affordable Care Act
    (ACA)
Obergefell v. Hodges, 61, 143, 171
O'Connor, Sandra Day, 31, 37, 44–45,
    46, 53, 57, 60–61, 122, 132
omnibus bills, 187
On Liberty (Mill), 15
online activism, 225
Operation Rescue, 21, 102–103, 105,
    106
oral contraceptives, 17, 207–208
O'Reilly, Bill, 226
originalism, 53, 139
Oswald, Lee Harvey, 26

Páez, Chiara, 228
paid parental leave, 213
pandemic, 114–115, 128, 202,
    212–213
parental consent/involvement, 44, 45,
    46, 89–90, 92–96, 187, 191
Parkland, Florida, shooting, 229
Parks, Rosa, 229
"partial birth abortions," 65, 120–122
Partial-Birth Abortion Ban Act, 121
Patel, Purvi, 197
Patient Protection and Affordable Care
    Act. *See* Affordable Care Act
    (ACA)
patriarchal legal system, 9–10
Peace Corps, 80
Pelosi, Nancy, 84
Pennsylvania's Constitution, 75
people of color

child care and, 213
clinic violence and, 101–102
infertility and, 209–210
maternal mortality and, 205–206
Medicaid and, 72
outsized impact of restrictions on,
    13
penalizing of, 11
prosecution of, 198
sex selection stereotype and, 126
support for, 220–221
teen pregnancy rate and, 90
See also racism/racial inequality
People of Praise, 10, 139
Pérez, 228
Personal Responsibility Education
    Program, 98
Phelps, Michael, 173–174
Plan C, 222
Planned Parenthood, 24, 104,
    108–109, 127, 194–195
*Planned Parenthood of Central
    Missouri v. Danforth* (*Danforth*),
    93
Planned Parenthood v. Casey (*Casey*)
    arguing of, 2, 53–55
    Blackmun and, 15, 36
    Court of Appeals decision on, 40,
        45–47
    decision on, 56–60
    family violence and, 16
    in federal district court, 44–45
    filing of, 42
    impact of decision on, 67
    June Medical Services v. Russo
        decision and, 136
    Kennedy on, 38
    shift toward state regulation and, 35
    strategy for, 47–52
    Supreme Court review of, 47–48
    *Thornburgh v. American College
        of Obstetrics and Gynecologists*
        and, 43
Plant, Morgan, 48

plurality opinions, 57, 136
Poland, abortion rights protests in, 227
Polish Constitutional Court, 227
Pollitt, Katha, 183
"post abortion syndrome," 45
potato boycott, 117–118
poverty. *See* low-income people
Powell, Lewis, Jr., 28
Preate, Ernie, 54
precedent, Barrett on, 141–142
pre-existing conditions, 83–84, 203
pregnancy
    domestic violence and, 216
    forced, 15
    health impacts of, 15
Pregnancy Discrimination Act (PDA; 1978), 215
Pregnant Workers Fairness Act, 215
pregnant workers, fairness for, 214–215
pre-K education, 212–213
prescription requirement for contraceptives, 207–208
presidential election (1992), 47–49
presidential election (2020), 61
preterm births, 205
prisons, federal, 80
privacy, right to, 12, 26, 29, 158, 161
private clinics, 108–109
Progressive Constitution, 179
"pro-life" stance, limitations of, 7–8
Protection of Life During Pregnancy Act (PLDPA), 165–166
providers, 100–101, 103–104, 105, 108, 110–113, 188
"pro-women's health" rhetoric, 7
public disclosure requirement, 44
Puerto Rico, statehood for, 193

race-selective abortions, 126–127
racism/racial inequality
    abortion rights movement and, 4
    impact of restrictions and, 13

in maternal and infant mortality, 205–207
mortality rate and, 23
structural, 13, 205–206
systemic, 68
See also people of color
Racketeer Influenced and Corrupt Organizations Act (RICO), 105, 106
ranked-choice voting, 224
rape
    crisis programs for, 216
    harassment after, 77–78
    statutory, 92
Rashbaum, William, 125
rational basis test, 55, 61
Reagan, Ronald, and administration of, 36, 41–42, 66
reason bans, 126–127
Reconstruction Era Civil Rights Act (1871), 105, 106
redistricting, 66
Rehnquist, William, 34, 50–51, 59, 60
reimbursement rates, 191
religion
    contraception access and, 143
    gender roles and, 10
    health care providers and, 110
    impact of on opinion of abortion, 8–9
    support from leaders and, 24
    See also Catholic Church
Reno, Janet, 106
representation, disproportionate for rural states, 193
reproductive freedom initiatives
    abortion and, 200–201
    affordable child care and pre-K, 212–213
    fairness for pregnant workers, 214–215
    family-friendly benefits in workplace, 213–214
    health care for all, 202–204

joining global women's human rights community, 217–218
reducing infertility, 209–211
reducing sexual abuse, violence, and harassment, 215–217
reduction in maternal and infant deaths and complications, 205–207
sexuality education, 211–212
widening contraception availability, 207–209
Reproductive Freedom Project, 116
Reproductive Health Access Project, 110
reproductive health centers, 189
Reproductive Health Equity Act (Oregon), 173, 187
Reproductive Health Protection Act (2020; Virginia), 184
Reproductive Health Services (St. Louis), 108
reproductive justice movement, 11, 91–92
Republican Party, 66, 84. See also individual politicians
Rescue America, 103
Risk Evaluation and Mitigation Strategies (REMS), 113–115, 195
Rittenberg, Bill, 118
Roberts, Dorothy E., 11, 70
Roberts, John, 66, 115, 136–137, 142, 144, 145
Robinson, Mary, 146
Roe, Jane, 20, 26, 28
ROE Act (2020; Massachusetts), 187–188
Roe v. Wade (Roe)
  attempts to overturn, 2–4, 36–37
  class certification for, 20
  context for, 21–26
  decision on, 28
  dissenting opinions on, 34
  history of, 20–21
  issue of standing in, 28–29

Louisiana ban and, 119
Planned Parenthood v. Casey (Casey) and, 51–52, 53–54, 57–61, 67
  reception of decision on, 33–35
  reliance of on physician's determination, 111–112
  right to privacy and, 12
  standards set by, 29–31
  strategy for overturning, 63–66
  trying of, 26–27
Roemer, Buddy, 118
Roman Catholic Diocese of Brooklyn v. Cuomo, 143
romantic paternalism, 9
Roosevelt, Eleanor, 154
Roosevelt, Franklin Delano, 28, 154, 193
Rosenblum, Victor, 63
Rosselle, Sue, 48
Rothrock, Michael, 1
Rothrock, Robin, 1, 119, 124, 125
RU-486 (mifepristone), 114
Ruby, Jack, 26
Rudolph, Eric Robert, 104
Rue, Vincent, 45
Ryder, Artis, 48

Salt-n-Pepa, 86
same-sex marriage, 61, 143, 170–171
Sanders, Bernie, 203
Sanderson, Robert, 104
Sanger, Margaret, 127
Sapag, Silvia, 228–229
Scalia, Antonin, 53–54, 60, 134, 139, 140–141, 143
Schlafly, Phyllis, 175
Schroeder, Pat, 39
self-managed abortion, 196, 197, 198–199, 222
sex discrimination, Brennan on, 9
sex selection, ban on abortions for, 126
sexual assault/abuse, 80, 215–217, 226
sexual harassment, 215–217, 226

sexual health programming, funding
    for, 98
sexuality education, 96–98, 211–212
Sexuality Information and Education
    Council of the United States, 212
Shannon, Shelley, 104
Sherry, 21–22, 221
Shuai, Bei Bei, 197
SIA Legal Team, 196
sick time, 214
Siegel, Reva, 35
Sirleaf, Ellen Johnson, 200
Slepian, Barnett, 103
Smeal, Ellie, 50
Smith, Priscilla, 122
Society for Adolescent Medicine, 96
Society for the Protection of Unborn
    Children, 158
Sotomayor, Sonia, 115, 131, 132–133,
    136, 144
Souter, David H., 57, 58, 60–61
South Africa's Constitution, 180
South Bend Tribune, 141
Specter, Arlen, 39–40
Starr, Kenneth, 54–55, 61
state constitutions, 75–76, 112, 179
state courts, 186
State of the Union address (Roosevelt),
    154
statehood for DC and Puerto Rico,
    193
state-level reforms, 185–187
statutory rape, 92
Steinauer, Jody, 109–110
Steinem, Gloria, 18–19
Stenberg v. Carhart, 122, 123
Stengel, Rusty, 48
sterilization
    forced, 16
    insurance coverage for, 209
Stevens, John Paul, 40, 50–51, 55, 59,
    60, 61
Stewart, Carmel, 159–160
Stewart, Ke'Arre, 104

Stewart, Potter, 28
strategies for future
    ballot initiatives, 186
    coalition allies and, 171–172
    electoral politics and, 184–185,
        192–194
    Gender Equity Amendment,
        174–182
    increasing number of providers, 188
    "kick it to the curb" list, 190–192
    questions to ask about, 169–170
    reproductive health centers, 189
    state-level reforms, 185–187
    telemedicine and, 190
    tribal governments and, 189–190
strict scrutiny, 29–30, 178
Stupak, Bart, 84
suicide risk/attempts, 151–152, 197
"Summer of Mercy," 102, 103, 106
super-precedents, 140
Supreme Court
    abortion as litmus test for, 6
    anti-abortion groups and, 105, 108
    conservative majority of, 129,
        130–131, 142–145
    courtroom of, 52–53
    Hyde Amendment and, 73–75
    "partial birth abortions" and,
        122–123
    potential reform of, 193
    pregnant workers and, 214–215
    REMS and, 114–115
    TRAP laws and, 131–132
    *See also individual cases; individual
        justices*
Swasey, Garrett, 104

Targeted Regulation of Abortion
    Providers (TRAP) laws, 65,
    131–132, 135–136, 142, 192
tax credits, child care and, 213
Taylor, Breonna, 172
Tea Party, 154
Teen Pregnancy Prevention Program, 98

teenage sexuality
    Hartford/Lane case and, 86–89
    parental consent/involvement and,
        92–96
    sexuality education and, 96–98
    statutory rape and, 92
    teen parents and, 90–91
    teen pregnancy rate and, 90–92
teenagers
    birth rate and, 90
    outsized impact of restrictions on,
        13, 25
    support for, 220
    two-trip requirement and, 43
    See also parental consent/
        involvement; sexuality education
telemedicine, 190
Terry, Randall, 102
textualists, 139, 144
Thomas, Clarence
    appointment of, 38, 66
    Barrett confirmation and, 138
    Bostock v. Clayton County and, 144
    confirmation of, 46, 134
    Hill and, 38–40
    June Medical Services v. Russo
        decision and, 136–137
    Planned Parenthood v. Casey
        (*Casey*) and, 60
    on race-selective abortion
        restrictions, 127
Thornburgh, Richard, 41
*Thornburgh v. American College of
        Obstetrics and Gynecologists*, 2,
        36–37, 41–42, 43
Tiller, George, 102, 103, 104, 107
TIME'S UP Legal Defense Fund, 226
Title VII, 144
Title X, 97, 194–195
Together for Yes, 166
Tometi, Opal, 172
transgender men and non-binary
    people (TGNB), 4. *See also*
    LGBTQ+ people

transphobia, 4, 107–108
tribal governments, 189–190
TRICARE, 79
trigger laws, 120
Trump administration
    abortion blocked by, 80
    ACA and, 173
    clinic violence and, 107
    extreme right and, 108
    "gag rule" and, 194–195
    judicial appointments and,
        134–135, 138
    opposition to, 19, 67, 225, 226
    sexuality education and, 98
two-trip requirement, 43

Ufot, Nsé, 185
Ultraviolet, 225
UN Women, 180
Underwood, Lauren, 207
undocumented immigrants
    health insurance and, 173, 203
    support for, 220–221
undue burden test, 46, 51, 58–60, 178
United Nations, 154, 217
United States v. Vuitch, 25
Universal Declaration of Human
    Rights, 154, 181
universal health care, 204
Unsoeld, Jolene, 39
urgent care centers, 189

Varadkar, Leo, 166
Vermont Constitution, 179
Veterans Health Administration, 79
viability, 30–31, 64
Violence Against Women Act, 67, 216
Vote Mama, 224
Vote Run Lead, 224
voter suppression, 193, 224
Vuitch, Milan, 25

Wade, Henry, 26
Waisman, Viviana, 148

waiting periods, 43, 45, 46, 191–192
Wall, Carole, 48
Washington, Sha-Asia, 205
Wattleton, Faye, 50
Watts, Tammy, 121, 221
Waxman, Henry, 97
*Webster v. Reproductive Health
    Services*, 37
Weddington, Sarah, 20, 27
Weems, Helen, 113
Weinstein, Harvey, 226
Whalen, Jennifer, 197
Wharton, Linda, 42, 48, 51, 102
Whelehan, Harry, 151
White, Byron, 34, 60, 119
White House Gender Policy Council,
    204
white supremacists/nationalists,
    107–108, 154
Whole Woman's Health v. Hellerstedt,
    131–133, 136
Wicklund, Susan, 111
Williams, Serena, 206
Wilson, Vicki, 121, 221

Winter, Aaron, 107
Winters, Faith, 214
Wolfson, Evan, 170–171
Women on Waves, 149, 189
Women's Division of the United
    Methodist Church, 73
women's equality, lack of legal
    guarantees for, 35–36
Women's Health Center (Duluth,
    Minnesota), 108
Women's Health Protection Act, 194
Women's Law Project, 41, 42
Women's Link Worldwide, 148
Women's March (2017), 19, 67, 225,
    226
Women's Suburban Clinic, 102–103
World Health Organization, 112,
    198
Wright, Angela, 40

Yard, Molly, 118

Zemaitis, Tom, 41, 42, 43, 48, 55
Zimmerman, George, 172